Arden of Faversham

ARDEN EARLY MODERN DRAMA GUIDES

Series Editors:

Andrew Hiscock, University of Wales, Bangor, UK and Lisa Hopkins, Sheffield Hallam University, UK

Arden Early Modern Drama Guides offer practical and accessible introductions to the critical and performative contexts of key Elizabethan and Jacobean plays. Each guide introduces the text's critical and performance history, but also provides students with an invaluable insight into the landscape of current scholarly research, through a keynote essay on the state of the art and newly commissioned essays of fresh research from different critical perspectives.

Titles published in this series:

A Midsummer Night's Dream: A Critical Reader, edited by Regina Buccola
Doctor Faustus: A Critical Reader, edited by Sarah Munson Deats
King Lear: A Critical Reader, edited by Andrew Hiscock and Lisa Hopkins
Henry IV, Part 1: A Critical Reader, edited by Stephen Longstaffe
'Tis Pity She's a Whore: A Critical Reader, edited by Lisa Hopkins
Women Beware Women: A Critical Reader, edited by Andrew Hiscock
Volpone: A Critical Reader, edited by Matthew Steggle
The Duchess of Malfi: A Critical Reader, edited by Christina Luckyj
The Alchemist: A Critical Reader, edited by Erin Julian and Helen Ostovich

The Jew of Malta: A Critical Reader, edited by Robert A. Logan
Macbeth: A Critical Reader, edited by John Drakakis and Dale Townshend
Richard III: A Critical Reader, edited by Annaliese Connolly
Twelfth Night: A Critical Reader, edited by Alison Findlay and Liz Oakley-Brown
The Tempest: A Critical Reader, edited by Alden T. Vaughan and Virginia Mason Vaughan
Romeo and Juliet: A Critical Reader, edited by Julia Reinhard Lupton
Julius Caesar: A Critical Reader, edited by Andrew James Hartley
The Revenger's Tragedy: A Critical Reader, edited by Brian Walsh
The White Devil: A Critical Reader, edited by Paul Frazer and Adam Hansen
Edward II: A Critical Reader, edited by Kirk Melnikoff
Much Ado About Nothing: A Critical Reader, edited by Deborah Cartmell and Peter J. Smith
King Henry V: A Critical Reader, edited by Karen Britland and Line Cottegnies
Troilus and Cressida: A Critical Reader, edited by Efterpi Mitsi
The Merchant of Venice: A Critical Reader, edited by Sarah Hatchuel and Nathalie Vienne-Guerrin
The Changeling: A Critical Reader, edited by Mark Hutchings
Coriolanus: A Critical Reader, edited by Liam E. Semler
Antony and Cleopatra: A Critical Reader, edited by Domenico Lovascio
Tamburlaine: A Critical Reader, edited by David McInnis
Richard II: A Critical Reader, edited by Michael Davies and Andrew Duxfield

Arden of Faversham

A Critical Reader

Edited by Peter Kirwan and Duncan Salkeld

THE ARDEN SHAKESPEARE
LONDON • NEW YORK • OXFORD • NEW DELHI • SYDNEY

THE ARDEN SHAKESPEARE
Bloomsbury Publishing Plc
50 Bedford Square, London, WC1B 3DP, UK
1385 Broadway, New York, NY 10018, USA
29 Earlsfort Terrace, Dublin 2, Ireland

BLOOMSBURY, THE ARDEN SHAKESPEARE and the Arden Shakespeare logo are trademarks of Bloomsbury Publishing Plc

First published in Great Britain 2023
This paperback edition published in 2025

Copyright © Peter Kirwan, Duncan Salkeld and contributors, 2023

Peter Kirwan, Duncan Salkeld and contributors have asserted their right under the Copyright, Designs and Patents Act, 1988, to be identified as the authors of this work.

For legal purposes the Acknowledgements on p. ix constitute an extension of this copyright page.

Cover image taken from the 1615 title-page of *The Spanish Tragedy*, by Thomas Kyd.

All rights reserved. No part of this publication may be reproduced or transmitted in any form or by any means, electronic or mechanical, including photocopying, recording, or any information storage or retrieval system, without prior permission in writing from the publishers.

Bloomsbury Publishing Plc does not have any control over, or responsibility for, any third-party websites referred to in this book. All internet addresses given in this book were correct at the time of going to press. The author and publisher regret any inconvenience caused if addresses have changed or sites have ceased to exist, but can accept no responsibility for any such changes.

A catalogue record for this book is available from the British Library.

A catalog record for this book is available from the Library of Congress.

ISBN: HB: 978-1-3502-7017-6
PB: 978-1-3502-7096-1
ePDF: 978-1-3502-7019-0
eBook: 978-1-3502-7018-3

Series: Arden Early Modern Drama Guides

Typeset by Deanta Global Publishing Services, Chennai, India

To find out more about our authors and books visit www.bloomsbury.com and sign up for our newsletters.

CONTENTS

Acknowledgements ix
Notes on Contributors xi

Introduction Duncan Salkeld and Peter Kirwan 1

1 The critical backstory Jane Kingsley-Smith 15

2 The performance history: 'Poor wench abused by thy misgovernance' – *Arden of Faversham* on stage Kath Bradley 41

3 The state of the art: Locating criticism of *Arden of Faversham*, 2000 to the present Catherine Richardson 67

4 New directions: Susan of Faversham: Staging subordination in *Arden* Emma Whipday 91

5 New directions: Mist opportunities: The play of the weather in *Arden of Faversham* Chloe Kathleen Preedy 117

6 New directions: 'What manner of man was he?' Will and the making of archival Blackness in *Arden of Faversham* Brandi K. Adams 143

7 New directions: Crimson snow: *Arden of Faversham* as golden age detective story Lisa Hopkins 169

8 Pedagogy: 'Now I take you': Approaches to teaching
   Arden of Faversham Kirsten N. Mendoza 191

Select Bibliography 219
Index 235

ACKNOWLEDGEMENTS

This book came together at a major time of transition for both editors and several of our contributors. Our most important thanks go to everyone who has participated in this book. Jane Kingsley-Smith, Kath Bradley, Catherine Richardson, Emma Whipday, Chloe Preedy, Brandi K. Adams, Lisa Hopkins and Kirsten N. Mendoza have been patient and generous collaborators, and we have learnt enormously from both their work and their collegiality. We would also like to thank Iman Sheeha, Lehua Yim and Carol Mejia LaPerle for their contributions to the development of this volume.

We would like to thank the team at Arden, especially Lara Bateman and Ella Wilson, for their professionalism and support from the initial commissioning of this volume. We are grateful to our anonymous readers and the series editors, Andrew Hiscock and Lisa Hopkins, for their support throughout.

Peter would like to thank his old colleagues at the University of Nottingham and his new colleagues at Mary Baldwin University (especially Doreen Bechtol, Kerry Cooke, Matt Davies, Finch, Paul Menzer, JP Schneider and Molly Seremet) for their support during the period of transatlantic displacement during which this book came to fruition. He would particularly like to thank Josh Caldicott and Simon Smith for many invaluable conversations about *Arden*'s epilogue, and the team behind *William Shakespeare and Others: Collaborative Plays* (Jonathan Bate, Eric Rasmussen, Will Sharpe and Jan Sewell) for helping engender his early interest in this play. This book, as with so many projects, wouldn't have happened without Susan Anderson's love and encouragement, and Peppermint's sobering disinterest.

Duncan would like to thank Darren Freebury-Jones, Charles Green, Jane Kingsley-Smith, Peter Kirwan, MacDonald P. Jackson, Pervez Rizvi and René Weis for many fruitful exchanges about *Arden of Faversham*. Nigel Morgan and Christine Smith of the

Faversham Society have been extremely generous with their knowledge regarding the Arden house and abbey. He thanks Mark Bick, Roger Cline, Neil Edington, Miles Leeson, Dave and Clare Mudie, and Peter Smith for their constant friendship, and Tom, Sam and Ellie for their love and support.

At the time of editing this book, many of our colleagues around the world, but particularly in the UK, are facing redundancy and/or precarity owing to threats to arts and humanities departments. This book is dedicated to all those fighting to keep the study of the arts alive.

CONTRIBUTORS

Brandi K. Adams is Assistant Professor of English at Arizona State University. Her research interests include the history of reading, the history of the book and premodern critical race theory of early modern England as well as modern editorial practices for early modern English drama. She has recently published on 'unbookishness' in *Othello* and Keith Hamilton Cobb's *American Moor* in the journal *Shakespeare* and has contributed a chapter to the volume *Shakespeare/Text* edited by Claire M. L. Bourne. She has begun working on her first monograph, tentatively titled *Representations of Books and Readers in Early Modern English Drama*.

Kath Bradley gained her MPhil in 'The Performance History of *Sir Thomas More*' from the Shakespeare Institute (University of Birmingham) and her PhD from Nottingham Trent University in 'Presentism, Politics and Contemporary Performance in *Arden of Faversham* and *King Edward III*'. She currently works as an independent researcher and is a regular contributor to *Cahiers Élisabéthains*. She co-edited the journal's special edition covering the RSC's Complete Works Festival. Her essays and reviews have also appeared in *Shakespeare, Linguaculture,* and on the *Blogging Shakespeare* website of the Shakespeare Birthplace Trust.

Lisa Hopkins is Professor Emerita of English at Sheffield Hallam University and co-edits *Shakespeare* (the journal of the British Shakespeare Association), *Journal of Marlowe Studies*, Arden Early Modern Drama Guides and Arden Studies in Early Modern Drama. She writes mainly on Shakespeare, Marlowe and Ford, but she has also published on Jane Austen, Bram Stoker, crime fiction and literature on screen. Her previous publications include *Shakespearean Allusion in Crime Fiction* (2016), *A Companion to* the *Cavendishes: Literature, Patronage, Material Culture*, co-edited with Tom Rutter (2020), *Burial Plots in British Detective Fiction* (2021) and *The Edge of Christendom on the Early Modern Stage* (2022). Her most recent project, *Ocular Proof and the Spectacled Detective*, will be published in 2023.

Jane Kingsley-Smith is Professor of Shakespeare Studies at the University of Roehampton, London. She is the author of three monographs: *Shakespeare's Drama of Exile* (2003), *Cupid in Early Modern Literature and Culture* (2010) and the first book-length study of the Sonnets' reception, *The Afterlife of Shakespeare's Sonnets* (2019). She has edited *Love's Labor's Lost* for the Norton 3 Shakespeare (2015) and *John Webster and John Ford: The Duchess of Malfi, The White Devil, The Broken Heart and 'Tis Pity She's a Whore* for Penguin (2014), and she will shortly be editing Shakespeare's Sonnets for the new *Cambridge Shakespeare Editions*.

Peter Kirwan is Associate Professor of Shakespeare and Performance at Mary Baldwin University. His research interests span textual history, performance history and the contemporary production of early modern plays. His monographs include *Shakespeare in the Theatre: Cheek by Jowl* (2019) and *Shakespeare and the Idea of Apocrypha* (2015). Edited volumes include *Shakespeare's Audiences* (with Matteo Pangallo, 2021), *The Arden Research Handbook of Shakespeare and Contemporary Performance* (with Kathryn Prince, 2021), *Canonising Shakespeare* (with Emma Depledge, 2015) and *Shakespeare and the Digital World* (with Christie Carson, 2014). He is the editor of *Shakespeare Bulletin* and a general editor of the Revels Plays Companion Library. He has written extensively on *Arden of Faversham* in the context of Shakespeare's 'apocrypha'.

Kirsten N. Mendoza is Assistant Professor of English and Human Rights at the University of Dayton. Her work, which focuses on early modern drama and literature, premodern critical race studies, sexual violence and consent, has been supported with grants from the Huntington Library, Folger Shakespeare Library and the American Council of Learned Societies. Her book, tentatively titled *A Politics of Touch*, examines the influences of the early modern stages and pages on shifting discourses of self-possession and race alongside changes in legal rights and protections. Her work has appeared or is forthcoming in *Renaissance Drama, Shakespeare Bulletin, The Oxford Handbook of Shakespeare and Race, Race and Affect in Early Modern English Literature* and *Teaching Social Justice through Shakespeare: Why Renaissance Literature Matters Now.*

Chloe Kathleen Preedy is Senior Lecturer in Shakespeare & Renaissance Literature at the University of Exeter. She is the author of *Marlowe's Literary Scepticism: Politic Religion and Post-Reformation Polemic* (2013), which won the Roma Gill Prize 2015, and sits on the editorial board for the journal *Marlowe Studies*. Her past and current publication projects include co-edited special journal issues on early modern stage space and the air's significance in contemporary performance; a forthcoming co-edited volume on Thomas Nashe; various individual articles and book chapters on early modern drama; and, with Professor William Sherman, a new Arden edition of Christopher Marlowe's *The Jew of Malta*. She is a principal investigator for the AHRC-funded project Atmospheric Theatre: Open-Air Performance and the Environment (2018–21) and her related monograph, *Theatres of the Air: Representing Aerial Environments on the Early Modern Stage, 1576–1609*, is forthcoming.

Catherine Richardson is Professor of Early Modern Studies at the University of Kent. She studies the history and representation of early modern material culture, writing articles and monographs about the stage and the household. She has written *Domestic Life and Domestic Tragedy in Early Modern England* (2006), *Shakespeare and Material Culture* (2011) and, with Tara Hamling, *A Day at Home in Early Modern England, The Materiality of Domestic Life, 1500–1700* for Yale (2016), and edited several books on material culture, including *Everyday Objects: Medieval and Early Modern Material Culture and Its Meanings* (2010) and *The Routledge Handbook of Material Culture in Early Modern Europe* (2016, also with David Gaimster). She is currently running an AHRC project on 'The Cultural Lives of the Middling Sort': https://research.kent.ac.uk/middling-culture/.

Duncan Salkeld is Professor Emeritus of Shakespeare and Renaissance Literature at the University of Chichester and Visiting

Professor at the University of Roehampton, London. He is author of three monographs: *Madness and Drama in the Age of Shakespeare* (1993), *Shakespeare among the Courtesans* (2012) and *Shakespeare and London* (2018). He is a co-editor for the New Variorum *Twelfth Night*. His latest publication is 'Q/F: The Texts of *King Lear*', *The Library* (March 2021).

Emma Whipday is Lecturer in Renaissance Literature at Newcastle University. Her first book, *Shakespeare's Domestic Tragedies: Violence in the Early Modern Home* (2019) explores domestic violence on the early modern stage, and is co-winner of the Shakespeare's Globe Book Award 2020. She is currently working on a book, funded by a Leverhulme Early Career Fellowship, on brother–sister relationships in early modern culture. Emma has also published on *Arden of Faversham, Titus Andronicus*, housework in Shakespeare, the lost play 'Keep the Widow Waking', domestic murder pamphlets and her 'practice as research' experiments; she regularly directs workshops, staged readings and productions of early modern plays. Emma is also a playwright; her play *Shakespeare's Sister* (2016) won the Theatre Royal Haymarket's Masterclass 'Pitch Your Play' award, and her play *The Defamation of Cicely Lee* won the American Shakespeare Center's 2019 'Shakespeare's New Contemporaries' prize.

Introduction

Duncan Salkeld and Peter Kirwan

'Thus have you seen the truth of Arden's death', says Franklin, at the beginning of the epilogue to *Arden of Faversham* (Epilogue 1). Franklin, similar to allegorical figures such as the Doctor who concludes the morality play *Everyman*, assumes a quasi-objective moral authority as he seeks to tie up the loose ends of the play. The voice of this epilogue is nuanced:[1] he is both a named character aligned with the titular Arden within the play and a distanced recounter of Arden's 'force and violence' (11). He is a speaker for the theatre company ('we hope you'll pardon this naked tragedy', 14) and also a moralist ('simple truth is gracious enough', 17). He recounts myths as facts ('in the grass [Arden's] body's print was seen / Two years and more after the deed was done', 13), yet also admits to uncertainty ('how [Clarke the painter] died we know not', 8). As Jane Kingsley-Smith remarks in her contribution to this volume, 'there will be no "simple truth" found in *Arden of Faversham*'.[2]

Such nuances of voice, even within one short speech, are testament to the complexity of the play that is the subject of this book. Indeed, *Arden of Faversham* might be characterized as a relatively straightforward story made difficult. Its central action – the murder of a landowner in Kent and the subsequent conviction of the murderers – is a simple one, given a conventional moral gloss by a title page that condemns lust and murder in categorical terms. However, at every turn, the play reminds us that the narrative is more complex than that. The murder itself succeeds only after multiple attempts, deferring the moralistic conclusion through moments of black comedy. The numbers of those involved in the murder swell throughout the play – at times, it seems that half the town is out for Arden's blood – and their varying motives create a much more nuanced tale of the social and fiscal relationships that tie together this community (as Brandi K. Adams discusses in this book in relation to the character of Black Will). The play's unusual insistence on the material and geographical conditions of this locale, from the fog that thwarts one of the murder attempts (see Chloe Preedy's chapter in this volume) to the physical business of cleaning the stage after the murder (as discussed by Emma Whipday), roots this story in the practical challenges that make murder so difficult both to commit and to hide.

What makes *Arden of Faversham* a drama, rather than a simple moral tract, is the role played by 'accidents' of all kinds. The long opening scene introduces its audiences to a close-knit community where chance encounters and local gossip lead to the forging of alliances and the development of conspiracies. The role played by happenstance is then accentuated by the slapstick disasters that befall the murderers Black Will and Shakebag as they attempt to waylay their mark, Thomas Arden, as he goes obliviously about his business. The various accidents, mistakes and revelations culminate in the characteristic dénouement of a morality tale or, as Lisa Hopkins argues in her contribution to this book, the detective story. If 'this accident . . . hath no success' (3.118–19), as the conspirator Greene notes of one failed murder attempt, a conclusion that audiences might draw from *Arden of Faversham* is that the relationship between 'accident' and 'success' is central to a play whose drama comes largely from plans going awry.

This *Critical Reader* is the first collection of essays devoted to one of the most frequently performed, studied and taught of all non-Shakespearean early modern plays – or, as a growing number of scholars are arguing, one of the least performed, studied and taught of all of Shakespeare's plays. The very fact that two such different emphases are simultaneously supportable is testament to the complexity offered by this play's truths and accidents, which the contributors to this volume explore in their surveys of the play's history and approaches to new readings. Far from being a 'naked tragedy', *Arden of Faversham* has been re-dressed in many new interpretive garments, as scholars of material culture, gender studies, economic history, cultural geography, and many more have turned their attention to it. In the course of this volume, our aim has been to represent the ever-widening scope of *Arden of Faversham*'s critical interest. Before that, however, we turn to the received 'true' history with which our play is inextricably intertwined – while noting that this is a history waylaid by accident.

(Not so) simple truths

At around 7:00 p.m. on St. Valentine's Day (14 February) 1551, Thomas Ardern, a gentleman of Faversham in Kent, sat down in his parlour to play a game of backgammon with a tailor, Thomas Morsby. In the moment his opponent moved a game-piece and declared 'Now I take you', Ardern was attacked from behind, dragged to the floor, struck on the head with a large 'pressing iron' and sliced with a knife in the throat.[3] His body was carried beyond the garden and left in snow not far from Faversham church. When the body was discovered by searchers at about 11:00 p.m., a trail of blood led back to the house and parlour. The murder was the culmination of a series of plots hatched by Ardern's wife and her lover Morsby, in collaboration with a number of associates who included hired killers Black Will and George Loosebag (later 'Shakebag'), a handful of acquaintances – John Green, Michael Saunderson, George Bradshaw and a painter named William Blackborne – and two women, Morsby's sister Cicely Ponder and Arden's serving-maid Elizabeth Stafford.

In later accounts of the crime, these names are regularized to 'Arden', 'Mosby', 'Shakebag' and 'Greene'. The authorities in Kent and London went to some lengths to track the offenders down and most of them were caught: only the painter and Shakebag escaped arrest.[4] A month after the murder, Alice was burned and Bradshaw hung in chains at Canterbury, Mosby and his sister were hanged in Smithfield, London, and in Faversham Saunderson was hanged, drawn and quartered and Stafford burned at the stake. On 15 June, the Privy Council acknowledged efforts to apprehend Black Will and bring him in under guard. In July, Greene was arrested in Cornwall and returned to Faversham to be hung there in chains. Black Will was apprehended at Flushing (Vlissingen) in the Low Countries for 'diverse murders', possibly including Arden's, and was there 'half-burned' or 'scorched' to death.[5]

The Faversham murder quickly became infamous. Henry Machyn recorded the executions of Alice and Mosby in his 'Diary'.[6] In 1577, the chronicle historian Raphael Holinshed included a detailed account of this murder, changing some names and adding to what we learn from the inquest, perhaps a little fancifully. Holinshed's account appeared again in the 1587 edition of his *Chronicles* with other minor changes and added marginalia. Holinshed claimed to have acquired his account of the murder from trustworthy sources, 'that have used some diligence to gather the true understanding of the circumstances'.[7]

Five years after Holinshed's second edition, this story was retold in the form of a sensational drama. In 1592, the play now known as *Arden of Faversham* was printed in black-letter quarto by Edward Allde and offered for sale in the London bookshop of Edward White.[8] This work seems largely to have been based on Holinshed's account, perhaps the second edition with marginalia.[9] The quarto bears a lengthy description on its title page:

> The lamentable and true tragedy of M. Arden of Feversham in Kent, who was most wickedly murdered by the means of his disloyal and wanton wife, who, for the love she bare to one Mosbie, hired two desperate ruffians, Black Will and Shakebag, to kill him. Wherein is showed the great malice and dissimulation of a wicked woman, the insatiable desire of filthy lust and the shameful end of all murderers.[10]

White evidently wanted to advertise the play's shock value but, as was customary for printed texts of the early 1590s, he omitted any mention of its author. The play was printed again in 1599 with minor corrections by John Roberts for White, and a third time by Allde's widow Elizabeth in 1633, once more without any assignation of authorship.

Emily O'Brien describes *Arden* as 'the original true crime drama'.[11] The play's unusual focus on recent domestic crimes developed over the following years into a distinctive genre. The anonymous *A Warning for Fair Women*, printed in 1599, tells the story of George Browne's attempts to murder George Sanders in order to gain his wife, and includes scenes set in London locations, including Newgate prison. Robert Yarington's *Two Lamentable Tragedies* (1601) interweaves the story of 'the murder of Master Beech a Chandler in Thames Street, and his boy' with the tale of 'a young child murdered in a Wood by two ruffians, with the consent of his uncle'.[12] The character of Homicide introduces these 'two tragedies in one': Master Beech is struck in the head with a hammer some 'fifteen times', and his boy is left clinging to life with the hammer still 'sticking in his head'.[13] The other 'young child' is run through with a sword by murderers who then kill each other. The 1605 case of one Walter Calverley, a Yorkshire gentleman who attempted to murder his family, killing two of his children and injuring his wife, inspired two separate plays in this genre: *A Yorkshire Tragedy* (printed 1608 with an attribution to W. Shakespeare, now thought to be by Thomas Middleton), which may well have been first performed before the murderer was even executed;[14] and George Wilkins's *The Miseries of Enforced Marriage* (published 1607). Other 'true crime' dramas, now lost, including *The Tragedy of Gowrie* and *Page of Plymouth* by Jonson and Dekker, are known to have been performed by Shakespeare's company.[15]

Even as the early modern stage began turning the stories of true crime into the material of dramatic fiction, Thomas Ardern's story recurred in other media. A ballad retelling the story was printed (possibly by Elizabeth Allde) for Cuthbert Wright in 1633 and titled *[The] complaint and lamentation of Mistresse Arden of [Fev]ersham in Kent, who for the love of one Mosbie, hired two certain Ruffians [a]nd Villains most cruelly to murder her Husband; with the fatal end of her and her Associates*.[16] The ballad appears to be based on the play rather than on the chronicle history: the title repeats wording from the 1592 quarto title page, and some of the poem's verses quote words and phrases from the play: 'There's something in' (line 23; 1.364), '*on the ground*' (l. 24; 1.366 SD), 'twenty more' (l. 50; 1.523, 568), 'watchword' (l. 148; 14.106–7), 'Thus have you' (l. 169; Epilogue 1) and 'on a stage' (l. 187, Epilogue 6). It also includes other elements found only in the play, including the character of Susan, Arden's disturbed dreams and Shakebag's murder in Southwark. Citing the language of a stage direction ('*on the ground*', l. 24), the ballad-writer seems to have been drawing on a reading rather than a performance of the play. This influence then returned the other way: a woodcut illustration at the head of the ballad shows Arden being attacked while playing a game of 'tables' (backgammon), and this woodcut was again used for the 1633 third quarto imprint of the play. As Tiffany Stern has shown, a number of Shakespeare plays were followed up with a ballad designed, it would seem, to advertise the play.[17] Perhaps coincidentally, the ballads of both *Titus Andronicus* (first printed 1661 but probably written earlier) and *Mistress Arden* (1633) were composed to be sung to 'Fortune My Foe', a melody known as 'the hanging tune' and popular at executions.[18]

Arden of Faversham and its intertexts create a complex network of variations on a subject as each version offers its own embellishments, emphases, judgements and implications. The 1592 play even seems to contradict itself; the heavy-handed emphasis of the title page on the 'disloyall and wanton', 'wicked' wife – who is not even accorded a name – and her 'great mal-lice and discimulation', 'unsatiable desire', 'filthie lust' and 'shamefull end', belies the complex and multifaceted treatment of Alice in the play itself. In the book that follows, our contributors reckon with *Arden*'s conflicting points of view and complex negotiations with truth, its critical histories and interpretive ambiguities, further extending the outcomes of the backgammon game left unfinished in 1551.

Critical and creative histories

In line with the structure of the *Critical Reader* series, this volume begins with three chapters assessing the play's history, with Kath Bradley's account of the play in performance bookended by Kingsley-Smith's critical survey of the play's fortunes up to the year 2000, and Catherine Richardson – the play's most recent editor – taking up the baton to explore more recent approaches to the play. With the auspices of the play so doubtful (no consensus has yet been found on the play's authorship, playing company or original venue), the surveys here concern instead what critics and theatre-makers have found in the play itself. As Kingsley-Smith's chapter illustrates, far from a depiction of 'simple truth', *Arden* is a play of dramatic tension, grim humour and nuanced characterization. While early criticism was dominated by the question of Shakespeare's involvement, more recent critics have focussed upon the character of Alice, the play's relations to historiography and Holinshed, its intertextual connections and generic complexity and its representations of murderous men for hire.

Aside from authorship, the question that most seems to vex critics of *Arden of Faversham* is that of the play's genre. As noted earlier, the play has become part of a canon of early modern 'domestic tragedies', the qualifier 'domestic' implying that the status and social class of the protagonists in this genre separates them not just by degree but by kind from the tragedies of kings and duchesses that continue to dominate curricula and stages. The relative critical neglect of this sub-genre has had important redress in recent years. Emma Whipday argues that it 'asserts the importance of the private world and shows that households outside the elite sphere can be performed on stage and taken seriously'.[19] Robert W. Daniel and Iman Sheeha note that 'the household emerges more often than not as a space of conflict, danger and anxiety rather than as one of refuge and comfort', their special issue of *Early Modern Literary Studies* offering an important moment for reflection on the growing critical significance attributed to the early modern household.[20] As Kingsley-Smith and Richardson's chapters both demonstrate, the renewed interest from the 1990s onwards in the ramifications and cultural valences of domestic plays intersected with new approaches to studies of material culture and cultural geography, locating the play ever more precisely in its historical moment and specifically in Kent. At the same time, readings drawing from new historicism and feminist theory picked up on the subversive potential that Whipday notes, seeing the play as staging a number of different ideological rebellions against feudal allegiances, incipient capitalism, master-servant relations, patriarchal authority and land ownership. The act of mariticide itself can be seen as an act of rebellion, with Catherine Belsey's landmark article 'Alice Arden's Crime' reflecting on Alice's 'challenge to the institution of marriage'.[21] Domestic tragedy makes the private public, and in doing so makes the personal political.

However, the critical emphasis on the affordances of domestic tragedy jars with much of the stage tradition, as outlined by Kath Bradley in her account of the play in performance. The reviewers of productions from across the twentieth and twenty-first centuries whom Bradley draws on repeatedly return to the language of comedy – though whether this is black comedy, Ealing comedy, screwball comedy, slapstick or something else, there is little consensus. Certainly, in the repeated bungled murder attempts that occur around the oblivious Arden, productions have often been able to strike a tone of cartoonish slapstick. However, as Bradley's account of the play in performance shows, the funnier a production is, the greater the impact of the sudden success of the final murder attempt. Whatever the auspices of *Arden of Faversham*, its careful management of tone and its expert subversion of generic conventions mean that its genre remains as elusive as its authorship.

The histories of criticism and theatre practice in these opening three chapters offer an invaluable resource for future scholars of the play; they also emphasize the areas that continue to make the play distinctive. Bradley notes that female directors have been particularly drawn to the play that offers one of the longest female roles in early modern drama, and Kingsley-Smith draws attention to the substantial body of work establishing Alice Arden not only as a complex and rewarding role in its own right but as an important intertext for Shakespeare's *Macbeth*. Richardson, meanwhile, suggests that the varied engagements with the play's different forms of 'locatedness' position it as an important vehicle for emergent fields, interrogating the relationship between cultural works, history and geography. Some of this work is begun in the second half of this volume.

New directions

In commissioning the research essays that make up the second half of this volume, we deliberately wanted to explore new perspectives in *Arden* scholarship and find intersections with critical practices and methods that have not been a traditional part of its critical history. The first of our 'new directions' essays, by Emma Whipday, combines close reading with practice as research to illustrate the ways in which an ostensibly minor character, Susan, can offer new and subversive perspectives. Drawing on experiments with actors' parts, Whipday allows us to see the play through Susan's eyes and highlights her paradoxical status: she is subordinated, silenced and threatened with homelessness, but also becomes a key figure in the murder case, especially as she attempts to wash away the evidence of the crime – a stage moment controlled by the apprentice actor who presumably first took on the role. As Whipday argues, the tragedy of *Arden of Faversham* is Susan's tragedy too.

Brandi K. Adams, in her chapter on the play's racial implications, similarly attends to a minor character and offers a challenge to what David Sterling Brown has referred to as 'the centrality of uncritiqued whiteness in studies of domesticity' by homing in on the 'blackness' of both Mosby and Black Will.[22] Drawing on work by other scholars of early modern race, including Kim F. Hall, Ian Smith, Ayanna Thompson and Patricia Akhimie, Adams points out that racial implications are coded in *Arden* in ways not limited to skin complexion alone. Turning to a historical archive replete with Black Wills, Adams asks what exactly it might mean to have been called Black Will and finds the name's implied darkness associated with a ghoulish otherworldliness that invites renewed critical attention.

As Richardson's chapter demonstrates, much has been done to 'locate' the world of *Arden of Faversham* in the solid material culture and landscapes of the play's historical setting. Chloe Preedy's contribution to this volume, though, draws on the more ephemeral aspects of cultural geography in her dynamic exploration of the play's climate and weather. Picking up on the typographical pun in Holinshed's *Chronicles* in which Black Will 'mist . . . his purpose' in the fog, Preedy shows how the tangible traces of the air – which may well have been evoked via pyrotechnics in the early modern theatre – create an enabling set of conditions which repeatedly thwart intention and invite questions of the intersection of divine providence with the mundane.[23] The play's anonymous, semi-comic Ferryman seems to emerge from the mouth of hell, like a version of Charon from Greek myth, further aligning natural and supernatural.

When Lisa Hopkins, in her chapter, writes that the mystery of the play's authorship is easily solved, she does so partly with her tongue in her cheek, but partly also to show affinities between the play's narrative structure and what we understand today as the detective story genre. For Hopkins, the play is a study in how individual guilt, original sin and societal pressures combine in the planning of the murder. Hopkins illustrates with several examples features that modern detective fiction consciously shares with early modern tragedy: footsteps in the snow, madmen, bodies in chains and plots for revenge. In so doing, Hopkins not only situates *Arden* within later middlebrow fictional models but also brings the volume back full circle to the question of *Arden*'s protean genre, in which attempts to fix categorization work against the play's own fluidity.

Many of the contributors to this book have found *Arden of Faversham* a hugely rewarding text to explore with students. Kirsten N. Mendoza, in the chapter that concludes this volume, begins by asking why we might teach this play, and suggests that its value lies in the 'vast array of issues' that it raises. Responding to recent work encouraging the teaching of social justice through early modern drama, Mendoza argues that the play's own depiction of inequities and uneven power relations offers rich potential for initiating discussion about history and the present. Mendoza offers a series of outlines for critical discussions with students on topics such as property, ambition, justice, genre and homicide, drawing attention as she does so to marginalized figures including women, servants, Black men and masterless men. Mendoza provides extensive bibliographies for each of these areas to support teachers in taking their own approaches.

It is hoped that this collection of essays on *Arden* will encourage critical interest in this remarkable play. Its significance for drama in the early 1590s and beyond and its diverse possibilities make it a thrilling text for study. The play has been criticized as the work of an amateur, as a patchwork reconstruction or as a brilliant failure. If *Arden* was the work of a playwright learning his trade, then the sardonic humour of killers who repeatedly screw up, the eerie intrusions of anxiety, dreams and foul weather, and the skill in using props all point to unusual dramatic ability. Early on, Arden sees Mosby as a threat, a tailor with unfamiliar skills in blackwork embroidery drawn from the Islamic world of Iberian Moors, and refers disparagingly to 'Your Spanish needle, and your pressing iron' (1.312). It is not entirely clear whether the 'pressing iron' was another prop used in early performances. Yet even at its start, the play hints at its ending as Arden suspects the means by which he will eventually, after several attempts, be killed. It is a work of unique craftsmanship.

'Sealed and subscribed with his name': A note on authorship

As Kingsley-Smith and Richardson's chapters note, much of *Arden of Faversham*'s critical history has been dominated by the question of authorship. While anonymity was a normal condition for drama printed in the late sixteenth century, *Arden* has since 1770 borne the mixed burden of an association with Shakespeare. As Janet Wright Starner and Barbara Howard Traister argue, 'if the creation of "Anonymous" is suddenly revealed as the lost child of a canonical author, that text undergoes a rags-to-riches rise in popularity, becoming the center of attention for a space, much cared for and about'.[24] Particularly in recent years, with the inclusion of the play in the *New Oxford Shakespeare* and a wide range of studies claiming Shakespeare's hand in at least the central section of the play, the Shakespeare connection has seen *Arden of Faversham* return to prominence in the wars over canonicity and attribution methods.[25]

The literature attempting to pin down the author(s) of *Arden of Faversham* is vast, as surveyed by Will Sharpe, Peter Kirwan and Catherine Richardson among others, as well as in Richardson's contribution to this collection.[26] While the obvious end point of attribution scholarship is to ascertain who wrote the text, the various quantitative and qualitative methodologies employed in the service of authorship claims have done a great deal to explore the structure and linguistic intricacies of the play, turning close reading into forensic reading. Key candidates at the time of writing other than Shakespeare include Christopher Marlowe, Thomas Kyd, Thomas Watson and Samuel Rowley, and a related set of arguments has advanced the possibility that the play is a collaboration between two or more authors.[27] It is perhaps apt that this book is published with a cover that includes the branding of the 'Arden Shakespeare' and a reproduction of an engraving taken from Kyd's *The Spanish Tragedy*, associating our play non-committedly with those two authors.

Yet as Kirwan has argued in his study of the critical fortunes of those plays consigned to the so-called 'Shakespeare Apocrypha', an overwhelming focus on authorship can lead to neglect of the plays on their own merits.[28] One of the most fascinating anomalies of *Arden of Faversham*, attested to in Bradley's chapter for this collection, is that no other anonymous play from the period has enjoyed so rich and full a stage history. Indeed, where the Royal Shakespeare Company has often felt the need to attach authors to its productions of rarely staged plays as part of its marketing strategy, the 2014 production of *Arden of Faversham* was unusually advertised without any claim of a Shakespeare connection. Whether the play was single-authored or collaborative and whether or not Shakespeare contributed to it, the play has consistently succeeded on its own terms as a theatrically vibrant black comedy. Further, while we offered no steer to our contributors about their own approach to questions of authorship, none found that attribution was essential (or even in many cases germane) to the arguments they wished to make.

The authorizing of documents with names is key to the action of *Arden of Faversham*; within the first few lines, Franklin passes to Arden the deeds to the Abbey lands, 'sealed and subscribed with his [the Duke of Somerset's name] and the King's' (1.6), the attribution so pointed that it gets its own fourteener in the middle of an iambic pentameter speech. However, as we noted at the start of this introduction, the ambiguous prints left by the bodies of those who have left us may be indicative of conflicting truths of ownership. With this in mind, and in the spirit of the play's own title page, this collection of essays advances no claim concerning the play's authorship. Instead, we encourage our readers to engage with the rich scholarship setting out the various hypotheses, while also acknowledging that one of the unique contributions made by *Arden*'s critical and theatrical history is to prove that a play needs no author – or other points of glozing stuff – in order to be 'gracious to the ear or eye' (Epilogue 16).

Notes

1 Josh Caldicott's forthcoming PhD thesis, *Audience Responses and Playhouse Epilogues: Staging the Labour of Early Commercial Theatre, 1578–1625*, offers an extensive survey of epilogue conventions in the period. Peter would like to thank Josh for many stimulating conversations about epilogues during the preparation of this volume.

2 See Kingsley-Smith, below, 16.

3 The wardmote inquest gives the date as 15 February 1551. See M. L. Wine, ed., *The Tragedy of Master Arden of Faversham* (London: Methuen, 1973), 160.

4 The play's epilogue claims that Shakebag was eventually murdered in a Southwark street as he made his way to the house of Edward Seymour, Lord Protector, in Greenwich (Epilogue 3–5).

5 Wine, *Arden*, 161–3.

6 Henry Machyn, *The Diary of Henry Machyn, Citizen and Merchant-Taylor of London, 1550–1563*, ed. J. G. Nichols (London: The Camden Society, 1848), 4.

7 Wine, *Arden*, 148.
8 The play had first appeared in print in a pirated form by Abel Jeffes. See Catherine Richardson, ed., *Arden of Faversham* (London: Bloomsbury, 2022), 92–3. All copies of the illegal edition were later destroyed.
9 See Wine, *Arden*, xl–xli.
10 *Arden of Faversham* (London, 1592), A1r, (modernized).
11 Emily O'Brien, '*The Tragedy of Master Arden of Faversham*, True Crime, and the Literary Marketplace of the 1580s', *Shakespeare Studies* 45 (2017): 113.
12 Rob[ert] Yarington, *Two Lamentable Tragedies* (London, 1601), A1r.
13 Ibid., B4r, C4r.
14 Stanley Wells, ed., *A Yorkshire Tragedy*, in *Thomas Middleton: The Collected Works*, ed. Gary Taylor and John Lavagnino (Oxford: Clarendon Press, 2007), 452.
15 Charles Nicholl, 'Fetch the Chopping Knife', *London Review of Books* 43, no. 21 (4 November 2021). Available online: https://www.lrb.co.uk/the-paper/v43/n21/charles-nicholl/fetch-the-chopping-knife (accessed 16 February 2022).
16 For the ballad with lineation, see Wine, *Arden of Faversham*, 164–70.
17 Tiffany Stern, 'Shakespeare the Balladmonger?', in *Rethinking Theatrical Documents in Shakespeare's England*, ed. Tiffany Stern (London: Bloomsbury, 2020), 216–38.
18 Una McIlvenna, 'The Power of Music: The Significance of Contrafactum in Execution Ballads', *Past & Present* 229, no. 1 (2015): 60–5.
19 Emma Whipday, *Shakespeare's Domestic Tragedies: Violence in the Early Modern Home* (Cambridge: Cambridge University Press, 2019), 16–17. On the implications of the way that scholarship has used this sub-genre to centre white characters and 'the critical implications of racial familiarity', see David Sterling Brown, '"Hood Feminism": Whiteness and Segregated (Premodern) Scholarly Discourse in the Post-Postracial Era', *Literature Compass* 18, no. 10 (2021).
20 Robert W. Daniel and Iman Sheeha, 'Introduction' to 'Door-bolts, Thresholds, and Peep-Holes: Liminality and Domestic Spaces in Early Modern England', *Early Modern Literary Studies* 29 (2020): 2.
21 Catherine Belsey, 'Alice Arden's Crime', *Renaissance Drama* 13 (1982): 84.
22 Brown, '"Hood Feminism"', 4.

23 Raphael Holinshed, *The Firste [Laste] Volume of the Chronicles of England, Scotlande, and Irelande* (London, 1577), 4M5r-4M5v.
24 Janet Wright Starner and Barbara Howard Traister, 'Introduction', in *Anonymity in Early Modern Drama*, ed. Janet Wright Starner and Barbara Howard Traister (Farnham: Ashgate, 2014), 4.
25 Gary Taylor, John Jowett, Terri Bourus, and Gabriel Egan, eds, *The New Oxford Shakespeare* (Oxford: Oxford University Press, 2016).
26 Will Sharpe, 'Authorship and Attribution', in *William Shakespeare and Others: Collaborative Plays*, ed. Jonathan Bate and Eric Rasmussen (Basingstoke: Palgrave Macmillan, 2013), 652–9; Peter Kirwan, *Shakespeare and the Idea of Apocrypha* (Cambridge: Cambridge University Press, 2015), 146–52; Richardson, *Arden of Faversham*, 37–51.
27 Though see Salkeld, 'Shakespeare in *Arden:* Pragmatic Markers and Parallels', *Shakespeare Survey* 76 (2023), forthcoming.
28 Kirwan, *Apocrypha*, 5.

1

The critical backstory

Jane Kingsley-Smith

There are no eyewitness accounts of the first performances of *Arden of Faversham* (written *c.* 1588, published 1592). The earliest critical response must therefore be found in the tragedy itself. In the opening line of the epilogue, the character Franklin observes to the audience: 'Thus have you seen the truth of Arden's death', and we might well imagine the actor leaning on that word 'truth'.

The facts of the historical murder on which the play is based, which had occurred some forty years earlier, could be found in a range of historical records, most famously in Raphael Holinshed's *Chronicles of England, Scotland and Ireland* (1577, 1587), where the author had gone to some lengths to emphasize the authority of his own account: 'having the instructions delivered to me by them that used some diligence to gather the true understanding of the circumstances'.[1] Franklin's onstage assertion of truth might thus be a celebration of the play's accuracy with regard to Holinshed, perhaps in contrast with other plays on the subject. In 1577, Edward White had entered in the Stationers' Register *A Cruel Murder Done in Kent*, which was probably based on the Arden story, and in 1579 *Murderous Michael* had been played before Elizabeth I.[2] Both plays, now lost, might have encouraged *Arden* to advertise itself as a more accurate account.

Alternatively, Franklin's 'Thus have you *seen* the truth' (italics mine) might take aim at those historical sources themselves, implying the superiority of a visceral, multisensory theatrical experience over cold chronicle reading. The sight (and perhaps the smell)[3] of Arden's blood, which 'cleaveth to the ground and will not out', despite Susan's best efforts at washing it away, or Alice's attempts to scrape it with her nails (14.259), created a more shocking effect than anything in the written account, where Holinshed describes a fairly easy process of stain removal.[4]

But perhaps the epilogue's most important critical reflection relates to the play's frustration of generic conventions:

Gentlemen, we hope you'll pardon this naked tragedy,
Wherein no filed points are foisted in
To make it gracious to the ear or eye;
For simple truth is gracious enough
And needs no other points of glozing stuff. (14–18)

Tragedy should be aimed at a noble audience, who will be pleased by rhetorical figures ('filed points') and visual spectacle – the OED cites 'to gloze' as 'to clothe with specious adornment' (3c). Not only has *Arden* lacked these but the epilogue is conspicuously awkward metrically: the trochaic rhythm of 'this naked tragedy', within this iambic speech, symbolizes the play's generic irregularity. The speech is also marked by repetition ('points . . . points', 'gracious . . . gracious'), which has sometimes been taken as evidence that the whole text is a memorial reconstruction – a potentially garbled version of the 'true' play[5] – but which also suggests a certain dogged insistence on plain fact, consistent with 'naked tragedy'.

It is, then, already clear that there will be no 'simple truth' to be found in *Arden of Faversham*. The critical history that follows takes a broadly chronological approach to the play's reception across 400 years, while arguing for a number of recurring themes or critical approaches. These are: the difference between *Arden* the play and 'The Tragedy of M. Arden' as a historical event; the inclusion of *Arden* among Shakespeare's apocryphal plays; the emergence of Alice as a tragic victim; the interpretation and reinterpretation of 'domestic tragedy'; and, finally, the sympathy between *Arden*'s murderers and Shakespeare's villains.

Notorious murder, obscure play

From its first publication, the distinction between what the play means and what the events that it portrays mean is unclear. The title page of the 1592 Quarto reads:

> The Lamentable and True Tragedie of M. Arden of Feversham in Kent. Who was most wickedlye murdered, by the meanes of his disloyall and wanton wyfe, who for the love she bare to one Mosbie, hyred two desperat ruffins [sic], Blackwill and Shakbag, to kill him. Wherin is shewed the great malice and discimulation of a wicked woman, the unsatiable desire of filthie lust and the shamefull end of all murderers.[6]

We cannot tell, here, what is meant by 'Wherin': the meaning of the events themselves or the play's interpretation of them? The notoriety of the real-life murder, and its interpretation as a tragedy of such momentous cultural importance that, even seventy years later, it would 'never be forgotten', overshadowed and partly obscured the critical response to the play.[7] When John Rainolds referred to Arden's murder in *A Defence of the Judgement of the Reformed Churches* (written *c.* 1597, published 1609), he asked 'how can [a husband] choose but live still in fear and anguish of mind, lest [his wife] add drunkenness to thirst, and murder to adultery – I mean, lest she serve him as *Clytemnestra* did *Agamemnon*, as *Livia* did *Drusus*, as Mrs Arden did her husband?'[8] As the author of *The Overthrow of Stage-Plays* (1599), Rainolds was unlikely to invoke a contemporary stage play as his authority, if he even knew about it. He cites 'Hollinshed. Chron. in K. Edward the Sixth' in the margin as his source.[9]

Similarly, the ballad, which seems to have derived from *Arden*, offers very little critical perspective on the play itself. *The Complaint and Lamentation of Mistresse Arden of Feversham of Kent* (1633) must have derived from the play, because of details they both share, not found in the main source. In the scene where Alice tries to poison her husband, for example, Holinshed reports that she contaminated the milk, and then when Arden complained about the taste 'she tilted it over with her hand'.[10] By contrast, the play and the ballad agree that it is broth that is poisoned, and the stage direction seems to prompt the poem: '*Then she throws down the broth on the ground*' (1.366 SD); 'At which inrag'd, I flung it on the ground'.[11] In both the play and the ballad, Alice suggests to Greene that he should not commit the murder himself, but hire some villains to do it for him; this is Greene's own idea in Holinshed. But perhaps most interesting is the way in which the ballad follows the play's epilogue, to bizarre effect, when the speaker suddenly reverts to the third person to produce the list of executions: 'His wife at Canterbury, she was burnt / And all her flesh and bones to ashes turn'd'.[12] Mrs Arden has briefly forgotten that she is speaking about herself.

If the ballad offers any critical response to the play, it does so by reducing its psychological and moral complexity. It avoids any discussion of Arden's avarice and his alienation of his neighbours through the withholding of land, rendering him more innocent, and his wife's betrayal more inexcusable. Furthermore, this Mrs Arden makes no attempt at self-defence, calling herself a 'vile wretch' and welcoming divine retribution for them all: 'For God our secret dealings soone did spy, / And brought to light our shamefull villainy'.[13] Hence, even a spin-off from the play, which purports to allow Mistress Arden to speak for herself, pulls the narrative back into its familiar shape, derived from Holinshed, whose marginal comments in the 1587 edition repeatedly emphasize the crimes of Mistress Arden without offering any attempt to understand them: 'O Importunate & bloody minded strumpet!'; 'Mark what a countenance of innocence and ignorance she bore after the murdering of her husband', 'This she did to colour her wickedness which by no means was excusable'.[14]

It has recently been argued that one of the reasons why Shakespeare might have been brought in to work on *Arden of Faversham* was his ability to write sympathetic (and long) speeches for female characters.[15] This would suggest a potential audience interest in Alice as something more than the stereotype of a monstrous woman, but there is no evidence of this in the 1590s–1630s. The final quarto of the play was printed in the same year as the ballad, 1633, and at the behest of a woman stationer, Elizabeth Allde, whose husband had entered it in the Stationers' Register on 29 June 1624, but who subsequently died (we presume of natural causes). The title page of Q3 includes the colophon: 'Printed by ELIZ. ALLDE dwelling neere Christs-Churche', but the play retains its moralizing title: 'Wherin is shewed the great malice and discimulation of a wicked woman, the unsatiable desire of filthie lust ...'. Presumably this remained a crucial selling point.

One final example of the extent to which the early history of *Arden* is overshadowed by the historical account is George Lillo's adaptation for the eighteenth-century stage. This play, which was written by Lillo and John Hoadley for performance in 1759, was printed posthumously in 1762 with a prologue which echoes *Arden*'s epilogue by focusing on the play's lack of grandeur and poetic artifice:

> *The Tragic Bard apes not the Epick fire,*
> *On Fancy's wing still aiming to aspire:*
> *In Nature's palace simple, great, and plain,*
> *Inrich'd and crowded* ornament *were vain:*
> Embellishment *does but distract the mind,*
> *Which* Art *should never to* minuteness *bind.*

But despite Lillo having obviously read *Arden of Faversham*, no mention of the earlier play is made in this prologue, which only focusses on its historical source:

> *To night, your Bard, from your own annals shews,*
> *A dreadful story of domestic woes:*
> *From facts he draws (his picture's from the life)*[16]

Recognition of the merits and otherwise of the Elizabethan play would emerge gradually as *Arden of Faversham* became a disputed part of Shakespeare's canon, although this authorship question brought with it its own critical limitations.

Arden and Shakespeare's apocryphal plays

The first hint that Shakespeare might have written *Arden* appears in 1656 – or nearly so. In a catalogue appended to a quarto of *The Old Law*, Shakespeare's name is listed next to *The Arraignment of Paris*, just above *Arden of Faversham*, but given the evidence of mislineation elsewhere in the list, it seems likely that the bookseller, Edward Archer, intended to place Shakespeare's name next to *Arden*.[17] There was otherwise no reason to connect the play with Shakespeare before 1770. The 1592, 1599 and 1633 quartos had all treated *Arden* as anonymous; it was not included by the King's Men in the First Folio of 1623; and although the third Folio (1664) 'added seven Playes, never before Printed in Folio', which would become the basis of Shakespeare's 'apocrypha', these did not include *Arden*.

The first printed assertion that Shakespeare was the play's author came from someone with a vested interest: Edward Jacob, a resident and local historian of Faversham, who published in 1770 *The Lamentable and True Tragedie of M. Arden, of Feversham, in Kent ... With a Preface; in which some Reasons are offered, in favour of its being the earliest dramatic Work of Shakespear now remaining. . . .* He begins by enlisting the posthumous support of an early eighteenth-century editor who had proven more open to the apocryphal plays:

> Mr. *Rowe*, in the Preface to his Edition of *Shakespear's* Plays, says it 'would be without Doubt a Pleasure to any Man curious in Things of this Kind, to see and know what was the first Essay of a Fancy like his'. It is therefore submitted to the discerning Critics to determine, whether this anonymous Tragedy of *Arden* is not the Thing so long wished for. The Reasons of this seeming extraordinary Proposition arise from the Similarity of this, with the later, and known Compositions of *Shakespear*, and the *Time* when it was printed, viz. in Quarto A. D. 1592.[18]

Jacob would be the first critic to identify verbal parallels between *Arden* and other Shakespeare plays. His brief list of comparisons is drawn overwhelmingly from the middle comedies; *Othello* is the only tragedy mentioned, and there are no allusions to the history plays.[19] In this respect, he fails to acknowledge the sympathy between *Arden* and *Macbeth* that subsequent critics would invoke. Nevertheless, Jacob identifies some Shakespearean connections that would gain traction later on:

> the very Name of *Arden*, from which Family he descended by the Female Line, might probably stimulate him to try his early Powers, on the Subject of this shocking Murder, so largely described by *Hollingshed*.[20]

The early date of the play also explains its lack of attribution:

> Why it never was printed with his other Plays, may be presumed to have happened, from its not having been acted in that House,

from whence his Plays were collected and published by his Brother-performers, so many Years afterwards.[21]

Jacob's attribution of *Arden* to Shakespeare did not initially gain many devotees, perhaps because it ran counter to the project of Bardolatry in the late eighteenth century. As Peter Kirwan explains, 'Jacob's *Arden* associated Shakespeare with a provincial and domestic register, only a year after the nationalisation of Shakespeare at the Jubilee and Garrick's subsequent mockery of provincial folk'.[22] What changed was the increased nineteenth-century appetite for Shakespeare biography, anticipated here by Jacob's desire to fill the gap in Shakespeare's early playwriting career with *Arden* and to gain a fuller sense of what 'a Fancy like his' might do first. Also significant to *Arden*'s critical discovery was a willingness to separate off the so-called 'apocryphal' plays from the authorized, undisputed canon, so that the former could be studied without danger of contamination; and the desire to add more and more plays to this 'apocryphal' canon on the assumption that the more 'pseudo-Shakespeare' one had the better.

After a period during which the forty-three-play canon had lost visibility and influence, editors in the latter half of the eighteenth century proved more willing to edit (and therefore engage critically with) the apocryphal plays. In 1760, Edward Capell made a case for *Edward III* as Shakespeare's work – despite lacking any external evidence other than a 1656 catalogue entry – and he provided the first critical edition of the play in his collection, *Prolusions, or, Select Pieces of Antient Poetry*. His subsequent edition of Shakespeare's dramatic works failed to include the apocryphal plays, but he was keen, nevertheless, to discuss the possible expansion of the canon, putting the number of plays either written by or associated with Shakespeare at fifty-eight, including 'seven . . . that were publish'd . . . in his life-time, and all with his name; and another seven, that are upon good grounds to be imputed to him'.[23] In the footnotes, Capell lists the latter as *The Arraignment of Paris*, *The Birth of Merlin*, *Fair Em*, *Edward III*, *Mucedorus*, *The Merry Devil of Edmonton* and *The Two Noble Kinsmen*. Perhaps if Jacob's attribution had predated *Prolusions*, *Arden* might have found a place in the list, though it would still not have made it into the edition. Capell argued that Shakespeare had been planning his own complete works before his death and had deliberately omitted all of these plays, as 'weak and idle pieces, the productions of his green years, wantonness or inattention'.[24]

Arden's fortunes would only start to change under the enthusiastic patronage of the German Romantic critics, Ludwig Tieck and August Wilhelm von Schlegel. Tieck had begun translating passages from early modern plays, including Jonson and Beaumont and Fletcher, as material with which to gloss his early translations of Shakespeare.[25] However, he became convinced of the legitimacy of the apocrypha, expanding the Shakespearean canon to as many as sixty-seven plays, among which was *Arden of Faversham*. He oversaw its translation into German by his daughter, Dorothea, and printed it in the first volume of *Shakspeares Vorschule* (1823). Tieck also lobbied Schlegel on behalf of the apocryphal plays in their correspondence, and in a lecture of 1810, Schlegel mentioned *Arden*, though he admitted to not having read it:

> It is said to be a tragedy on the story of a man from whom the poet descended by the mother's side. This circumstance, if the quality of the piece be not too directly at variance with its supposed authorship, would afford an additional probability in its favour. For such motives were not without their influence on Shakespeare: thus he treated with a manifest partiality, Henry VII, who had bestowed lands on his forefathers for services performed by them.[26]

But if the influence of Schlegel and Tieck would garner *Arden* more serious critical attention than it had yet enjoyed, this was achieved negatively at first, with English critics hastening to read the play so that they might more comprehensively reject the German expanded canon and repudiate German aesthetic judgement. Thus, we find William Hazlitt quoting from Schlegel in his section on 'Doubtful Plays' in *Characters of Shakespeare's Plays* (1817), but also forming his own qualitative judgement: '*Arden of Feversham* contains several striking passages, but the passion which they express is rather that of a sanguine temperament than of a lofty imagination; and in this respect they approximate more nearly to the style of other writers of the time than to Shakespeare's'.[27]

By mid-century, *Arden* was starting to make further claims upon the Shakespeare canon and upon mainstream critical studies, partly because no one could agree who else might have written it. When

Charles Knight included *Arden* in the 'Doubtful Plays' volume of *The Pictorial Edition of Shakspere* (1838–41), he agreed with the *Edinburgh Review*, that 'both in conception and execution it is quite unlike even [Shakespeare's] earliest manner', but he was less sure that 'its date cannot possibly be removed so far back as the time before which his own style had been demonstrably formed'.²⁸ Knight continued:

> Do we then think that *Arden of Feversham* belongs to the early manhood of Shakspere? We do not think so with any confidence; but we do think that, considering its date, it is a very remarkable play, and we should be at a loss to assign it to any writer whose name is associated with that early period of the drama, except to Shakespeare.²⁹

Henry Tyrrell took up the question when he too published *Arden* in *The Doubtful Plays of Shakspere* (1853), part of J. O. Halliwell's *The Complete Works of Shakespeare* (1851–3). He asked himself, 'does this drama possess those qualities which are to be expected in an early work of Shakspere's? Has it his sweetness and grace of language, his depth of thought, his knowledge of character, his occasional aphorisms, rhyming couplets, and frequent quibbles?'.³⁰ He answered in the negative – 'I do not assert this tragedy to be the work of Shakspere; my belief is rather on the other side' – but he, nevertheless, admired 'this powerful drama, the work of a poet of no common power, whoever he was'.³¹ Perhaps most decisive and influential was A. C. Swinburne, who included *Arden* in his section on the 'Comic and Romantic' period in *A Study of Shakespeare* (1880), thereby ostensibly extricating it from any 'Doubtful' category. Swinburne began by berating J. P. Collier for suggesting that *A Warning for Fair Women* might be by Shakespeare, and for 'rejecting without compromise or hesitation the belief or theory which would assign to the youth of Shakespeare the incomparably nobler tragic poem in question [i.e. *Arden*]'.³² He went on to demolish Collier's argument, while building up the merits of *Arden*, particularly its characterization, so that 'I cannot but finally take heart to say, even in the absence of all external or traditional testimony, that it seems to me not pardonable merely nor permissible, but simply logical and reasonable, to set down this poem, a young man's work on the face of it, as the possible work of no man's youthful hand but Shakespeare's'.³³

At the turn of the century, C. F. Tucker Brooke's *The Shakespeare Apocrypha* (1908) would as confidently assert the opposite opinion. But by identifying the plays as a discrete collection, which illuminated the qualities of the acknowledged canon, he alleviated much of the anxiety that had surrounded these plays and opened them up to further analysis on their own terms. *Arden* is one of the five plays whose Shakespearean authorship one might seriously entertain – indeed, Tucker Brooke identifies it with *The Two Noble Kinsmen* as being in the 'very first rank of the extra-Shakespearian drama'[34] – but although there are 'gorgeous poetic passages that grip the imagination and overwhelm the reason', none of these five plays has the necessary consistency: 'There is nothing fitful or transitory about the true Shakespearean quality'.[35] There are other objections to *Arden*, which illuminate things that Shakespeare does not do. For example, *Arden* is one of the seven apocryphal plays which represent dramatic genres in which Shakespeare did not write, 'and which there is inherent reason for supposing he would have avoided'.[36] *Arden* and *A Yorkshire Tragedy* may be 'remarkably fine instances' of 'the dramatic record of contemporary crime', but this is a category which, 'because it concerns itself primarily with actual physical horror, can scarcely rise to the level of high art'.[37] Similarly, although Alice Arden is 'a character of the first magnitude' who speaks 'the finest poetry . . . in the play', Tucker Brooke finds her to be 'vulgarised and degraded by the two vices which are most distinctively un-Shakespearean, and which, perhaps, it is hardest of all to pardon in a tragic heroine: purposeless revolting deceit and coarseness of feeling'.[38]

Looking back, Tucker Brooke's response to *Arden* is prophetic in at least a couple of ways. Through his willingness to see the apocryphal plays as composed by many hands, with Shakespeare as a 'reviser or elaborator' – 'During his long and many-sided connexion with the stage, the poet-manager would doubtless have had occasion to retouch and refine much of the inferior work which came to his company'[39] – Tucker Brooke bridged the gap between 'real' Shakespeare and pseudo-Shakespeare and paved the way for *Arden's* admission into the Shakespearean canon in the twenty-first century. His critical focus on Alice Arden as a cynosure, holding together a play that is 'otherwise hopelessly disjointed and ineffective',[40] and speaking the most Shakespearean parts of the text, was likewise important. However, Tucker Brooke's insistence that

Alice 'has little of the sustained delicacy of tragic feeling'[41] would not be the final word on Alice's character. An important aspect of *Arden*'s critical history is the perception that her tragedy might yet transcend the faults of her play.

The tragedy of Alice Arden

The incomprehensibility of Mistress Arden was an intrinsic part of her notoriety from the earliest historical accounts of the murder, but it would be some time before the enigmatic personality of the dramatic character, Alice Arden, received its due. Two of the nineteenth-century critics discussed earlier, Henry Tyrrell and A. C. Swinburne, were among the first to devote attention to her predicament.

In *The Doubtful Plays of Shakspere*, Tyrrell is moved to rapturous flights of rhetoric by the struggle that he finds in Alice, whose resemblance to Lady Macbeth, though not directly invoked, clearly underpins his vision of her as demonically possessed:

> Alice is in a waking dream of sensuality and horror all through the play; she is haunted by an ever-present and tyrannical suggestion. These whisperings of savage and revolting desires breed a kind of wolf-like madness in her, an impatient thirst for her husband's blood. Nor does this hideous dream vanish until after the murder is accomplished; then the darkness of soul in which she has been so long enveloped, suddenly disappears; the gibbering phantoms who have tempted her, fade away in the departing gloom, like shrouded ghosts into their graves, and she awakes to a sense of her guilt and the horrors of her situation.[42]

For Tyrrell, the dramatist's achievement is to make the murderess 'still look like a woman', so that after her confession 'we experience for her a sensation of pity'.[43] This was a striking contrast with other critiques, which had argued that the crime and the criminals were so disgusting that there could be no elevated, tragic sensations provoked by their fall. Tyrrell disagrees, however, singling out Alice's appeal to Mosby, when she anticipates their disaster: 'I pray thee, Mosby, let our springtime wither; / Our harvest else will yield but loathsome weeds. / Forget, I pray thee, what hath passed betwixt us, / For now I blush and tremble at the thoughts' (8.66–9). For Tyrrell, this is a moment of intense psychological and eschatological drama:

> It is the crisis of her fate, the hallowed moment when a light from heaven seems to show the wanderer her way back into the right path; her better angel beckons her from that sad vale of pitfalls and ruin; she hesitates, her eyes fall again upon her paramour; the evil influence returns in all its overwhelming force, the struggle is over; – a star has fallen from heaven, and a soul is lost.[44]

Various aspects of this critique bode well for *Arden*'s future. First, although he does not think Shakespeare wrote the play, Tyrrell's language is inflected by Sonnet 144 and its 'better angel', thereby drawing an unconscious connection with other parts of the canon. His use of the present tense and his attention to Alice's gestures ('her eyes fall again upon her paramour') also make a strong case for the play in performance. Tyrrell did not have a chance to see it on stage – he laments the fact that only Lillo's has been recently performed[45] – but he clearly encourages his readers to think that it would be powerful and affecting in performance. And finally, his choice of a passage from scene eight anticipates its importance to *Arden*'s reputation, as the scene which seems to have the strongest Shakespearean imprint and which would become the foundation of the play's inclusion in the Shakespeare canon.

For Swinburne, the characterization of Alice is the bedrock of his argument for the play's Shakespearean authorship. He observes the elevation 'to the tragic height of the situation and the dramatic level of the part . . . unfalteringly sustained from first to last by the wife and the murderess of Arden'.[46] To Tyrrell's picture of Alice's moral struggle, however, Swinburne adds a deeper sense of her victimhood. He condemns Mosby's behaviour to Alice after his wounding in the quarrel with Arden (13.84): 'Such an exhibition of currish cowardice and sullen bullying spite increases rather our wondering pity for its victim than our wondering sense of her degradation.'[47] He uses the comparison with Lady Macbeth, and Dionyza from *Pericles*, to reinforce Alice's sympathetic appeal:

> Deeply dyed as she is in bloodguiltiness, the wife of Arden is much less of a born criminal than these. To her, at once the agent

and the patient of her crime, the victim and the instrument of sacrifice and blood-offering to Venus Libitina, goddess of love and death – to her, even in the deepest pit of her deliberate wickedness, remorse is natural and redemption conceivable. Like the Phaedra of Racine, and herein so nobly unlike the Phaedra of Euripides, she is capable of the deepest and bitterest penitence – incapable of dying with a hideous and homicidal falsehood on her long polluted lips. Her latest breath is not a lie but a prayer.[48]

Alice Arden's victimization, by her own passions or by other people, seems to be a theme that has particularly endured the passage of time, and it is worth looking ahead to the modern reinvention of this trope before we return to the missing century in the following sections.

Catherine Belsey's essay, 'Alice Arden's Crime' (1982), differs in many ideological and methodological respects from the work of Tyrrell and Swinburne, but it is also their heir in its focus on Alice's subjection. For Belsey, this is not attributable to supernatural soliciting, or the desires of the flesh, but the religious and political institution of marriage, found to be in crisis during the 1590s when the debate about divorce was particularly intense: 'Alice Arden, held in the chain of bondage which is marriage, in a period when liberty is glimpsed but not authorized, is caught up in a struggle larger than her chroniclers recognise.'[49] *Arden*'s inconsistencies make more sense in this historical context: both condemning the murdering wife, who 'blush[es] not at [her] husband's death' (14.256), and praising her for her heroism in arranging the murder: 'Wherein, trust me, you show a noble mind / That rather than you'll live with him you hate / You'll venture life and die with him you love' (1.267–71). And the compulsive reiteration of Alice's crime, of which the play is just one example, hints at the cultural work performed by her scapegoating.

Belsey's argument would have a long critical reach, inspiring a range of feminist interpretations of Alice's victimization, including the suggestion that the historical Alice was raped.[50] Belsey's assertion that the murder of Arden is 'a defiance of absolutism'[51] also encouraged a more sustained engagement with *Arden* as a political play, discussed in the next section. But there was a sense in which this victimization might have gone too far. One curious lacuna in Belsey's argument is the fact that Alice, as a character in the *Chronicles* and in the play, does not simply 'procure and witness the murder of her husband'[52] but also repeatedly stabs him herself. Frank Whigham later corrected this oversight, arguing of the play's murder scene that

> it is Alice's reaction that is most striking of all. She is unwilling, in the end, to leave the actual killing to her hirelings or even to Mosby. Arden's groan seems to infuriate her: perhaps she is angry that he still needs killing, or perhaps it is his agony and its uncomprehending claim on her that enrages her. For whatever reason, she seizes the weapon in her own hands, and curses Arden as she strikes, for *hindering* her: his greatest offence is that of having dared to think to limit her will, to exercise marital authority over her (who is to rule herself).[53]

Other critics have complicated Alice's depiction as a victim by stressing her manipulation of her own self-image. Frances E. Dolan compares *Arden* with contemporary murder pamphlets which attempted to justify the wife's behaviour by describing her experience of domestic abuse. This is something Alice does herself, insisting to Greene that 'When he is at home, then have I froward looks, / Hard words, and blows to mend the match withal', and that he keeps 'in every corner trulls' (1.493–6). However, the play provides no evidence to support this: '*Arden* presents Alice as a skilful performer who manipulates possible versions of the murderous wife narrative ... in order to secure sympathy and avoid blame.'[54] Julie R. Schutzman expands this perspective to argue that the play itself, between the conception and execution of the murder, creates a suspended moment which 'functions for Alice as a limited realm of freedom and agency, a realm of autonomy made possible by the very fact of its impermanence'.[55] Alice's skillset includes her manipulation of spectatorial control, redirecting her neighbours' attention towards Arden as cuckold: 'While Mosby sees Alice's tendency to "acquaint each stranger with our drifts" [1.576] as a severe threat to their safety, Alice seems intuitively to understand both the impossibility of relegating their affair to a strictly private realm and the benefits to be derived from its inevitably "public" nature.'[56] Alice loses control of the spectators' gaze and therefore their judgement, when Arden the cuckold is replaced by 'Sweet Arden, smeared in blood and filthy gore' (14.333).[57] Nevertheless,

Schutzman notes that the absence of Alice's execution onstage implies that her 'earlier freedom and the disorder it engendered' is not ultimately erased.[58]

What both Dolan's and Schutzman's critiques depend on is not just the feminist, revisionist reading offered by Belsey, but a new investigation of domestic tragedy, which further enhanced the status and visibility of *Arden*, and it is to this development that we must now turn.

Arden as political–historical–domestic Tragedy

In 1943, Henry Hitch Adams argued that 'domestic tragedy' was a more reputable dramatic genre than had previously been thought, with a canon of more than twenty lost plays. It was 'a tragedy of the common people, ordinarily set in the domestic scene, dealing with personal and family relationships, rather than with large affairs of state, presented in a realistic fashion, and ending in a tragic or otherwise serious manner'.[59] Among those that had survived, *Arden* was declared 'the most famous of all Elizabethan domestic tragedies'.[60]

In Keith Sturgess's subsequent collection, *Three Elizabethan Domestic Tragedies* (1969), *Arden* appeared alongside *A Yorkshire Tragedy* and *A Woman Killed with Kindness*, on the basis of the same shared features: 'A domestic tragedy . . . is a play with a sad end which seriously depicts crime and punishment in the lives of ordinary men, often dwelling on the disruption of normal family relationships. It is set in London or the provinces, and it teaches a simple moral lesson.'[61] The simplicity of its message would later be called into question, as would Sturgess's insistence that the ephemeral, journalistic nature of these plays meant that 'Nothing could be more different from the noble intentions of high tragedy or the durability of serious art'.[62] Nevertheless, Sturgess defended reading these plays as part of a tradition of 'warning literature', in which 'writers happily combined the triple intention of reporting, moralizing and titillating, and produced a wealth of sub-literature of considerable interest to the literary specialist and the social historian'.[63]

In the 1990s, a series of monographs would extend considerably the cultural value and political significance of domestic tragedy.[64]

Key to these studies was an understanding of the post-Reformation 'reinvention of the household as a unit of social control, the empowerment of the householder as defender of political order, and . . . the promulgation of an enabling ideology of domestic patriarchalism'.[65] This function of the early modern household was brought into sharp relief when it became a space of domestic crime. As Dolan explained, where a man killing his wife or servant was accused of murder, a wife or servant who killed their husband/master was accused of 'petty treason' – treason because 'killing a husband or master challenged patriarchal hierarchical social order, as killing a wife or a servant did not'.[66] If this understanding of the politics of the domestic would alter perceptions of *Arden*, the play was also attributed with reshaping the landscape of early modern drama. Lena Cowen Orlin describes the play as

> proceed[ing] from the early modern principles that there was no unimportant household and that, by virtue of analogy, Alice Arden's crime achieved a notional parity with the opening of trade with Moscovy, the defeat of the Spanish Armada, and, most especially, the assassination of an anointed king. It established the precedent that found private matters fit for dramatic representation and institutionalised in a new medium an operative domestic ethos.[67]

Richard Helgerson takes these historiographic implications further in his essay, 'Murder in Faversham: Holinshed's Impertinent History' (1996). He demonstrates the movement in the early modern period from an expansive kind of chronicle history, including sensational 'domestic' murders, to Thomas Blundeville's more exclusive definition in 1574: 'Histories be made of deeds done by a public weal or against a public weal, and such deeds be either deeds of war, of peace, or else sedition and conspiracy.'[68] For Helgerson, Thomas Arden's murder becomes 'a point of intersection for a whole range of once marginalised and still suspect historical interests, interests that were repressed by the post-Holinshed redefinition of history but that have lately returned in force to call that humanist enterprise into question'.[69] In fact, the story of Arden has an equally strong case for being included in the category of 'public' or state history, thereby demonstrating the fragility of these distinctions. Drawing on Orlin's extensive research into the real-life murder, Helgerson points out that Alice was the stepdaughter of Sir Edward North (though this fact is suppressed in both the *Chronicles* and the play), who became Lord Chancellor of the Court of Augmentations, which administered land coming from the dissolution of monasteries. It was from Sir Thomas Cheyne that Arden purchased Abbey lands and a house near the Abbey gate, which set him at enmity with his neighbours in Faversham. Either North or Cheyne was probably responsible for Arden's gaining the post of King's customs officer for the port of Faversham. Arden is thus 'a public man, a servant of the Crown, a man whose participation in the royally dictated dissolution of church property and in nationally determined partisan and sectarian conflict may have helped bring on his death'.[70]

This re-evaluation of Arden's murder had two major impacts on the reception of the play. On the one hand, *Arden* gains status as a historiographic intervention: 'First brought to the London stage at the same time as the earliest "chronicle history" plays, Alice's murder of Arden has continued to stand for an alternative history of England, a history focussed not on the court and the battlefield, as were those other plays, but on the household and the local community.'[71] On the other hand, those socioeconomic and class tensions which laid the ground for the real-life murder are increasingly detected in the play. Chief among these is the play's concern with land. The play opens with Franklin congratulating Arden on being given 'All the lands of the Abbey of Faversham' (1.5) and ends with Arden occupying 'that plot of ground' as a bloody imprint (Epilogue 10). This preoccupation partly reflects a change in the perception of land and the duties of the landlord, as explored by Garrett A. Sullivan,[72] but it also alludes specifically to the historical act, which allowed land to become the property of men like Arden in the first place.

In *Seizures of the Will in Early Modern English Drama* (1996), Frank Whigham avers that '*Arden of Faversham* is a history play. It situates various local seizures – of land, of wife, of life, of self – in the aftermath of Henry VIII's seizure of the monasteries in the 1530s ... *Arden of Faversham* seems to me a direct dramatic study of the fruits of the Dissolution'.[73] For Whigham, this act 'unleashed a deluge of social flux deriving from the suddenly moveable status of hitherto rock-solid land, once the uncirculating sign of the aristocracy, now increasingly a commodity',[74] and it underpins the chaos that marks the lives of all three protagonists. Whigham is one of the first to observe the parallelism between Arden and Mosby, as social upstarts, advanced by patronage, who 'use women's bodies for their promotion'.[75] He also notes the language of property and legal bonds which shapes Alice's relationships to both men. His observation that 'The actions of the lovers are not simply erotic, but social and political and ideological. Or, perhaps, better to say, we must ask once again about the *range* of the category for the erotic for Elizabethans'[76] would prove extremely influential.

Michael Neill acknowledges his debts to Whigham, not least in his perception that 'Readings of *Arden of Faversham* that concentrate on the sexual intrigue between Alice and Mosby . . . habitually overlook the imbrication of erotic desire (and indeed of affective relations generally) with the appetite for property and status that is everywhere apparent in the play'.[77] Giving the text the same level of meticulous attention as Whigham, Neill explores how the play's unstable status relationships are figured by the careful use of personal pronouns 'you' and 'thou', and allusions to the gentle status of characters. 'Master Mosby', for example, is used by Alice 'not only to deceive her husband by suggesting a properly courteous distance between herself and their visitor, but (more subversively) to imply an equality of status between lover and husband'.[78] Neill argues powerfully for the value of close reading as a historicist tool, and its ability 'to reveal the sheer linguistic density of [*Arden*'s] dramatization of conflicts over rank and status'.[79] However, this close reading approach, by critics schooled in the complexities of the Shakespearean text, also had another consequence for *Arden*. Not only did such a forensic level of discussion heighten the status of the play, it was also the case that the more critics attended to the text of *Arden*, particularly the dialogue between Mosby and Alice in scene eight, the more Shakespearean it sounded.

Arden and Shakespearean villainy

In 1963, Sarah Youngblood published an essay which asserted that '*Arden of Feversham* is one of the most remarkable dramas of the sixteenth century, and yet it has suffered the neglect of critics for over 300 years'.[80] She attributed this neglect partly to an underestimation of its tragic effect. While the play undoubtedly fulfils the definition of tragedy 'as a death or retribution for sin', she argues that

> the nature of tragic retribution in the play is complicated by the psychological and mental form which it takes in the lives of the two secondary tragic characters, Alice and Mosbie. And it is at this level of psychological action that the play achieves its most impressive effects, since it is, like *Macbeth* (a play which it resembles in striking ways), a study of the effects of evil on the personalities of those who perpetrate it.[81]

Youngblood goes on to draw detailed comparisons between the language of Mosby and Macbeth, particularly the former's opening soliloquy in scene eight: 'The whole passage is a dramatically effective delineation of the way in which "blood will have blood", and evil will seed evil'.[82] At the end of the play, Mosby is 'in the same state of emotional paralysis that marks the end of Macbeth's tragedy. Macbeth's apathetic "I have liv'd long enough" is paralleled by Mosbie's final statement: "But bear me hence, for I have lived too long".'[83]

Also convinced of the similarities between *Arden* and *Macbeth* was MacDonald P. Jackson, as developed initially in his BLitt thesis, 'Material for an Edition of *Arden of Feversham*' (Oxford, 1963), and then in a number of articles published over the next five decades.[84] Like Youngblood, Jackson focusses his attention on scene eight and the parallels between Mosby and Macbeth, not only the sense both men have of the irrevocability of their actions, 'I am in blood stepped in so far . . . ',[85] but also Mosby's misconstruing of Alice's comment, 'It is not love that loves to murder love' (8.59) in light of his recent plan to kill her:

> This portrayal of the workings of a guilty mind is so subtle that most actors and directors fail to register the subtext here. . . . There is a similar effect in *Macbeth*. After Duncan's murder, Macbeth's startled question 'Whence is that knocking?' (2.2.54) as the noise sounds 'within' (that is, offstage within the tiring house; see 2.2.53 SD), reflects his guilty fear that the murder has no sooner been performed than discovered.[86]

Beyond the *Macbeth* connections, Jackson offered a wealth of evidence for the similarity in verbal style between *Arden* and

Shakespeare's early work; for example, Mosby's description of his anxiety that 'nips me, as the bitter north-east wind / Doth check the tender blossoms in the spring' (8.5–6) is identified as peculiarly Shakespearean, echoed in *The Taming of the Shrew*, *The Rape of Lucrece*, *Love's Labour's Lost* and the *Sonnets*.

Jackson's thesis was absorbed and frequently referred to by M. L. Wine in his 1973 edition of the play; he noted, for example, that the former's 'detailed analysis of scene viii confirms the Shakespearean quality of its language'.[87] Jackson's discussion of another Shakespearean image cluster on muddied fountains also encouraged Wine to alter the text of *Arden* (8.132–4) in a way that strengthened the Shakespearean parallel. But Wine's edition altered the perception of *Arden* in other ways too. *Contra* Sturgess, he distinguished it from the 'Other "news plays" . . . [which] do point a simple moral in a very heavy hand', arguing that 'one of the more remarkable features of *Arden* . . . is its lack of didacticism', and quoting Louis Gillet:

> What is most astonishing is that the author refrains from judging: he never declaims nor moralizes in any way. In this horrible affair of conspiracy and murder, he keeps throughout the unified and transparent tone of simplicity; he shows all these impurities, these follies, as they appear in the bright light of intelligence. We are astonished to find them so natural.[88]

Wine also commented on the sensitivity and realism with which all the characters are sketched: 'there is hardly even a minor character, let alone a major, whom he has not enlivened in some way, sometimes by just a brief touch',[89] and this applied particularly to the hired villains, Black Will and Shakebag.

The entry for the play in the Stationers' Register, dated 3 April 1592, had defined the play as 'The tragedie of Arden of Feuersham & blackwill', suggesting the importance of the latter villain. Nevertheless, both he and Shakebag had been habitually dismissed by critics as 'stage-murderers, painted from the outside, rather than portrayed with personal and psychological difference'.[90] Wine contextualized these villains as Elizabethan masterless men, and therefore of historical interest, and paved the way for Frank Whigham's extraordinary close reading of Black Will. Whigham not only revealed the villain's fantasies of bestowing hospitality and enjoying professional employment but also illuminated the text's surprisingly subtle insights into Black Will's mental and physical suffering: 'we need to register how softness and anguish survive within this brutal and degraded man before we can hear him truly'.[91]

By the close of the twentieth century, criticism of *Arden* still has some way to go before it addresses Sturgess's desire for a critique that 'keeps its artful theatricality fully in view'.[92] The incorporation into the Shakespearean canon proposed by Jackson in 1963 will also have to wait until the next century, when *Arden* comes to reshape the perception of Shakespeare's early career.[93] In the meantime, the play has travelled a considerable critical distance from its early obscurity and can now boast of showing more – much more – than 'the great malice and discimulation of a wicked woman, the unsatiable desire of filthie lust and the shamefull end of all murderers'.

Notes

1 Quoted in Martin White, ed., *Arden of Faversham* (London: Bloomsbury, 2007), 113.

2 Arthur F. Kinney, 'Authoring *Arden of Faversham*' in *Shakespeare, Computers, and the Mystery of Authorship*, ed. Hugh Craig and Arthur F. Kinney (New York: Cambridge University Press, 2009), 79.

3 On the olfactory nature of the early modern theatre experience, and on the use of animal blood as an effect, see Holly Dugan, '"As Dirty as Smithfield and as Stinking Every Whit": The Smell of the Hope Theatre', and Lucy Munro, '"*They eat each others' arms*": Stage Blood and Body Parts', both in *Shakespeare's Theatres and the Effects of Performance*, ed. Farah Karim-Cooper and Tiffany Stern (London: Bloomsbury, 2013), 73–93, 195–213.

4 'Then they made clean the parlour, and took a clout and wiped where it was bloody', *Chronicles*, quoted by White, *Arden of Faversham*, 119.

5 See M. L. Wine's argument: 'To an extraordinary degree the play repeats itself; whole lines and phrases, sometimes with only the slightest variation, recur. . . . Repetitions contribute significantly to one of the most characteristic features of reported texts: the poor state of their versification.' *The Tragedy of Master Arden of Faversham* (London: Methuen, 1973), xxvii. An alternative argument is made by Goran Stanivukovic, who notes that repetitive figures of speech are a particular feature of Shakespeare's early plays and

that he exploited 'his period's propensity for, and love of, iterative rhetoric'. See 'The Language and Style of Early Shakespeare', in *Early Shakespeare, 1588–1594*, ed. Rory Loughnane and Andrew J. Power (Cambridge: Cambridge University Press, 2020), 81.

6 *Arden of Feversham* (London, 1592), STC (2nd ed.), 733.

7 John Taylor takes examples of murders linked with adultery from 'Our English Chronicles', including '*Arden of Feversham* and *Page of Plinmouth*', whose 'Murders are fresh in memory, and the fearfull ends of their Wives and their Ayders in those bloudy actions will never be forgotten'. *The Unnaturall Father, of the Cruell Murther Committed by [one] John Rowse . . . upon two of his owne Children* (London, 1621), n. p.

8 *A Defence of the Judgement of the Reformed Churches. That a Man may Lawfullie not Onlie Put Away his Wife for her Adulterie but also Marrie Another* (1609), 88.

9 Ibid.

10 *Chronicles*, quoted by White, *Arden of Faversham*, 114.

11 *The Complaint and Lamentation of Mistresse Arden of Feversham* (London, 1633), STC 732, 156.

12 Ibid., 157.

13 Ibid.

14 *Chronicles*, quoted by White, *Arden of Faversham*, 118–20.

15 See Terri Bourus, '*Arden of Faversham*, Richard Burbage, and the Early Shakespeare Canon', in *Early Shakespeare, 1588–1594*, ed. Rory Loughnane and Andrew J. Power (Cambridge: Cambridge University Press, 2020), 213.

16 *Arden of Feversham: An Historical Tragedy: Taken from Holingshead's Chronicle* (London, 1762), A2.

17 See W. W. Greg, 'Shakespeare and *Arden of Feversham*', *Review of English Studies* 21, no. 82 (1945): 134–6.

18 Edward Jacob, ed., *The Lamentable and True Tragedie of M. Arden, of Feversham, in Kent* (Faversham: J & J March, 1770), iii.

19 Ibid., vi.

20 Ibid., iii.

21 Ibid.

22 Peter Kirwan, *Shakespeare and the Idea of Apocrypha: Negotiating the Boundaries of the Dramatic Canon* (Cambridge: Cambridge University Press, 2015), 44.

23 Edward Capell, ed., *Mr William Shakespeare his Comedies, Histories, and Tragedies* (London, 1768), 1.9–10.
24 Ibid., 47.
25 See Edwin H. Zeydel, 'Ludwig Tieck as a Translator of English', *PMLA* 51, no. 1 (1936): 222.
26 A. W. Schlegel, *A Course of Lectures on Dramatic Art and Literature*, trans. John Black (London: Henry G. Bohn, 1846), 445–6.
27 William Hazlitt, *The Round Table and Characters of Shakespeare's Plays* (New York and London: J. M. Dent & Sons, 1936), 357.
28 Charles Knight, ed., *The Pictorial Edition of Shakspere* (London: Charles Knight & co., 1838–41), 260.
29 Ibid.
30 Henry Tyrrell, ed., *The Doubtful Plays of Shakspere* (London: John Tallis & Co., 1853), 374.
31 Ibid., 376, 373.
32 A. C. Swinburne, *A Study of Shakespeare* (London: Chatto & Windus, 1880), 129.
33 Ibid., 141.
34 C. F. Tucker Brooke, ed., *The Shakespeare Apocrypha: Being a Collection of the Fourteen Plays Which Have Been Ascribed to Shakespeare* (Oxford: Clarendon Press, 1908), vi.
35 Ibid., xiv.
36 Ibid., xii.
37 Ibid.
38 Ibid., xv.
39 Ibid., xii.
40 Ibid., xv.
41 Ibid.
42 Tyrrell, *Doubtful Plays*, 375.
43 Ibid.
44 Ibid., 376.
45 Ibid., 373.
46 Swinburne, *A Study of Shakespeare*, 134.
47 Ibid., 139.
48 Ibid., 140.
49 Catherine Belsey, 'Alice Arden's Crime', *Renaissance Drama* 13 (1982): 98.

50 Lena Cowen Orlin, *Private Matters and Public Culture in Post-Reformation England* (Ithaca: Cornell University Press, 1994), 79–84.
51 Belsey, 'Alice Arden's Crime', 100.
52 Ibid., 83.
53 Frank Whigham, *Seizures of the Will in Early Modern English Drama* (Cambridge: Cambridge University Press, 1996), 117.
54 Frances E. Dolan, *Dangerous Familiars: Representations of Crime in England, 1550–1700* (London: Cornell University Press, 1994), 52.
55 Julie R. Schutzman, 'Alice Arden's Freedom and the Suspended Moment of *Arden of Faversham*', *Studies in English Literature, 1500–1900* 36, no. 2 (1996): 290.
56 Ibid., 302.
57 Ibid., 310.
58 Ibid., 311.
59 Henry Hitch Adams, *English Domestic or, Homiletic Tragedy, 1575 to 1642* (New York: Columbia University Press, 1943), 1–2.
60 Ibid., 101–2.
61 Keith Sturgess, ed., *Three Elizabethan Domestic Tragedies* (Harmondsworth: Penguin, 1969), 14.
62 Ibid., 9.
63 Ibid., 10.
64 See, for example, Dolan, *Dangerous Familiars*; Orlin, *Private Matters*; and Viviana Comensoli, *Household Business: Domestic Plays of Early Modern England* (Toronto: University of Toronto Press, 1996).
65 Orlin, *Private Matters*, 17.
66 Frances E. Dolan, 'The Subordinate('s) Plot: Petty Treason and the Forms of Domestic Rebellion', *Shakespeare Quart*erly 43, no. 3 (1992): 317.
67 Orlin, *Private Matters*, 76.
68 Thomas Blundeville, *The True Order and Methode of Wryting and Reading Hystories* (London, 1574), 147.
69 Richard Helgerson, 'Murder in Faversham: Holinshed's Impertinent History', in *The Historical Imagination in Early Modern Britain: History, Rhetoric and Fiction, 1500–1800*, ed. Donald R. Kelley and David Harris Sale (Cambridge: Cambridge University Press, 1997), 135.
70 Ibid., 153.
71 Ibid., 157.

72 Garrett A. Sullivan, '"Arden Lay Murdered in that Plot of Ground": Surveying, Land, and *Arden of Faversham*', *ELH* 61, no. 2 (1994): 231–52.
73 Whigham, *Seizures of the Will*, 63.
74 Ibid., 77.
75 Ibid., 69.
76 Ibid., 73.
77 Michael Neill, '"This Gentle Gentleman": Social Change and the Language of Status in *Arden of Faversham*', *Medieval & Renaissance Drama in England* 10 (1998): 90–1.
78 Ibid., 87.
79 Ibid., 76.
80 Sarah Youngblood, 'Theme and Imagery in *Arden of Feversham*', *Studies in English Literature* 3, no. 2 (1963): 207.
81 Ibid., 208.
82 Ibid., 210–11.
83 Ibid., 212–13.
84 See, for example, 'Shakespearean Features of the Poetic Style of *Arden of Faversham*', *Archiv fur das Studium der reveren Spracher and Literaturen* 230 (1993): 279–304, and 'Shakespeare and the Quarrel Scene in *Arden of Faversham*', *Shakespeare Quarterly* 57, no. 3 (2006): 249–93.
85 Jackson, 'Shakespeare and the Quarrel Scene', 250, n. 3.
86 Ibid., 251.
87 Wine, *Arden of Faversham*, lxxxix.
88 Ibid., lx–lxi.
89 Ibid., lxvi.
90 John Addington Symonds, *Shakspere's Predecessors in the English Drama* (London: Smith, Elder & Co., 1884), 357.
91 Whigham, *Seizures of the Will*, 96. See also Martin Wiggins's acknowledgement: 'At 270 lines, Black Will's part is one of the longest in the play' and his discussion of the character's complexity in *Journeymen in Murder: The Assassin in English Renaissance Drama* (Oxford: Clarendon Press, 1991), 62, 80–1.
92 Sturgess, *Three Elizabethan Domestic Tragedies*, vii.
93 See *Arden*'s role in the redefinition of Shakespeare's early career in *Early Shakespeare, 1588–1594*, ed. Rory Loughnane and Andrew J. Power (Cambridge: Cambridge University Press, 2020).

2

The performance history

'Poor wench abused by thy misgovernance' – *Arden of Faversham* on stage

Kath Bradley

Regrettably, as with so many plays of the time, little is known of *Arden of Faversham* in performance during the early modern period. The wide-ranging interest generated by the scandalous events of 1551 is evidenced by both the unprecedented inclusion of such 'a private matter' in Holinshed's *Chronicles* and the proliferation of ballads such as '[The] complaint and lamentation of *Mistresse Arden* of *[Feu]ersham* in *Kent* . . . ' (1633). It is, therefore, reasonable to assume that the play, written approximately thirty-seven years after the event and within living memory for some, would have been performed and revived on a regular basis. M. L. Wine's suggestion of an association with Pembroke's Men is supported by Roslyn Lander Knutson, who convincingly argues that ownership of the play probably moved from Pembroke's Men to the Chamberlain's Men during the early 1590s.[1] Martin Wiggins too asserts that 'it seems very likely that the role of the

Ferryman was written for the same actor who played the Mower in *Edward II* and Dr Pinch in *The Comedy of Errors*, and who was a hired man in Pembroke's Men'.² However, in the absence of further documentary evidence, all theories about the play's earliest stage history remain conjectural. Despite Catherine Richardson's reference to a local newspaper, *The Kentish Post*, dated Christmas Eve 1729 reporting '[we] hear from Feversham, that a Company of their Townsmen design to Act the Tragedy of ARDEN, at the Roe-buck joining that Place', the earliest documented professional staging is of a single performance of Lillo and Hoadley's sanitized adaptation at Drury Lane on 12 July 1759.³ Tom Lockwood further notes that 'the play was regularly performed in Faversham itself at least from the eighteenth century', with the most recent production taking place in the garden of Arden's house.⁴ This was staged by the What You Will Theatre Company in 2000, directed by Ian Garner, and was rather harshly judged by Ian Shuttleworth, who saw no value in the production other than the frisson of the setting itself.⁵

The modern performance history of *Arden of Faversham* is often almost as obscure as the play's origins. While there have been a handful of professional productions, the play's performance history has largely been amateur and provincial, leaving sparse records. However, as this chapter will show, the play has still provided rich material for companies exploring the wider canon of early modern drama. During the twentieth and twenty-first centuries, *Arden*'s generic fluidity has offered a variety of options to directors and performers alike, whether addressing contemporary social issues or emphasizing the play's comic potentialities. The 1592 quarto describes it as 'The Lamentable and True Tragedie of M. Arden of Feversham in Kent', but since that time there has been a movement away from presenting what Peter J. Smith describes as 'a rather dry morality tale, reinforcing the importance of a well-governed (that is, patriarchal) family'.⁶ Instead, Emma Whipday considers it 'offers a potent challenge to the conventional ideal of early modern femininity: Alice is neither chaste nor silent, and the play grants her the opportunity of a vocal defence of her own unchastity'.⁷ The humour inherent in the many failed attempts to kill Alice's unwanted husband has also, increasingly, been a feature of modern productions.

Arden and post-war feminism

It is surprising that such a dramatized account of a horrific domestic tragedy, albeit with strong comic elements, lay dormant until the twentieth century. There are no recorded performances in the UK until a BBC radio broadcast produced by Raymond Raikes in September 1952, followed by a 1953 production by the student dramatic society Worcester Buskins, directed by Michael Hughes, in the grounds of Worcester College, Oxford.[8] Beyond these early productions, however, *Arden* has since proved to be of particular interest to female directors, and issues of gender have been at the forefront of most post-war theatrical productions of a play that places a woman centre-stage while examining her disruptive role within a patriarchal society. Throughout the post-war period, coinciding with the inception of what became the Women's Liberation Movement, productions were generally set within the medieval or early modern period, with heavily corseted costuming designed to reflect the constraints placed on women of the time. Reacting against such constraints, female directors have reflected the times of political and social change in which they were staged, presenting Alice as a woman struggling for self-determination. This struggle led J. C. Trewin to describe Adrianne Finch's Alice for the Margate Stage Company in 1963 as a 'she-devil', possibly reflecting his personal misogynistic concerns about the rise of the feminist movement during the early 1960s.[9] The most influential of these post-war productions was Joan Littlewood's 1954 staging at the Theatre Royal, Stratford East, London for the newly created left-wing Theatre Workshop. Littlewood's textual choices reflected her ongoing concerns with issues of class and gender. Removing the denouement in which Alice is arrested, tried and sentenced, the production challenged the image of a repentant woman accepting her fate; instead, Littlewood presented no clear binary distinction between right and wrong, leaving the audience to weigh the play's moral ambiguities. Critics were divided by such textual emendations. While Trewin considered it 'no doubt wise ... to do away with all the straightening-out and clearing up at the end', Kenneth Tynan recorded his shock that 'the retribution scene was omitted', thus excising the title page's promise to demonstrate 'the shameful end of all murderers'.[10] Littlewood's production successfully transferred to the Paris Festival and toured Scandinavia, but critical focus remained on Barbara Brown's Alice throughout. *Le Figaro* felt 'we can understand the lover who gives in to her, and the husband who lets himself be deluded', while *Combat* evoked the Garden of Eden when describing Alice as 'whirling around her husband like a serpent'.[11]

When offered the opportunity to direct *Arden* for the RSC at London's Roundhouse, Buzz Goodbody seized the opportunity to disrupt ongoing patriarchal assumptions about the narrative, placing emphasis not on the murder attempts but 'on the sensual energy of the text and individual passion, particularly that of the character of Alice Arden', described by Eric Porter as 'a wife compounded of lust and cruelty'.[12] John Peter of *The Sunday Times* considered Dorothy Tutin's Alice 'full of finely controlled frenzy' while bemoaning Goodbody's fear of 'wholehearted histrionics'.[13]

The suppression of women's sensuality by early modern religious pressures was highlighted in Katie Mitchell's 1990 staging with Classics on a Shoestring at the Red Lion, London. Mitchell, possibly influenced by Alice Arden's transgressive offer to burn a prayer book (8.116), chose not to highlight the play's relevance to feminist struggles within the twentieth century. Instead, she used Alice to present the difficulties faced by early modern women, emphasizing the religious pressures that have supported patriarchal suppression of women throughout history. The intimacy of the studio at the Red Lion, along with candlelit scenes illuminating frescoes of haloed saints, created a sense of claustrophobic religious intensity, further emphasized by the murderers muttering together while kneeling side-by-side in church. The year 2006 saw another small London venue, the White Bear, host a Skin and Bones Theatre production, directed by Samantha Potter, again with an almost bare, candlelit staging that created the sense of a morality play in which 'Zoe Simon's Alice, smiling cruelly through the gloom, left Chris New's Mosby alternating between ecstasy and self-doubt'.[14]

In 2014, *Arden* returned to the RSC, and to parallels with the feminist movement, as part of a *Roaring Girls* season described by Emma Whipday as 'designed to foreground strong female characters and to engage with questions of gender in contemporary society'.[15] Reflecting a theatrical zeitgeist that saw Maxine Peake play Hamlet at Manchester's Royal Exchange and Phyllida Lloyd's all-female company stage *Henry IV* at London's Donmar that year, the Swan season comprised four plays illustrating a theatrical history of transgressive women: Webster's *The White Devil*; Ford, Dekker and Rowley's *The Witch of Edmonton*; *The Roaring Girl* by Middleton and Dekker; and an unattributed *Arden of Faversham*. Despite the season's overt feminist agenda in staging plays featuring strong women challenging societal, that is patriarchal, strictures defining acceptable female behaviour, Polly Findlay transposed the action into the recognizably modern world of reality TV. Rather than an independent woman, Sharon Small's Alice was presented as merely a sexy trophy wife and Mosby a social-climbing Cockney wide boy, with jacket sleeves rolled up, swaggering across the stage before briefly removing his ever-present chewing gum to kiss his lover passionately. Despite costuming that emphasized Alice's reliance on her sexuality in order to achieve fulfilment, in giving her the epilogue, Findlay offered Alice the opportunity to accept her fate and acknowledge the consequences of her quest for self-determination for her fellow conspirators.

Wider social issues

Until this production, readings of the play had tended to underplay Arden's cruelty to his neighbours, the social impact of the enclosure of previously communal land and the concomitant wider social issues. The 2014 RSC production's emphasis on the commodification of human life was prefigured in a pre-show sequence set in an Amazon-like warehouse where workers robotically packed consumerist tat into boxes bearing Alice's image, while Arden sat aloof counting his profits. While the updated setting attempted to find a modern equivalent for the devastation of early modern enclosure, the trivialization of the play's economic underpinnings failed to evoke the impact of Arden's capitalist practices on the lives of others. The production did, however, encapsulate images of toxic capitalism, female empowerment and a sense of divine justice in a single scene. Findlay's casting of Lizzie Hopley as 'Mrs Reede', passing the powerful and prophetic curse to the widowed Mistress Reede rather than her husband, emphasized the danger in which single mothers, often the most vulnerable in society, find themselves. Wearing a cross around her neck, she implored 'God, I beseech thee, show some miracle / On thee or thine in plaguing thee for this. /

That plot of ground that thou detains from me ... / Be ruinous and fatal unto thee' (13.30). In response, replacing the word 'knave' with the specifically gendered (and inherently more dangerous) term 'witch' when dismissing her as 'the railingest witch in Christendom', Franklin not only invoked disastrous consequences for Reede but also ironically accorded her curse more power.[16]

Terry Hands, who has directed *Arden* three times, had prefigured Findlay's emphasis on the power of the curse, albeit in less gendered terms. His first production was staged in 2004 at the RSC's Other Place, then little more than a tin shack. The claustrophobic nature of the venue became an integral part of the mise-en-scène, emphasized by actors 'prowling around and speaking outside the auditorium itself, thus immuring the audience too'.[17] There were clearly supernatural forces at work, and his Dick Reede (Ken Bones) recalled that 'the whole production was imbued with a sense of otherworldliness'.[18] Bones also recalled that Hands considered the curse to be pivotal, 'sealing Arden's fate and emphasizing the personal and political fact that, despite Arden's claim "By letters patent from his majesty" to previously held common land ... the stakes were high for Reede; his need and sense of injustice palpable'. Despite Hands's concerns with the political and social issues surrounding class distinctions, many critics, reflecting the casual sexism of the period, still conflated actor and role in assessing to what extent Jenny Agutter's Alice failed to live up to male expectations of the character's sensuality. John Barber described Agutter as creating a 'swift-moving impression of gleaming malevolence' which missed 'the full sensuality of the young voluptuary'.[19] In contrast, Irving Wardle considered her Alice 'a radiantly honest young wife, full of wide-eyed admiration for all the strong men around her'. Some critics overlooked the political and societal concerns of the production, considering that Hands had directed the play 'as a genial farce', making 'no attempt to articulate the social element, nor Alice's feminist position as a woman determined to "rule myself"'.[20] *The Spectator* compared the failed assassination attempts of Black Will and Shakebag to 'the latest Ealing comedy *The Ladykillers*, with bungling thugs describing what dreadful deeds they will perform next time'.[21]

In 2010, Hands again directed *Arden*, this time as Artistic Director of The Emlyn Williams Theatre (now Theatr Clwyd Cymru). Once more, the 'black comedy' was, as Victor Hallett for *Theatre in Wales* confirmed, 'the strongest thread emerging from Terry Hands' fast-moving production'.²² Hands placed the emphasis firmly on the contrast between the murderous passion of the lovers and the humorous ineptitude of their hired assassins. Despite his analysis of the play's achievement of its aims 'to interest, to instruct, and occasionally to amuse', it was amusement which was foregrounded in critical responses.²³ Interviewed by Peter Kirwan, Hands described each murder attempt as 'a masterpiece of comic invention'.²⁴ Kirwan's own review considered Hands's direction as conceptualizing 'the play as black comedy, emphasising the ludicrous nature of the repeated failed murder attempts while allowing us to mock the more severe evil-doers'.²⁵ Despite this, elements of Hands's RSC production remained, with one reviewer noting that 'muted set and lighting . . . added to the eerie atmosphere and lawlessness of sixteenth-century England', but the production merely hinted at the causes for such social unrest with a brief mention of 'disgruntled farmers'.²⁶ Hands had previously been invited to direct the play in Zürich in 1992, with Gerhard Mack dismissively reporting 'there is little to see on stage', while Alice is merely a 'one-dimensional furie'.²⁷

The struggle between comic and serious treatments that divided responses to Hands's productions also afflicted other directors' versions. Findlay's 2014 production over-emphasized the text's comic potential, to the detriment of the play's subtleties. As Eoin Price highlighted, 'the assassination attempts, orchestrated by Black Will (Jay Simpson) and Shakebag (Tony Jayawardena) were . . . brilliantly funny' but the humour 'sometimes felt over-egged'.²⁸ The humour extended through the final, barbaric murder and even beyond the epilogue. In a hurried attempt to hide Arden's body, the lovers rolled it into a packing case bearing Alice's image and hauled it above the sightline of the arriving dinner guests. As Mosby toasted the arrivals, his champagne glass caught blood dripping from the suspended 'coffin'. Undermining the sombre tone of the epilogue, the dark humour of the production was reinforced as Joe Cocker and Jennifer Warnes's *Up Where We Belong* echoed around the auditorium as the audience exited.

Humour was also a key feature of Em-Lou's 2010 production at the Rose Theatre, Bankside, London, as emphasized by the omission of the word 'Tragedy' in promotional literature, although the strapline described it as 'The oldest tragic comedy'. Kirwan accepted that 'tragic comedy . . . is not a bad description of a play which is unavoidably funny for much of its first three quarters'. Although fully embracing the play's comic potential, director Peter Darney did so without sacrificing the final tragedy, while Kirwan considered that playing Clarke as a 'much older painter... drooling over a diminutive [Susan]' reminded the audience that 'this is primarily a play about transactions in which women are treated as just one more desirable commodity'.[29]

Non-anglophone productions

For this very English domestic tragedy, overseas productions, particularly those in translation, are literal outliers. Interestingly, for such a localized, domestic and suburban tragedy with its specific English place names and customs, the play has a performance history in mainland Europe beyond that of Hands's Swiss production, and IMDb contains brief details of a French language 1960 TV movie entitled *Arden de Faversham*, directed by Marcel Bluwal.[30] A 1984 production at the Theatre de Ville, Paris, directed by the controversial Romanian Lucian Pintilie was entitled *Arden din Kent*. In addition, two productions have taken place in Romania itself.

The first, *Arden din Kent*, was directed by Aureliu Manea at the Ploieste State Theatre in 1978. The second, entitled *Arden din Feversham*, was directed by Dragoş Galgoţiu at the Odeon Theatre, Bucharest, in 2003. The theatre's website gives a detailed history of the original narrative and its transmission through Holinshed, Stow's *Chronicles* and Faversham's Wardmote Book. It also outlines the authorship question and addresses the play's generic fluidity, stating '*Arden of Feversham* is the first domestic tragedy in English literature, inspired by common people's lives. It can be regarded also as the first comical thriller, because of the grotesque actions of Black Will and Shakebag, that are a counterpoint to the passionate relation [sic] of Alice and Mosby'.[31] This passion is clearly demonstrated in images of Alice available on the website's photo gallery. She is partially clothed throughout and is often in physical contact with her male accomplices. Cristina Iamandi's review for *Gardianul*, quoted on the website, describes the impact of the production:

> *Arden of Feversham* captivates the audience by the spectacular style of stage directing. Dragoş Galgoţiu is helped by Vittorio

Holtier's Renaissance-like setting . . . A great admirer of Shakespeare, Galgoţiu emphasises Shakespearean elements: the lust ending in murder, the deep fog, the premonitory dreams, all of them meant to trouble the spectator.[32]

In keeping with Romanian theatrical tradition, Holtier's images confirm the spectacular nature of the production, while the political resonances of the text in Romania during this period are apparent. The set comprised a 'robust and sophisticated wooden structure' combining 'the idea of London Bridge and also the mediaeval atmosphere' of the production.[33] A stage covered in heavy eiderdowns represented the suffocating domestic environment in which Alice was confined, while hinting at the passion that drew her to murder. This narrow world was dominated by images of rural work embodied in an immense waterwheel. The combined forces of Alice's confinement in this domestic world and the impact of Arden's ownership of the land on which the farm workers depend collided to bring about the play's ultimate tragedy. *Arden*'s concern with the commodification of common land and human labour to further enrich the powerful must have resonated in a country that had suffered the consequences of Ceauşescu's systematization of rural land. Over 3,000 villages were deemed non-viable and phased out, while 'over eight square kilometres in the heart of Bucharest were destroyed . . . and some 40,000 people were forced to leave their homes with only a twenty-four-hour notice'.[34]

Amateur and academic explorations

In 1978, the Bristol Revunions, described in 2014 as 'the University of Bristol's premier (and only) sketch comedy troupe', took their production to the Edinburgh Fringe Festival, directed by Martin White, whose edition of the play was first published in 1982.[35] He had previously directed *Arden* in Manchester, though there is little further archival detail about either production. The programme comprised a cast list, including future RSC artistic director Gregory Doran (who later commissioned Findlay's RSC production) as Clarke, and a brief synopsis of the original narrative alongside a statement that

> *Arden of Faversham* . . . has mainly been the quarry of authorship seekers, and while Shakespeare's claims may still be worthy of

serious consideration, the play is strong and rich enough to stand examination – and performance – for its own sake.[36]

White's edition, however, offers no authorial attribution, ascribing the play to 'Unknown'.

Other productions, particularly in the United States, have also focussed on the authorship question. Appropriately, the first full US production was staged by the Shakespeare Society of America in 1985, at the Globe Playhouse, Los Angeles, alongside *Edward III* and *The Puritan* as part of an ongoing project to present all fourteen plays in C. F. Tucker Brooke's *The Shakespeare Apocrypha* (1908). Joseph H. Stodder's *Shakespeare Quarterly* review is naturally, given the nature of the project, concerned with authorial attribution. He speculates that audience members may have found the text's episodic nature reminiscent of Thomas Kyd, identifies possible traces of Marlowe's 'mighty line' and suggests that 'the poetry, as well as the innovative realistic characterisation, could also have been Shakespeare's', concluding that such tentative possibilities would leave many 'convinced of the hazards of asserting attribution, exciting though the prospects might be'.[37] Stodder also records that director Bennett E. McClellan 'retained the integrity of the play's text, period, and dramatic conventions'. Emphasizing the importance of performing lesser-known texts, he concludes that 'the action of *Arden*, which in reading often appears uneven and disjointed, was satisfyingly fluent in performance'.[38] Stodder was impressed by Melodee Spevack's Alice, whom he describes as revealing 'the elemental passion that fires her unrelenting efforts to murder her husband' conveying her 'revulsion for the one man and desire for the other'. Ultimately, though, he felt that 'some of the most memorable scenes' were those involving Black Will and Shakebag. Acknowledging the difficulty for directors and actors in presenting the contrast between their previous farcical failures to commit murder and the ultimate tragedy of their success, he accepts that the culmination of their efforts proved 'sensational, if not altogether tragic'.[39]

In 2014, a North American audience was offered the opportunity to see three further productions of *Arden*, again with an academic impetus: the first by Willing Suspension Productions, sponsored by Boston University English Department and the Center for Humanities, and available on YouTube.[40] The company, comprising graduate and undergraduate students from the department, is dedicated to producing rarely seen early modern plays while also stressing their relevance to contemporary social issues. With a majority of female actors, some male roles (Michael, Greene) were played by women as men, while other male roles were presented as women: Adam Fowle, landlord of the Flower-de-Luce, became a landlady named Ada, while Shakebag was played as a young woman who flirted with Bradshaw while pickpocketing his wallet. The Jack Hylton Band soundtrack and the costuming was clearly inspired by Jack Clayton's 1974 film *The Great Gatsby*, a period setting selected not to investigate the status of women in the United States at that time but rather to reflect wider social and economic issues. Describing the 1920s as a decade that 'carries connotations of excess and social inequality in the American cultural imagination', Emily Gruber Keck (one of three co-directors) explained it was intended also to draw parallels with the then-current Occupy Wall Street protests by examining 'the play's imaginative investment in economic inequality'.[41] The production also emphasized the comedy of the many failed murder attempts right up to the point of the conspirators' success. At that point, the murder was shockingly graphic, in order to raise the dramatic and moral stakes for both the characters involved and an audience complicit in their enjoyment of the previous failures.

In the same year, The Hidden Room in Austin, Texas combined fully blocked and costumed staged readings of *Arden* alongside *Mucedorus* and *The Merry Devil of Edmonton* as part of *The Apocrypha Project: A Sampling of Suspected Shakespeare*, echoing the Shakespeare Society of America's earlier project to examine Shakespeare's putative links to all three. *Arden* was revived in 2020 as a full production available on Vimeo.[42] Although the other two plays were staged in their own period, director Beth Burns presented *Arden* within a specific non-Renaissance setting, choosing like Findlay to produce a recognizably twenty-first-century aesthetic, with 'a modern feel of self-as-celebrity about it'. She explained, 'Alice certainly exemplifies many aspects of those modern celebrities, such as Kim Kardashian, who rely on social media to validate their decisions and, indeed, their very existence'.[43] Like Kardashian's Twitter posts, Alice reveals her inner thoughts to servants and selected neighbours, placing herself at the centre of the world she inhabits, while simultaneously decrying how 'these my narrow-prying neighbours blab' (1.135) like contemporary internet trolls.

The final US production of 2014 was performed by the Hoosier Bard Group, based at Indiana University-Purdue University, Indianapolis (IUPUI), and directed by Terri Bourus with Gary Taylor as dramaturg. The company was created as an experimental theatre research group in order to support the work of the *New Oxford Shakespeare*, with Bourus explaining that 'every play we do has an editorial crux linked to it: a crux that can only be solved through performance'.[44] The title, *Arden of Fevershame*, drew on the spelling used throughout the quarto, which the editors in their edition argue 'suggests an allegorical place of fever and shame'.[45] Bourus linked the play to 1940s and 1950s film noir as a way of demonstrating the play's generic fluidity:

> It has all the elements of that genre: suspense, a femme fatale, the first detective in English drama, fog, professional killers, amateurs out of their depth and a brutal onstage murder. . . . It's the first domestic tragedy and the very first black comedy in English drama.[46]

Bourus's production (available on YouTube) joined a limited number of other outliers in addressing the role of Susan.[47] This often-overlooked minor character affords productions the opportunity to explore the differences in attitude towards a high-status woman like Alice and a woman of lower status who could be bartered in marriage. Unlike Findlay, whose Susan (Elspeth Brodie) was so passive as to appear catatonically unaware of the murder plots taking place around her and for which she was condemned, Bourus drew her into an overt awareness of the conspiracy. Rather than present her wishes for her husband's death in soliloquy, here Alice addressed her lines directly to Susan:

> Sweet Mosby is the man that hath my heart,
> And he usurps it, having nought but this:
> That I am tied to him by marriage.
> Love is a god, and marriage is but words,
> And therefore Mosby's title is the best. (1. 97–101)

Within the same scene, however, she offered Susan's hand in marriage to both Michael and to Clarke, both of whom had agreed to assist in Arden's death as long as the promise was kept, thus portraying Alice as complicit in the patriarchal society against which she was rebelling.

In November 2017, Bourus and Gary Taylor's *New Oxford Shakespeare* edition inspired a further US production, for which Bourus contributed a programme note describing the role of Alice as the first woman's role to dominate the English stage. The Resurgens Theatre Company, in collaboration with the Atlanta Shakespeare Company and University of North Georgia Department of English, presented the play at the Shakespeare Tavern, Atlanta. Like Hoosier Bard, Resurgens had been established to support academic research, particularly the artistic director Brett Griffin's interest in the prosody of early modern drama, and *Arden* was selected in order to capitalize on the recent canonization of the play. The production was later restaged for their 2018 *Death and Domesticity* conference alongside Heywood's *A Woman Killed with Kindness*. While not attempting to recreate an authentic Renaissance experience, the production did offer minimal staging, original pronunciation, Renaissance costuming and music, and minimal cuts to the text.

North American interest in the play continued the following year, with two further productions aimed principally at exploring both its Shakespearean links and its comic potential. Inspired by the 2013 publication of *William Shakespeare & Others: Collaborative Plays*, edited by Bate and Rasmussen, John Ciccarelli's Hudson Shakespeare Company toured open-air venues in New Jersey and Connecticut with what was billed as a 'lost' Shakespeare play entitled *The Murder of Thomas Arden of Faversham*. Like Hidden Room, this production found contemporary relevance and was presented in a recognizably modern period with a strong emphasis on its inherent humour. Ciccarelli commented, 'the play is billed as a tragedy by its title page, but really it's a screwball comedy ... unlike many plays that are serious dramas that have comedic relief, *Arden* is a comedic farce that has dramatic relief'.[48] Setting the play in the 1950s, he drew inspiration from US sitcoms of the period such as *The Donna Reed Show* and the production was punctuated with pop songs of the era, with characters underscored by specific motifs. Black Will and his female Shakebag, dressed like characters from the film *Grease*, were introduced by Elvis singing *Jailhouse Rock*, while their failed murder attempts echoed the pre-show playing of Dean Martin's *Ain't That a Kick in the*

Head, with the ultimately ironic opening line, 'How lucky can one guy be?'. Despite the comic aspects of the play stressed in both pre-performance advertising and in performance, Ciccarelli joined other directors in briefly altering the tone with a shocking staging of the murder itself. As with the Willing Suspension production, the final, successful attempt on Arden's life involved the victim being dragged to the ground by Black Will who suffocated him while Alice, Mosby and the other conspirators took turns to make deep and violent stabs to his body. However, the comedic tone of the production was re-kindled immediately as the body was disposed of and then discovered, before becoming darker once again with the inclusion of Franklin's epilogue describing in graphic detail the fates of the murderers. Particularly with productions that emphasized the comedy, such as Willing Suspensions and Polly Findlay's RSC production, these sudden changes of tone reflect the play's generic fluidity, which only in the final minutes becomes *The Tragedy* of the title.

US popular culture and social commentary

Both professional and amateur companies in North America continued to find contemporary relevance. The only fully professional staging in the United States to date was directed by Alex Roe at the Metropolitan Playhouse in 2004 and demonstrated the flexibility of the text in reflecting US society. Roe was influenced by what *Vanity Fair* described as a 'Made-for-Tabloid Murder', the trial of Laci Petersen's husband for the murder of his wife and unborn child.[49] The gruesome details and subsequent guilty verdict generated a number of accounts for both TV and cinema release. A further example of spousal murder also received a great deal of publicity at the time. The production opened in the year of the tenth anniversary of the murder of O. J. Simpson's ex-wife, Nicole, which was commemorated with a number of television documentaries and interviews that reignited public interest. It was this sense of ongoing public prurience that informed the production, as Roe sought to challenge his audience's belief that media exploitation of personal tragedy for entertainment is a modern, peculiarly American phenomenon. Although fully embracing the play's comic elements, there were also hints of an ongoing political debate concerning the treatment of homecoming veterans. Black Will's co-conspirator, Shakebag, became a bloodied wooden staff bearing the image of a skull which Will talked to and through. Giving rise to much slapstick comedy, this decision also indicated a darker, inner conflict for Will, whom Roe describes as a 'split-personality braggart'.[50] Both he and Shakebag were survivors of a bitter war, and the bloodied skull may have represented a lost comrade or a slain enemy, the memory of whom haunted Black Will and influenced his violent tendencies: a revenant acting as a permanent reminder of the impact of war and opening up the possibility of PTSD-induced aggression. Such a reading gave added weight to his response to Bradshaw's 'Ay, Will, those days are past with me' with the words 'Ay, but they be not past with me' (2.27–8). Attempting to draw a distinction between the early modern religious sensibility addressed by Mitchell and Potter and contemporary sensibilities, Roe 'incorporated an actor to play an "angel" who took on the role of every passing, one-scene character who saved Arden, up to the moment he appeared as a retributive authority in the person of the Mayor'.[51]

Brave Spirits Theatre presented *Arden* at the Atlas Performing Arts Center in Washington, DC, in 2015. As part of the company's commitment to redressing the gender imbalance of Renaissance drama, director Dan Crane cast two women as Black Will and Shakebag, thus altering the dynamics between the lovers and their suborned accomplices; two female characters agreeing so readily to kill an unwanted husband hinted at a sympathy for Alice's plight that went beyond their need for money. The politics of class and status were also highlighted by Crane's decision to have his actors use British accents, which to Eric Minton 'not only provides the local colour of a Kent market town – fitting, given the amazing geographical detail in the script – but also helps in delineating the social strata that are a central element of the play'.[52] The *Washington Post*'s reviewer also commented on this sense of 'class conflict (the low birth of Mosby is a matter for repeated comment)', noting that 'the most vivid characters come from opposite ends of the social spectrum'.[53] Despite the strong social and political elements of this production, Crane also played to the full the comedy of all five incompetently failed murder attempts, balancing both the ineptitude of the murderers and the violence of the final deed. Minton's comprehensive review details the staging of this multiplicity of failures:

> Their first attempt fails when a shopkeeper lowers his awning on the hiding Black Will's head. For the second attempt, they get locked out of the house by Michael. For the third attempt, their ambush is foiled when another Kent nobleman spots them and orders them to go home. The English fog messes up their fourth attempt. They finally manage to spring an attack in their fifth attempt, but end up outdueled by Arden and Franklin. 'Sirrah Greene, when was I so long in killing a man?' Black Will complains.[54]

In addition to the Hidden Room's restaging in 2020, wider social concerns surrounding class and status, as well as the suppression of women, were also highlighted in the two most recent US productions, both staged pre-pandemic in 2019. Neither were staged in contemporary dress, choosing instead, like Bourus, to reflect the American noir filmic tradition of a post-war period that saw the early burgeoning of the women's movement, albeit from a greater distance than the mid-century British directors discussed earlier in this chapter. The Classical Actors Ensemble of Minneapolis emphasized the period parallels through a cross-gendered casting of Reede, who was no longer a sailor but a Rosie the Riveter-like shipyard worker. Just as the post-war period forced women back into the home, depriving them of financial independence, so Arden's withholding of land left Reede unable to feed her family. Douglas Green notes that staging, rather than merely reporting, Shakebag's rape and murder of the widow Chambley 'forced the audience to witness, as the #MeToo movement has, the consequences of evil', and describes *Arden* as possibly 'the perfect play for the Trump era – unbridled lust and avarice, under the guise of love and business' while also underscoring 'the constraints on women's will and satisfaction'.[55] Franklin's overt misogyny would certainly have recalled Trump's attitude to women, and Arden's business dealings were made to seem even more dubious when Arden appeared wearing the dark suit and red tie of the ex-president.

Also in 2019, the American Shakespeare Center, based in Staunton, Virginia staged the play as part of its regular Actors' Renaissance Season, in which productions are mounted with no director or production team and only six days' rehearsal for each play. Taking place at the Blackfriars Playhouse, the production used the theatre's usual conventions of universal lighting and a thrust stage on which audiences were seated on gallant stools. These original practices did not, however, preclude a modern aesthetic for *Arden*, again adopting a film noir setting and highlighting contemporary social issues. Music was a key element, although the selection of pre-show and interval music covered a more eclectic range of periods and styles: cover versions of Talking Heads' *Psycho Killer,* Bill Withers's *Use Me* and I'm with Her's *Game to Lose* reflected the tone of the narrative. Arden was an entrepreneur and real estate developer, and his musical motif was an ominous double bass soundtrack with a jazz-tinged groove. This choice of profession drew parallels with Arden's original withholding of previously public land and also reflected ongoing twenty-first-century concerns about the lack of affordable homes in the United States following the sub-prime mortgage crisis some ten years earlier. Although Black Will and Shakebag quarrelled and adlibbed to provide the laughs, it was the passionate relationship between Alice and Mosby that remained the focus of the production. Taking a cue from the pair of silver dice with which Alice recalls 'we played for kisses many a time, / And when I lost, I won, and so did he' (1.123–4), dice were the lovers' own motif, appearing at key moments throughout the play to symbolize the gamble they were taking in plotting Arden's death.

International adaptations

The most intriguing of all adaptations of *Arden of Faversham* took place in New York some fifteen years before the Shakespeare Society of America's full production. The Romanian director, Andrei Serban, staged a version at La Mama Experimental Theatre in 1970, prior to its transfer to London's Royal Court the same year. Running in repertory with *Ubu Roi*, both of which were heavily cut, it apparently evoked 'more giggles and humorous comments from the audience' than Jarry's comedy. One reviewer concluded that the adaptation was 'calculated to give pleasure to anyone with a liking for full-frontal male nudity accompanied by sadistic ritual castration'.[56]

The earliest two productions outside the UK and US were staged in the Antipodes. Both were presented by amateur groups in university theatres, the first at the Little Theatre, Auckland, in 1984 and the second at the School of Drama, Victorian College of the Arts, Melbourne, in 1999. These were followed by a further, highly adapted, version staged by the Hayloft Project, Melbourne, in 2013.

MacDonald P. Jackson's review of the Little Theatre production appreciated the 'simple and imaginative set' of hanging ropes which represented doors, walls, trees, etc. The ropes 'hung in web-like clusters, [and] foreshadowed Arden's dream ... of being entangled in a deerstalker's net'.[57] Costuming was generally monochromatic, using black, white, grey and brown for the central characters, although Alice's gown was inset with a panel of red 'declaring the scarlet woman within'.[58] With the use of freeze-frame effects to highlight her emotions when arguing with Mosby, the focus of this production was clearly on Alice.

The Victorian College of Art production was adapted and directed by Kim Durban, a student working towards her Master of Dramatic Art (Direction) degree. The text was extensively reworked from a specifically feminist perspective and entitled *Alice Arden*. This amended title emphasized Durban's interest in the gendered roles within the play, in line with her stated intention to address textual elements that 'are problematic for a late twentieth-century sensibility, particularly the representation of women'.[59] Durban adopted a collaborative approach, working with a number of actors to investigate the material and experiment with multiple representations of characters and cross-gender castings of Alice and Mosby. The production used back projections to show the idealized presentation of Elizabethan women within their own period. These contrasted with Durban's Alice, who appeared to be in the process of donning this acceptable conventional appearance, but whose facial expression betrayed an unwillingness to do so. This Alice was in a state of undress, which revealed the constrictions placed upon the actor by a tightly laced corset and bumroll, designed to help transform her into a classically fetishized womanly shape. Her ruff was not yet sufficiently restrictive to impact on her bearing, as if signalling her unwillingness to accept her defined role. Instead, she glowered out into the audience in defiance of the conventions of submissive feminine behaviour imposed by patriarchal society.

Cross-gendered casting has become an increasingly recurrent theme in twenty-first-century productions, reflecting not only the gender imbalance often found in smaller, amateur acting companies, but also a general movement towards inclusivity in the theatre. A further highly adapted text was staged in 2003 by The Hayloft Project, Melbourne, this time renamed *Arden v. Arden*. A first half re-written by director Benedict Hardie was set in suburban Australia and incorporated cross-gendered casting in order to create contemporary parallels. Innovations included a female Greene as 'a single mother made homeless when her rental house is sold', and a female Black Will and a male Shakebag who were presented as 'dishonourably discharged veterans from Afghanistan'.[60] From the only available review, it would appear that this adaptation proved ultimately to be an unsuccessful attempt to address contemporary political issues through the medium of a lesser-known collaborative play.

Finally, in 2009 and again in 2013, students of the Grupo Filologica Inglesa at the Universidad de Sevilla, Spain, staged *Arden of Faversham*, with both productions being presented in English by actors in contemporary casual dress, again available on YouTube. The course convenor confirmed this was an optional course 'taught as part of the degree in English Philological Studies', intended for students 'interested in performance rather than simply as play text'. He chose *Arden*, not because of its authorship, but because he felt that 'the conflicts of marriage and property and the exercise of violence at different levels set an interesting ground for the students to consider'.[61] The students were divided into small groups and given free rein to adapt the text. The first of these productions, both of which were performed in modern dress, was presented as a radio broadcast episode in the ongoing story of *Alice of Faversham*, in which Alice was presented as 'a lonely, romantic housewife, totally ignored by her rich husband, Arden ... an ordinary woman whom passion and boredom lead astray.[62] This was an interestingly gendered and contemporary reading of the basic elements of the original narrative, with a greatly reduced cast. There was no indication that hired assassins were involved, nor was there reference to their many failed attempts on Arden's life. Instead, Alice alone was driven by omnipresent Fates to try to take control of her own destiny. In an apparent contrast to this extremely free textual adaptation, the 2013 production by a new student group began by adhering more closely to the original text. However, the language soon became as colloquial as the earlier production, although bearing no other major similarities. This production featured a larger cast of characters, many of whom, including Mosby, Michael and Greene, were played by (but not as) women. Black Will and Shakebag were present, but only the failed murder attempt thwarted by the locked door of Franklin's London home and the successful knifing of Arden by his wife were staged. On learning of the murderers' first failure, Alice informed Mosby 'if you want something done, you have to do it yourself'. Although Alice was shown stabbing her husband to death, taking control of the disposal of his body and the clear-up, this production echoed the conclusion of Littlewood's earlier production by disclosing no details of her arrest or punishment.[63]

Conclusion

Despite the specificity of time and place, and its limited performance history until the twentieth century, *Arden of Faversham* has proved of interest to both feminist directors and those wishing to address wider social issues around the world. Offering the longest role for women in Renaissance drama, a wide range of generic possibilities and no great weight of audience expectation, companies have been able to appropriate and radically adapt the play to examine contemporary concerns about class, gender, power and wealth. It is particularly notable, further, that while the UK, with the notable exception of Findlay's RSC production, has generally remained wedded to costuming the play within the early modern period, international productions have largely pursued the play's potential to remark on contemporary concerns through modern dress and music. And with the increasing presence of the play within new editions of Shakespeare's canonical works, the recent upsurge of productions around the world suggests a rich future life in theatrical repertoires.

Notes

1 Roslyn L. Knutson, 'Shakespeare's Repertory', in *A Companion to Shakespeare*, ed. David Scott Kastan (New York: John Wiley, 1999), 346–61.

2 Martin Wiggins, personal communication, 8 August 2021.
3 Catherine Richardson, '"Scene of the Murder": *Arden of Faversham* and Local Performance Culture', *Early Modern Literary Studies* 28 (2019): 6.
4 Tom Lockwood, 'Introduction', in *Arden of Faversham,* ed. Martin White (London: A & C Black, 2007), xxiv–xxv.
5 Ian Shuttleworth, '*Arden of Faversham*, Arden's House, Faversham, Kent', *Financial Times*, undated. http://www.cix.co.uk/~shutters/reviews/00139.htm (accessed 23 March 2022).
6 Peter J. Smith, 'Inaugurating the Complete Works (again): Shakespeare Nation, Doranism and Literalism in the Royal Shakespeare Company's 2014 Summer Season', *Cahiers Élisabéthains* 89, no. 1 (2016): 68.
7 Emma Whipday, 'The Picture of a Woman: Roaring Girls and Alternative Histories in the RSC 2014 Season', *Shakespeare* 11, no. 3 (2015): 276.
8 'An Elizabethan Tragedy', *The Stage,* 4 September 1952, 7; '*Arden of Faversham*', *The Stage*, 18 June 1953, 10. Coincidentally, the two most recent UK productions (at the time this goes to press) were also a BBC radio broadcast (Radio 3, aired 20 January 2019 and repeated on 17 January 2021) and a student production at the ADC theatre in Cambridge in 2017, promising 'coercion, classism and patriarchy'.
9 J. C. Trewin, 'The World of the Theatre: Fun and Games', *Illustrated London News,* 23 February 1963, 28.
10 Trewin, 'The World of the Theatre, Our Critic's First Night Journal', *Illustrated London News*, 21 May 1955, 936; Kenneth Tynan, 'Part 1: The British Theatre – *Arden of Faversham*', in *Curtains: Selections from the Drama Criticism and Related Writings* (London: Longmans, 1961), 82.
11 Elizabeth Schafer, 'Troublesome Histories: Performance and Early Modern Drama', in *The Cambridge Companion to Shakespeare and Contemporary Dramatists*, ed. Ton Hoenselaars (Cambridge: Cambridge University Press, 2012), 259.
12 Eric Porter, 'Dorothy Tutin Brings Off a Taxing Role', *Daily Telegraph*, 7 November 1970.
13 John Peter, 'Review', *Sunday Times,* 8 November 1970.
14 John Thacker, '*The Tragedy of Master Arden of Faversham* review at White Bear, London', *The Stage,* 15 August 2006.
15 Whipday, 'The Picture', 272.

16 *Arden of Faversham*, ed. Polly Findlay and Zoé Swensen (London: Nick Hern Books, 2014), 82.
17 Stephen Wall, 'Black Will and Shakebag', *Times Literary Supplement*, 16 April 1982.
18 All quotations attributed to Ken Bones are taken from personal emails to the author during 2018.
19 John Barber, 'Agutter's Star Quality', *Daily Telegraph*, 1 April 1982.
20 Irving Wardle, 'Brutality as genial farce', *The Times*, 1 April 1982.
21 Mark Amory, 'Botched Butchery', *Spectator*, 10 April 1982, 26.
22 Victor Hallett, 'Arden of Faversham', *Theatre in Wales*, 19 February 2010.
23 Peter Kirwan, ed., 'From Script to Stage', in *William Shakespeare and Others: Collaborative Plays*, ed. Jonathan Bate and Eric Rasmussen (Basingstoke: Palgrave Macmillan, 2013), 750.
24 Ibid., 747.
25 Peter Kirwan, 'Arden of Faversham @ The Emlyn Williams Theatre, Theatr Clwyd', *The Bardathon*, 20 February 2010. Available online: http://blogs.nottingham.ac.uk/bardathon/2010/02/20/arden-of-faversham-the-emlyn-williams-theatre-theatr-clwyd/ (accessed 16 February 2022).
26 Francesca Elliott, 'A Tale of Lovers with Murderous Intent', *Flintshire Chronicle*, 25 February 2010.
27 Gerhard Mack, 'Räuber Hotzenplots: Terry Hands inszeniert in Zürich *Arden von Faversham*', *taz*, 13 February 1992.
28 Eoin Price, 'Review of *Arden of Faversham* (directed by Polly Findlay for the Royal Shakespeare Company)', *Shakespeare* 11, no. 3 (2015): 320.
29 Kirwan, '*Arden of Faversham* (Em-Lou Productions) @ The Rose Theatre Bankside', *The Bardathon*, 23 June 2010. Available online: http://blogs.nottingham.ac.uk/bardathon/2010/06/23/arden-of-faversham-emlou-productions-the-rose-theatre-bankside/ (accessed 16 February 2022).
30 '*Arden de Faversham*', *IMDb*, n.d. Available online: https://www.imdb.com/title/tt6525354/?ref_=nv_sr_1 (accessed 16 February 2022).
31 '*Arden of Feversham*', *Teatrul Odeon*. Available online: http://istoric.teatrul-odeon.ro/spectacol/arden-of-feversham?lang=en (accessed 16 February2022).
32 Ibid.

33 Luminita Batali, 'Vittorio Holtier, "The Tower and the Island, a Shakespearean Universe, an Attempt at Approach by means of centrality archetypes"', *Romanian Scene Designers*, 2005. Available online: http://www.romanian-scene-designers.org/Vittorio-Holtier-The-Tower-and-the-Island-a-Shakespearian-Universe-an-Attempt-at-Approach-by-Means-of-Centrality-Archetypes-s122_a4.htm (accessed 16 February 2022).

34 Ronald D. Bachman, 'Systematization: A Settlement Strategy', in *Romania: A Country Study*, ed. Ronald D. Bachman (Washington: GPO for the Library of Congress, 1989). Available online: http://countrystudies.us/romania/39.htm (accessed 16 February 2022).

35 *Arden of Faversham*, ed. Martin White (London: New Mermaids, 1982)

36 *Arden of Faversham* theatre programme (Edinburgh: Bristol Revunions, 1974).

37 Joseph H. Stodder, 'Three Apocryphal Plays', *Shakespeare Quarterly* 38, no. 2 (1987): 244.

38 Ibid., 245.

39 Ibid.

40 Boston University, 'Willing Suspension Productions Presents Arden of Faversham Written by Anonymous', *YouTube*. Available online: https://www.youtube.com/watch?v=Oe7-c-EqoOk (accessed 16 February 2022).

41 Emily Gruber Keck, personal communication, 7 February 2018.

42 Hidden Room, Austin, Texas *Arden of Faversham*. Available online https://vimeo.com/452896852 (accessed 24 March 2022).

43 Beth Burns, personal communication, 12 November 2014.

44 Terri Bourus, quoted in 'IUPUI Hoosier Bard presents *Arden of Fevershame*: Shakespeare's Clever Spin on a Real-Life Crime', *IUPUI Newsroom* Press Release, 25 March 2014. Available online: http://archive.news.iupui.edu/releases/2014/03/shakespeare-arden-play.shtml (accessed 16 February 2022).

45 Terri Bourus and Gary Taylor, ed., '*The Tragedy of M. Arden of Faversham; or, The Tragedy of M. Arden of Fevershame*', in *The New Oxford Shakespeare*, ed. Gary Taylor et al. (Oxford: Oxford University Press, 2016), 121.

46 'Student Spotlights', *Indiana University Inside UI: Spotlights and Profiles*, 2 April 2014. Available online: http://archive.inside.iu.edu/spotlights-profiles/student/2014-04-02-ah-students-fevershame-iupui.shtml (accessed 8 October 2017).

47 New Oxford Shakespeare, 'Hoosier Bard's Arden of Fevershame', *YouTube*, 6 May 2016. Available online: https://www.youtube.com/watch?v=OXQD3H4zYWA (accessed 16 February 2022).

48 'A Lost Shakespeare meet[s] Desperate Housewives 1950s Style', *New Jersey Stage*, 30 June 2015. Available online: http://www.newjerseystage.com/articles/getarticle.php?ID=5508 (accessed 16 February 2022).

49 Maureen Orth, 'A Made-for-Tabloid Murder', *Vanity Fair*, 1 August 2003. Available online: https://www.vanityfair.com/culture/2003/08/laci200308 (accessed 25 March 2022).

50 Alex Roe, personal communication, 18 April 2017.

51 Ibid.

52 Eric Minton, 'Shakespeare or Not, This is a Good One', *Shakespeareances.com*, 14 April 2015. Available online: http://www.shakespeareances.com/willpower/onstage/Arden_Faversham-01-BST15.html (accessed 16 February 2022).

53 Celia Wren, '*Arden of Faversham*: Killing Time (and a man) in an Entertaining Way', *Washington Post*, 10 April 2015. Available online: https://www.washingtonpost.com/entertainment/theater_dance/arden-of-faversham-killing-time-and-a-man-in-an-entertaining-way/2015/04/08/eacbc186-dc84-11e4-b6d7-b9bc8acf16f7_story.html?utm_term=.e2c67b6d8850 (accessed 16 February 2022).

54 Minton, 'Shakespeare or Not'.

55 Douglas Green, '*Arden of Faversham* (review)', *Shakespeare Bulletin* 38, no. 2 (2020): 265, 263.

56 L. G. S., 'Café la Mama', *Stage and Television Today*, 28 May 1970, 15.

57 MacDonald P. Jackson, 'Review of *Arden of Faversham*, Little Theatre, Auckland, University Theatre Workshop, *Research Opportunities in Renaissance Drama* 28 (1984): 127.

58 Ibid.

59 Kim Durban, 'Research Topic', *Alice Arden* (unpublished Master's thesis, University of Melbourne, 2000), 2.

60 Alison Croggon, '*Arden v. Arden,* The Hayloft 'Project – Review', *The Guardian*, 24 November 2013. Available online: https://www.theguardian.com/stage/australia-culture-blog/2013/nov/25/arden-v-arden-hayloft-project-review (accessed 16 February 2022).

61 Manuel J. Gómez Lara, personal communication, 20 December 2017.

62 Elizabeth Guerrero, 'Arden of Faversham (Part 1)', *YouTube*, 18 March 2012. Available online: https://www.youtube.com/watch?v=GVAREjn7xLg (accessed 16 February 2022).

63 Estela Haro Puertas, 'Arden of Faversham (Grupo Filologia Inglesa Sevilla 2013-2014)', *YouTube*, 30 January 2014. Available online: https://www.youtube.com/watch?v=qihP7UVujwo (accessed 16 February 2022).

3

The state of the art

Locating criticism of *Arden of Faversham*, 2000 to the present

Catherine Richardson

Director Findlay takes ingenious swipes at the Amazon-style retail culture. She successfully plugs a 21st century audience into the play's concerns about over-mighty landlords. Alice's gang are chavs, Arden's lot are yuppies. . . . Miss Small is a sparkler. For all its topicality and interest to feminists, however, this remains, when compared to proper Shakespeare, a two-dimensional work. Even with skilful acting, we do not sympathise with the characters. They stroll before our eyes, flash their blades, accept their punishments and that is that. A footprint in the snow may make more impression.[1]

So said Quentin Letts of the RSC's 2014 production of *Arden*, directed by Polly Findlay. The review gives a flavour of two decades of reassessment of this play that could be seen as representing a step change in understanding of *Arden* – Letts's take on the production, for all its problematic language and sweeping stereotypes of value, draws attention to changing attitudes towards the play's interest in material culture and the way it intersects with pressing social questions, to growing interest in characterization and to questions of authorship. In other ways, however, scholarship of the past two decades journeys on roads very clearly recognizable from Jane Kingsley-Smith's astute identification of pre-millennium strands in the criticism earlier in this volume: 'the difference between *Arden* the play and Arden the historical event; the inclusion of *Arden* among Shakespeare's apocryphal plays; the emergence of Alice as a tragic victim; the political reading of domestic tragedy; and, finally, the sympathy between *Arden* and Shakespearean villainy'. Polly Findlay's was probably the highest-profile production of the play since the turn of the century, but there have been several others; and the past two decades have seen three new major editions of *Arden* and a substantial revision, several monographs, a special issue of *Early Modern Literary Studies* on the genre of domestic tragedy which includes extensive discussion of the play and many articles besides.[2] Across the different areas of critical attention, this has been a period of separating the play out from other versions of the story of Arden's murder, exploring its theatricality more fully and rebalancing what Kingsley-Smith calls the 'overshadowing' of the play by the historical account.

Topography

A key aspect of recent criticism of *Arden* has been an interest in different aspects of the play's locatedness. Partly as a result of the use it makes of place and journey, critics have responded to it as a play whose narrative is glued to place. Its action is firmly positioned within named spaces that reference real-world locales, springing from the nature of its physical locations and their concomitant social relationships. Régis Augustus Bars Closel describes it (alongside Richard Brome's *Jovial Crew*) as 'topographical'.[3] Building on the earlier work of Frank Whigham and Garret A. Sullivan on the redistribution of land at the Reformation and its impact on the moral and social ties that bound landlords to tenants, understanding of the play is starting to be connected to the ecological practices of early modern England. Within a wider interest in ecocriticism and the literary geography of early modern drama, this kind of work unpicks resonant connections to early modern practice, lived experience and economic and cultural investment in environment and place.[4] Elizabeth D. Gruber argues, connecting *Arden* to *King Lear*, that it illuminates 'the ecopolitics of tragedy, the way in which questions of identity are inextricably bound up with shifting apprehensions of the natural world'. This reorientation of understanding of land nevertheless continues to be moralized: 'Operating with the cautionary logic of a morality play', she points out, '*Arden of Faversham* indicates that notions of community are intimately tied to ecological concerns, such as how natural resources are distributed'.[5]

Bars Closel argues that the play is 'concerned with the physical place in which problems arise and how the resulting social space is recomposed'. He reads the play in the light of More's *Utopia*, where the number of existing relationships, 'regulated by customs, within a social space determined the impact of such changes', highlighting the relationship 'between density and the enclosing process'. Concepts of social density relate to the depiction of society in Faversham and London in interesting ways, and Closel suggests that *Arden* is 'possibly the most comprehensive play on the changes in the relationship between people and land'.[6] That is quite a bold statement, and it makes it possible to see this play as a trailblazer for tragic engagements with place. He reflects some of the novelty of this situation for early modern audiences, reinstating a sense of a social situation still in progress, with all the attendant raw emotions that arise, and of a play that facilitates exploration of social transformation.

Gina Bloom's cultural reference points are very different – she examines how the play engages with the dynamics of early modern board games – but she maps out a cognate territory in order to explore questions of spatial control. Arguing that 'the murderers' desire for "place" – in both geographic and social terms – is an overriding feature of their plot to kill Arden',[7] she builds on post-feudal conceptions of land with her understanding of the power structures that underpin movement in games, with their interplay of commanding knowledge and chance. She explores parallels between de Certeau's theorized practices of urban walking and the various perspectives on action taken up by board game players, theatre spectators and characters, culminating in an analysis of the final successful attempt on Arden's life, which she dubs the 'backgammon plot'. Here, he 'will not simply be an object of surveillance, subjected to the observation of others; as Arden plays backgammon, he will partake in a god's-eye view of himself, gazing down on the game board', a position which gives him a false 'sense of power and security' similar to that of his murderers.[8] It is possible to see the play, through such analysis, as connected to forms of entertainment newly available to just the social groups that this play concentrates on, and understand its focus on social mobility.[9]

As well as offering a different interpretation of the reasons for the final plot's success, Bloom offers a clarification of the theatrical tension of this key scene. Historical accounts of the murder merely place it in the context of a game, but in the play, in theory, 'Arden may preserve his life if he manages to keep his blots from being captured by Mosby', and theatrical pleasure therefore demands that the audience use their senses to play along, 'becoming involved cognitively and emotionally with its unpredictable risks and aggressive interactions'.[10] Both audience and characters have more skin in the game in the drama than they do in the narrative accounts. As this argument suggests, there is much scope for further consideration of how the play's strong interest in spatial dynamics plays out in performance. In my own work on local performance histories of *Arden*, for instance, I have begun to think through how plays that make insistent reference to the geographical and material locations for action might work as site-specific drama – performed in the locations in which the murder took place.[11]

In previous criticism on the play's topography, control of land has been seen as key to Arden's identity as a gentleman. Ann Christensen, however, offers a rebalancing of scholarly ideas about the links between Arden's identity and the spatial practice and social designation that goes with landowning status, by focussing on his commercial activities as an active man of business rather than a leisured landowner.[12] Her wider argument is about the genre of domestic tragedy as a whole, which she nuances by suggesting a renaming to 'something like absent-husband or separate-spheres dramas', seeing them as 'a dynamic and critical cultural form that used householders' disruptive commercial travel to resist the emerging ideology of the separation of the spheres'. About *Arden* in particular, she points out how much more comfortable scholars are discussing Arden's landowning than his (equally prominent) commercial activity. Her take on his restless movement across the county of Kent and London figures itinerancy as part of Arden's identity, pointing out that 'other characters, both in his household and in the community, expect his mobility and exploit his absence'.[13] Seeing him in this way allows her to make interesting connections between the characters across status lines; Arden and Black Will, for instance, both come across as restless travellers along the road to the city.

Christensen's focus gives new insights into the play's rootedness, equally embedded in a specific geographic and economic climate, but complicating response to the relative status of the characters and the activities their status generates, issues that together form the tense net of the spatial mapping of the murder attempts. She argues that the commercial world is given dramaturgical form via two particular 'theatrical stratagems': first, 'separation scenes' that are set on thresholds, and second, the 'spilt-screen effect', in which domestic and extra-domestic passages of action are intercut with one another in a technique that demonstrates both simultaneity and distinction. As these techniques suggest, travel over the landscape becomes the 'other' to domestic life, and the male-focussed ownership issues that preoccupied previous scholarship open up to find a place for women's economic agency; Christensen explores Alice's economic role in the play alongside her husband's. Social and economic perspectives spin out from the way the play configures its characters' movements within space.

Household

Domestic life in *Arden* has also seen an explosion of critical interest in this century, one that we can trace back to the previous century, with Lena Cowen Orlin's foundational book *Private Matters and Public Culture* (1994) and Viviana Comensoli's *Household Business: Domestic Plays of Early Modern England* (1996), discussed in Kingsley-Smith's chapter in this volume. These books claimed new ground in the significance of the domestic, as a political project involving the recovery of quotidian actions, often specifically motivated by an interest in women's agency. Orlin's reconstruction of the prescriptive advice around domestic life and its political consequences in particular unlocked a rich seam of printed material about the theory of household activity and gendered behaviour within it, and both books went a long way to more subtly defining the genre as one that takes 'the household as its fulcrum', in Comensoli's words.[14]

In this century, critics have continued to piece out scholarly knowledge of the significance of the household, the genre of domestic tragedy and *Arden* in particular in relation to one another. In my own book on *Domestic Life and Domestic Tragedy*, I aimed to reach beyond the proscriptive writing about household life and explore its practice, using manuscript documentary sources in particular to reconstruct the material culture of early modern buildings – their structures and the furniture and fittings with which they were filled – in order to understand more fully the way they figured familial identity and the impact of their staged representation on audiences. I analysed a range of court depositions in which ordinary people spoke about their quotidian activities in relation to wrongdoings, in order to get to grips with the reality of domestic behaviour, and then considered them in relation to the portraits of idealized domestic obedience given in advice manuals such as William Gouge's *Of Domesticall Duties* – what women's actions as wives were like day-to-day, for instance, and the impact this had on their husbands' authority. Although these documents too were mediated and indirect representations of household practice (written by male scribes for particular legal reasons), the snapshots of contemporary practice, fragmented, fraught and very far from the ideals of the proscriptive literature, nevertheless made it possible to construct an argument that moved from lived experience to theatrical practice by connecting dramaturgy and the imagination of audience members, examining the relationship 'between the spatial containment which is an essential feature of a house, and the dynamics of representation on a comparatively "bare" stage'.[15] Within the context of opening chapters that laid out the material and moral dynamics of middling provincial households, the book aimed to 'trace the meanings of the household through to their finale as the location of Arden's demise', doing so through a mixed analysis of both 'verbal images of the shared intimate household in which threat is firmly transcribed in the closeness of space' and physical features of staging: for instance, stage doors, Arden's chair and the 'sureness with which all take up their positions', which rests upon the 'palpable impropriety' of their familiarity with the murder space.[16]

More recent work has been material in a much broader sense, moving out beyond the specifics of object and room to consider the house as a material environment for murder. Iman Sheeha, in her article in the 2019 special edition of *EMLS*, explores the physical engagement of murder and household. She argues that the house, 'as both a physical entity and an ideological institution', is at the centre of the play, 'turning into a character in its own right towards the end'.[17] After the murder, however, the house becomes the remaining reliable witness of its former owner's fate, 'an extension of the master's body, his tongue, revealing truths that the man can no longer speak'.[18] Her reading of Mosby and Arden's competition for control of assets, material and human, leads her to assert that 'Against all claims for ownership, the house chooses its master', and the active role so assigned increases as 'the house displays Master Arden's blood in the place where the master used to sit . . . asserting the permanence of patriarchal authority even when its representative in the play has been eliminated'.[19] This pairing of man and house has a clear role to play in the discovery of the crime, and her readings of their intermingled fates is epitomized by the statement that 'just as the house retains elements of Master Arden's body, the master's body retains elements of the house' in the form of the rushes stuck in his shoe.

Ariane M. Balizet's 2014 *Blood and Home in Early Modern Drama* works in a similar way, considering how blood moves between material property and conceptual trigger to patriarchal thinking in *Arden*. On stage, she argues, 'dramatists harnessed the figurative power of the embodied home by linking a husband's bodily integrity to his household's security (and vice versa)', exploring how 'the actor's body stands in for the embodied household' in ways that make for morally confusing patterns of strength and weakness.[20] Balizet connects up the 'blood on the towel, knife, and floor – along with the blood under Alice's nails', suggesting that together they give 'visibility to the degradation of domestic order', as 'legible' properties.[21] In doing so, she makes important visual and material connections across the play that were missed in earlier criticism that was more textually focussed. And this 'spectacle' of bleeding, most formally realized in the corpse's cruentation (an invention of the writer, she points out), but also visible in the scene of futile floor washing, has a clearly gendered element. Arden's inability to provide proper household management leads to a shame that is made manifest in his 'uncontrollably leaky corpse', which offers 'the bizarre image of a menstruating man'.[22] The tracing of such 'intricate connections between blood, shame, power, and gender' has given a new edge to a wider understanding of the power of the play's material investment and its connections to wider social meaning.

Props

The richly metaphorical nature of these material understandings is only fully realized in an analysis that explores how they are seen by an audience, then, and it is a rare analysis of *Arden* in these two decades that makes no mention of a stage property. In his *British Drama Catalogue*, Martin Wiggins lists some thirty-nine objects in total as being required in the play, including what were apparently (looking across the contemporary plays he lists) relatively unusual combinations of tables and seating, in the context of a wide range of other things that indicate the sophisticated nature of the play in performance.[23] Work has often focussed on domestic properties, considering the ways in which they structure the interior scenes and foreground the issues of hospitality and authority that such objects communicated both on and off the stage. In my own recent edition of *Arden*, I looked at the contribution that dining goods make to the definition of community in the play, in both early modern and contemporary performances. Such goods offer an economical and flexible means of indicating how comfortable the guests feel with Arden's hospitality and aim to evoke for the audience either 'conventional hospitality perverted by lust and murder', or, particularly in twenty-first-century performances, 'a social configuration uncomfortable from the start in a more structural way'.[24] Visiting one another's homes offers a moment of social clarity about cultural and economic similarity and difference.

A focus on a range of the play's props threads through the analyses mentioned earlier, often leading to metatheatrical thinking. Backgammon in particular, Bloom argues, is used 'to take up questions of visual surveillance and the navigation of space', because it offers 'direct analogies to theatergoing to suggest that theatergoer

pleasure and power come not from abstract, visual surveillance of
– but rather, risky, engaged interaction with – the ludic world of the
boards'.[25] Mary Floyd-Wilson traces bewitchment and enchantment
from the poisoned objects proposed as murder weapons: Clarke's
proposed remote poisoning provides 'a horizontal circulation of
eye-beams, spirits and passions. Perfectly suited to its spectatorial
genre, the theatricalised version of Arden's story suggests an ocular
theory of tragic causation'. But then she takes the argument a step
further, into the nature of drama itself:

> The poisoned portrait recalls, for example, the complaints
> of Stephen Gosson, who warns against seeking cures in the
> enchantment of the stage and equates such behaviour with
> patients who leave physic for the 'witchcraft' of cunning folk.
> Just as the poison of drama infects its audience 'secretly', a
> presentation of Clarke's painting might harm not just Arden but
> all eyewitnesses.[26]

Scholars have also begun to explore how these props contribute
to processes of characterization. The prayer book provides an
instructive example. Elizabeth Williamson traces female domestic
use of prayer books in a post-Reformation context, arguing
for contemporary impact both on our understanding of Alice's
character and on attitudes towards prayer in material form: 'When
they turned books – especially prayer books – into stage properties,
the playing companies drew attention to the physicality of the
Protestant codex and the practices associated with it.' This made,
she argues, a clear connection to larger theological questions: it
revealed 'a pre-existing but often unacknowledged rift between
the ideal of an immaterial faith and the realities of daily life in
the late sixteenth and early seventeenth centuries'.[27] Alice's prayer
book is also involved in a soliloquy-like investigation of her moral
and spiritual condition as she threatens to tear it: 'Rather than
serving' as Williamson describes it, 'as proof of her piety, the prayer
book becomes the focus of her rejection of the ideals explored' in
contemporary piety manuals. Object and female body and spirit
are analogously vulnerable, and the prop allows the playwright to
'bring [Alice's] unholy thoughts to light'.[28]

John Henry Adams explores material/immaterial connections
through assemblage theory, as it 'clarifies how human behavior can

be structured by inhuman agency: objects possess agency because they manifest social pressures'. In the way he conceives of the connection to characterization, the book was at the centre of Alice's conversion, and so her 'virtue endures only as long as the book itself is incorporated into her assemblage. Remove the physical object and she reverts to her previous sinful behavior'. Because of 'objects' agentive potential as a social reality', their identity-forming qualities are inherently dangerous: 'all objects used to help shape personal identity carried the threat of idolatry with them'.[29]

The thread that ties these interests together is a developing sense of the significance of the material qualities of performance as a whole, criticism focussed on both the sixteenth and twenty-first centuries. As the prayer book analyses show, in early modern England, objects were part of an everyday culture that provided an important imaginative way of engaging with truly lasting, spiritual issues via their contrast and engagement with the ephemeral. In the last twenty years, however, *Arden*'s foregrounding of things has been read in the context of twenty-first-century consumer lifestyles. Reviews of productions such as the one with which this chapter opened draw attention to a throw-away culture in order, Michael Billington suggests, 'to show how murder is the logical outcome of a society based on commodification'. He notes how Arden's business activities extended, in Findlay's production, into the mass-manufacture of cheap toys, Mosby's costuming as 'a sharp-suited arriviste swathed in bling', and 'Merle Hensel's design, in which the white stuffing that lines Arden's factory packing cases is visually echoed by the snow in which his body is finally abandoned'.[30] Ironically, the emptying out of moral, spiritual and familial significance that material culture has undergone has given it a renewed prominence as a part of the experience of the play in performance.

Performance histories are also becoming an important element in our understanding of characterization in *Arden* and should be more significant and better integrated in these arguments than is often the case. Elizabeth Shafer's 2012 chapter aims to increase the profile of specifically feminist performance histories of less canonical plays, in order to produce new insights into their dramaturgy. As she points out (and as Kath Bradley pursues in her chapter for this volume), a significant number of female directors, including Joan Littlewood, Buzz Goodbody and Katie Mitchell (to which we might now add Findlay), 'have been drawn to

Alice's story'.³¹ Schafer traces the representation of Alice through Littlewood's 1954 decision to cut the end of the play, including Alice's repentance (a decision that saw her character as 'far less contained, less penitent, and . . . offered a far more challenging vision of female criminality'). She also interrogates the language of reviewers, including, for example, a Parisian review of Littlewood's production which described Alice as 'whirling around her husband like a serpent which encircles its victim in rapid . . . enveloping, provoking, sensual, versatile; perversity itself'.³² These fascinating responses to female gesture and movement as interpreted by largely male critics invite engagement with the way they react to the character's power in performance.

In Mitchell's production in 1990, however, rather than Alice, critical attention was instead focussed on the role of Susan: 'the *Evening Standard* (10 August 1990) detected excess when Susan 'is obliged to pirouette wildly, scattering earth as she whirls', and Jeremy Kingston in *The Times* commented acerbically that Susan 'crouches, keens, throws sand on her hair and crawls under a table'.³³ Where Alice's role was cut in the 1950s, Susan's role in both the 1990s and 2014 was expanded: her extended mime of cleaning in the latter ran behind much of the scripted action, dusting, adjusting and then cleaning up blood.³⁴ When I asked the contributors to this book which character they would most like to play in performance, it was Susan and Michael who came up most frequently – the former now has her own chapter – showing how important the servants' view from the edge has become to our understanding of the play's power dynamics. Such a long view through *Arden*'s production history elucidates the play through changing responses to it, by working with the impact it has on audiences as embodied drama. There is ample scope in the future to develop other trajectories – the modern performances of masculinity in relation to the play's overtly homosocial overtones and its patterns of comic and tragic violence, for instance, have yet to be explored in any great detail.³⁵

History and drama

The question of *Arden's* dependence on and relationship with sources continues to be considered. Tom Lockwood's neat formulation –

that the play 'is constructed with the special kind of artfulness that can look like apparent artlessness' – is instructive here. 'Rather than turn its fidelity to a real-life narrative into a formal restriction', he argues, *Arden* 'opens out into delaying, formal innovation within the limits that are imposed by its closed formal structure'.[36] Critics have seen *Arden*'s precociousness in turning historical material into theatre in the wider context of changing ideas of truth and evidence. A key tension between restriction and innovation is visible in Melissa Rohrer's argument that 'The theatrical medium encouraged playwrights to invent, elide, and present alternative viewpoints to a "known true story".'[37] It was the 'act of transferring well-known, fact-based crime narratives to the stage', she suggests, that 'gave rise to a new kind of dramatic storytelling, premised on accepting the simultaneity of fact and fiction in a narrative which claims truthful origins'.[38] The patterning of 'accepted facts' – in *Arden*'s case the heavily stressed locations for action, crime and punishment for instance – with the 'speculation and invention' needed 'to adequately dramatize the characters involved' is seen by Rohrer (in relation to developing legal practice) as modifying the truth value of drama itself. Such subtle considerations of a shifting relationship between 'literature' and 'culture' are placing *Arden* at the centre of generic novelty in the early modern theatre. They build on Helgerson's earlier opening up of a role for the play in shaping such genres as murder play and crime pamphlet.[39]

Key twenty-first-century currents of criticism on the play have moved away from analyses that read it against its historical analogues and towards a fuller accounting for its theatricality that explores characterization on its own theatrical terms. As Ian McAdam puts it, previous 'attempts to historicize *Arden of Faversham* have multiplied rather than clarified the possible meanings of the play-text', leaving 'the actual artistic and psychological details of the text under-examined'.[40] Work on narrative tales of the murder has been invaluable in understanding what is at stake in the story, but it has had the implication of calling into question its specifically theatrical narratives.

There are sophisticated challenges here too to the original view of domestic tragedies as homiletic. Understanding more fully how they pull apart from the single viewpoint of the historical sources to offer moral complexity has encouraged an investigation of their plurality of perspective that focuses mainly on characterization.

As Carol Mejia LaPerle points out, 'The change from historical account to dramatic representation – from generic and moral certainty to theatrical serialization and deferred outcome – undercuts . . . efforts at regulating reception.'[41] Glenn Clark, for instance, aims to show that *Arden* reflects 'a serious Calvinist vision of the agonizing experience of reprobation'.[42] He explores the different ways in which Alice and Mosby respond to sin, the former as 'sweetness' and the latter as 'painful and inescapable', from the point of view of a contemporary hot topic – the doctrine of double predestination – which 'demands the imagination of an arbitrarily cruel God and inappropriately ambiguates the location of moral responsibility for sin'.[43] As well as a contextualized reading of the excess of the character of Alice, this analysis offers us a fundamentally different idea of the material world that features so strongly in the play through props and the processes of leisure, interpreting it as the source of the 'embodied desires' and frenetic activity on which the daily experience of the reprobate is based, and which takes their concentration away from their spiritual life'. When the lived experience of reprobate life was being explored in pulpit and print, the intense representations of Alice and Mosby's compulsions speak to a complex but extremely significant spiritual context for the drama.

Clark's article is one of several that resituate the play in relation to contemporary discourses of and attitudes to sin and crime, often focussing on the character of Alice. He argues that she 'is easily understood in terms of fully liberated passion and appetite . . . a figure of freedom whose cultural origins lie in the demonically appetitive and manipulative reprobate of popular sermons and Puritan tracts'.[44] Sandra Clark, in a related article on 'The Problem of Sin and Crime in Domestic Tragedy', also considers how the play's homiletic elements 'operate in relation to the contemporary conceptualisation of sin and crime, forming a nexus where what is contemporary and contingent comes to terms with what is deemed eternal and immutable'.[45] Her reading, however, is a broader one, going beyond the intensely realized passion of Alice and Mosby: 'No character in *Arden of Faversham* is without moral culpability or free of criminal responsibility.' She gives attention to the differently realized motivations of the murderers. Shakebag, she says, 'brings to the play a commitment to criminality untroubled by any consciousness of sin, and effectively comic in its relish of sordid detail'[46]. Such work suggests a complex moral drive for the play and insists those working on it consider the way it acts on its audiences in the round.

In contrast to the realist appeal to lived experience that Glenn Clark finds in the play, Cheryl Birdseye states that she is breaking away from the 'critical tendency to respond to Alice as a psychologically plausible character'.[47] She identifies the variety of 'testimonial styles' that Alice uses throughout the play, analysing their different audiences and finally concluding that her 'increasingly unconventional authority within the theatre as an unreliable narrator ... is revealed, presenting serious challenges to the audience's willingness to believe'.[48] This is one of several arguments that consider the way *Arden* draws in and then implicates its audiences in response to the characters. Birdseye asks, 'what responsibility [playhouse audiences] have to question the testimonies laid before them, particularly as Alice is not a fictional character but, rather, the dramatization of an historical figure?'[49] LaPerle asks what portrayals of a female character 'who does not have formal access to rhetorical devices but is persuasive and effective nonetheless, have to say about the production of persuasion?; About what counts as eloquence?'[50] Her answer is that, as a rhetorical agent, 'Alice asserts a sense of self that depends upon the improvised and limited manipulation of external forces', and this allows her to consider the gendering of agency: 'The play reveals that the female subject is an agent only within situations – in this case, only through an overarching historically determined narrative – that she neither authors nor controls.'[51] Reading these articles alongside one another reveals an *Arden* more plural and multi-vocal than has sometimes been supposed. It is a malleable drama that has drawn large contemporary themes into play for its audiences from the start.

Arden's distinctiveness and the question of authorship

Authorship has been a key area of contention for scholarship on *Arden* in the twenty-first century, providing both a positive stimulus to reconsideration of the play's status, verse and dramaturgy, and some occasionally ill-tempered disagreements. Peter Kirwan provides important context for scholarly arguments concerning how *Arden* may or may not fit into the canon of Shakespeare's work, tracing the role that its provincial setting played in its banishment to the apocrypha.[52] And several authors have explored parallels of various kinds between *Arden* and Shakespeare's plays. Emma Whipday takes the most holistic view of such connections, setting out to see how *Arden* (and other domestic tragedies) 'interact with Shakespeare's tragedies in significant and previously unconsidered ways'.[53] Taking *Macbeth* as an example, she notes that 'both plays stage the antecedents and aftermath of a treasonous household murder' and traces patterns of action and dramaturgical trope between the plays, establishing a significant string of events: 'neighbourhood surveillance of the boundaries of the home, followed by the detection of a crime, leading to the entry of neighbours into the home to apprehend the criminals'. In the passages following Duncan's death, she finds meaningful correspondences with *Arden* including fruitless attempts to clean away blood.[54]

Also interesting here is Whipday's analysis of how previous critics have responded to their awareness of such parallels: 'Many critics have observed that *Arden* foreshadows *Macbeth*, yet critical attention has primarily focussed on linguistic echoes, in relation to the question of *Arden*'s authorship.' Whipday takes critics to task for the direction of their analytical gaze, because 'in the majority of work on the subject, there is a reluctance to discuss *Arden* as an influence or literary model'. The word 'foreshadowing', she suggests, avoids 'the question of agency' and implies 'that Shakespeare's artistic achievement in *Macbeth* somehow reaches back in time, illuminating earlier plays'.[55] In contrast, Whipday argues that '*Macbeth* appropriates, expands and transforms many of *Arden*'s narrative features', redirecting attention to the play's generic novelty.

Many recent discussions of *Arden*'s authorship come from attribution scholars who have to make much more stark pronouncements as their method is a quantitative one, based on computer-aided stylistics work that has developed considerably in the twenty-first century. Authorship is determined by comparison of details of word usage and structure in the play with the corpus of writing of other authors. Such computational stylistics tests have been undertaken on *Arden*, which then rank how likely a selection of candidates are to have written a particular passage, producing a hierarchy of possible authors. This type of analysis is most valuable for giving a broad sense of probability, which takes our understanding beyond a scholar's inevitably subjective sense of connection between individual passages, giving textual connections a context within the whole range of dramatic writing of a given period. Analyses that compare only two playwrights to one another do not advance our sense of this too far – they have been described as 'one horse races'.[56]

Despite particular provisos around the paucity of writing available for comparison in such an early period, itself one of swift linguistic change, possible corruption in the 1592 quarto and a potentially larger percentage of quotidian language in domestic tragedy, there is nevertheless a broad consensus among attribution scholars on two points: first, that *Arden* exhibits two distinct patterns of writing, with the play's central scenes distinguished from its outer ones; and second, that those central scenes exhibit stylistic traits which resemble those in other plays by Shakespeare. This pattern appears to map onto the common early modern practice of co-authorship in which a more mature writer worked with a less experienced one; in this scenario, Shakespeare would be cast as the junior partner.

Such sustained stylistic analysis, more holistic and less idiosyncratic than the poetic game of 'snap' of earlier practice in which passages of text written by different authors are matched, began in the last century, with MacDonald P. Jackson's early identification in his 1963 BLitt thesis of Shakespeare's possible hand in the play, and his ongoing involvement with the question has shown the greatest methodological variety over the following decades, taking in both computer-aided analysis and detailed analysis of Shakespeare's verse form.[57] In his 2014 book, Jackson presented his work on scenes six and eight and summarized the recent debates, suggesting that Shakespeare's portion lies within scenes four to nine.[58] Shakespeare's presence has also been detected by methods as diverse as Jonathan Hope's sociolinguistic approach, Arthur F. Kinney's primary component analysis of function and lexical words and Marina Tarlinskaja's metrical tests.[59]

As a result of this work, *Arden* has entered into a belated process of canonization. Scene eight was included in Bate and Rasmussen's *Complete Works* volume, and the whole play in *William Shakespeare and Others: Collaborative Plays* in 2013, where Will Sharpe describes, 'whoever wrote *Arden of Faversham*' as 'one of the most innovative and daring talents the Renaissance theatre ever saw'.[60] In

2016, the play also found a place in its entirety in the *New Oxford Shakespeare Complete Works*. In their 'Canon and Chronology of Shakespeare's Works' for that edition, Gary Taylor and Rory Loughnane justified its inclusion by stating that both collaboration and Shakespeare as the junior partner 'are now supported by extensive, independent, interlocking evidence'.[61] The edition not only gives a uniquely elevated status to the play by including it in a highly respected and much used Complete Works of Shakespeare but brings together a large amount of scholarship from the previous two decades that pertains to *Arden*'s authorship. Its accompanying *Authorship Companion* includes two chapters on the subject in its Case Studies section: one by Jack Elliott and Brett Greatley-Hirsch, which tests *Arden* against a database of thirty-four 'well-attributed, sole-authored texts of sound provenance' first performed between 1580 and 1594, and one by Jackson, who counts the incidence of Shakespeare-plus-words and Shakespeare-minus-words: those whose Shakespearean and non-Shakespearean usage is most sharply differentiated in the plays in the Literature Online database between 1580 and 1600.[62]

But Shakespeare has not been the only candidate for authorship of *Arden*. Brian Vickers, the general editor of a *Complete Works of Thomas Kyd* currently in preparation (for which *Arden* is being edited by Darren Freebury-Jones), aims to expand his writer's canon as Taylor has done for Shakespeare, and *Arden* has been the subject of a recent, sometimes intemperate, tug of war between the two editors. The same computer-aided tests that showed Shakespeare to be a major contributor to the play, however, tended to exclude most other known dramatists as possible collaborators. Jackson concludes, for instance, that 'Even the blocks of text other than 4–9 proved . . . to be more closely associated with Shakespeare than with either Marlowe or Kyd', both previous hot contenders, as Jane Kingsley-Smith shows above, and the works by Kinney, Elliott and Greatley-Hirsch, Jackson and Tarlinskaja indicate that Kyd was not the author of 'any significant part of the play'.[63] There is currently little research published in academic journals that uses techniques of comparison between multiple authorial candidates to defend Kyd's authorship. Rather, Vickers and Darren Freebury-Jones have used more partial techniques to argue for their candidate's authorship of the whole play. Although much energy has been expended criticizing the methods of other scholars (Vickers' article in *Studies in Philology* spends only four pages of thirty-four laying out a positive case for Kyd[64]), both critics do note some very interesting verbal and dramaturgical parallels 'encompassing verse style, the prosodic features of function words, rhyme forms, vocabulary, stage direction formulae, verbal links, and overall dramaturgy' between *Arden* and, for instance, *The Spanish Tragedy* and *Soliman and Perseda*.[65]

To date, the only other candidate for authorship who has seen much traction is Thomas Watson, a poet and translator, and a friend of Lyly, Peele, Marlowe, Kyd and Greene who is known to have written plays, but none of whose dramatic output survives. Michael J. Hirrel has argued that he was 'among the first to intermix comedy and tragedy' within a play.[66] Gary Taylor has published articles analysing a range of aspects of Watson's extant works in relation to *Arden* and identifies 'evidence for Watson in scenes 1–3, 9–10, and 12–Epilogue: all the scenes (except 11) that seem least likely to have been written by Shakespeare', although these claims have been vigorously disputed by Vickers.[67]

The information the attribution scholars have generated about different styles within the play is useful for purposes other than direct discussion of authorship. In the Arden Early Modern Drama edition, I considered how its careful dramaturgical patterning might map onto the proposed units of authorship, helping us to understand *Arden*'s theatrical power and its conception as an artistic whole: for instance, scenic patterning such as the pairing of scenes set on the Kent-London road, scenes of prophetic dreaming in London or scenes of threating by the murderers; or distinct ways of representing place and action across the scenes, alternative modes of geographical precision and scenic structure and distribution of groups of characters. Analysing the way such formal shaping of the dramaturgy provides a unified whole across different styles also suggests contemporary models of co-authorship.

In these first two decades of a new century, then, *Arden*'s status has shifted considerably. The discussions of authorship, although not always constructive, have given it a prominence in scholarly debate that is unprecedented in its history, and its inclusion in the Shakespearean canon will, whatever new evidence for authorship is revealed in the coming decades, doubtless lead to further analysis and more high-profile productions that will clarify its contributions to our wider cultural concerns in the twenty-first century.

Understanding of the impact of *Arden's* characters is growing, and the new ways of understanding its fundamental 'locatedness' that appear in this volume stand testament to its power. In my discussions with my fellow contributors, it transpired that this is not a play that leaves the imagination easily, once one has encountered it; *Arden's* growing prominence is likely to ensure that it develops ever firmer roots in the twenty-first-century cultural consciousness.

Notes

1 Quentin Letts, 'Rough Justice of a 16th Century Sort: Quentin Letts Reviews *Arden of Faversham*', *Daily Mail*, 6 May 2014.

2 The editions are by Martin Wiggins in *A Woman Killed with Kindness and Other Domestic Plays* (Oxford: Oxford University Press, 2008), Terri Bourus and Gary Taylor in *The New Oxford Shakespeare* (Oxford: Oxford University Press, 2016) and Catherine Richardson for Arden Early Modern Drama (London: Bloomsbury, 2022). Tom Lockwood has contributed a new introduction to the New Mermaid edition, edited by Martin White (London: A & C Black, 2007).

3 Régis Augustus Bars Closel, '*Utopia* and the Enclosing of Dramatic Landscapes', *Renaissance and Reformation* 41, no. 3 (2018): 91.

4 See, for instance, the inspiring work of Julie Sanders, including *The Cultural Geography of Early Modern Drama, 1620–1650* (Cambridge: Cambridge University Press, 2011).

5 Elizabeth D. Gruber, 'Nature on the Verge: Confronting "Bare Life" in *Arden of Faversham* and *King Lear*', *Interdisciplinary Studies in Literature and Environment* 22, no.1 (2015): 99, 104.

6 Bars Closel, '*Utopia*', 70, 72, 80.

7 Gina Bloom, *Gaming the Stage: Playable Media and the Rise of English Commercial Theater* (Ann Arbor: University of Michigan Press, 2018), 106.

8 Ibid., 112.

9 For more on leisure opportunities for the middling sort in relation to *Arden*, see Tara Hamling and Catherine Richardson, *A Day at Home in Early Modern England* (New Haven: Yale University Press, 2017), chapter 5.

10 Bloom, *Gaming*, 114.

11 Catherine Richardson, '"Scene of the Murder": *Arden of Faversham* and Local Performance Cultures', *Early Modern Literary Studies* 28 (2019).

12 Ann C. Christensen, *Separation Scenes: Domestic Drama in Early Modern England* (Lincoln: University of Nebraska Press, 2017).
13 Ibid., 4, 41.
14 Lena Cowen Orlin, *Private Matters and Public Culture in Post-Reformation England* (Ithaca: Cornell University Press, 1994); Viviana Comensoli, *Household Business: Domestic Plays of Early Modern England* (Toronto: University of Toronto Press, 1996), 7.
15 Catherine Richardson, *Domestic Life and Domestic Tragedy in Early Modern England: The Material Life of the Household* (Manchester: Manchester University Press, 2006), 4, 6.
16 Ibid., 106, 109.
17 Iman Sheeha, "'Looke in the place where he was wont to sit / See see his blood it is too manifest': Domestic Space and Patriarchal Authority in The Tragedy of Master Arden of Faversham', *Early Modern Literary Studies* 28 (2019): 3.
18 Ibid., 11.
19 Ibid., 14.
20 Ariane M. Balizet, *Blood and Home in Early Modern Drama* (London: Routledge, 2014), 125.
21 Ibid., 152.
22 Ibid., 153.
23 Martin Wiggins, *British Drama 1533–1642: A Catalogue*, vol. III (Oxford: Oxford University Press, 2013), no. 846, 9–12.
24 Catherine Richardson, ed., *Arden of Faversham* (London: Bloomsbury, 2022), 86.
25 Bloom, *Gaming*, 101.
26 Mary Floyd-Wilson, '*Arden of Faversham*: Tragic Action at a Distance', in *The Cambridge Companion to English Renaissance Tragedy*, ed. Emma Smith and Garrett A. Sullivan (Cambridge: Cambridge University Press, 2010), 197.
27 Elizabeth Williamson, 'The Uses and Abuses of Prayer Book Properties in *Hamlet, Richard III,* and *Arden of Faversham*', *ELR* 39, no. 2 (2009): 372.
28 Ibid., 392. Conversely, in a carefully argued passage on the moment of book tearing, Sophie Duncan suggests, 'the textual evidence for tearing is inconclusive'; Mosby does not look at Alice during the passage, and a comparative study of cognate moments indicates that it may be a future threat rather than a performative action. *Shakespeare's Props: Memory and Cognition* (London: Routledge, 2019), 200.

29 John Henry Adams, 'Agentive Objects and Protestant Idolatry in *Arden of Faversham*', *Studies in English Literature, 1500–1900* 57, no. 2 (2017): 247.
30 Michael Billington, 'Arden of Faversham Review – Elizabethan Tragedy Goes Modern', *The Guardian*, 7 May 2014.
31 Elizabeth Schafer, 'Troublesome Histories: Performance and Early Modern Drama', in *The Cambridge Companion to Shakespeare and Contemporary Dramatists*, ed. Ton Hoenselaars (Cambridge: Cambridge University Press, 2012), 258.
32 Ibid., 259.
33 Ibid., 262.
34 Ian Shuttleworth, for the *FT*, described her 'wealth of wordless drudgery that is by turns comical and exquisitely agonising', 7 May 2014.
35 See Martin Wiggins, 'Introduction', *Domestic Plays*, xi, for an interesting start; such work has an important history of analysis of models of masculinity in the play on which to build, for example, Randall Martin's 'Arden winketh at his wife's lewdness, & why!': A Patrilineal Crisis in *Arden of Faversham*' *Early Theatre* 4, no. 1 (2001): 13–33; and Ian McAdam, 'Protestant Manliness in *Arden of Faversham*', *Texas Studies in Literature and Language* 45, no. 1 (2003): 42–72.
36 Lockwood, 'Introduction', x.
37 Melissa Rohrer, '"Lamentable and True": Remediations of True Crime in Domestic Tragedies', *Early Modern Literary Studies* 28 (2019): 2.
38 Ibid., 2.
39 Richard Helgerson, 'Murder in Faversham: Holinshed's Impertinent History', in *The Historical Imagination in Early Modern Britain*, ed. Donald R. Kelley and David Harris Sacks (Cambridge: Cambridge University Press, 1997), 133–58.
40 McAdam, 'Manliness', 42.
41 Carol Mejia LaPerle, 'Rhetorical Situationality: Alice Arden's Kairotic Effect', *Women's Studies* 39, no. 3 (2010): 179.
42 Glenn Clark, 'Hurried to Destruction: Reprobation in *Arden of Faversham* and *A Woman Killed with Kindness*', *Renaissance and Reformation* 41, no. 4 (2018): 111.
43 Ibid., 120–1.
44 Ibid., 119.
45 Sandra Clark, 'The Problem of Sin and Crime in Domestic Tragedy', *Early Modern Literary Studies*, 28 (2019): 4.
46 Ibid., 9.

47 Cheryl Birdseye, '"Let death make amends for all my sins": (In)Sincere Confessions in *Arden of Faversham*', *Early Modern Literary Studies* 28 (2019): 2.

48 Ibid., 21.

49 Ibid., 7.

50 Laperle, 'Rhetorical', 176.

51 Ibid., 191.

52 Peter Kirwan, *Shakespeare and the Idea of Apocrypha* (Cambridge: Cambridge University Press, 2015), 44, 146–52.

53 Emma Whipday, *Shakespeare's Domestic Tragedies: Violence in the Early Modern Home* (Cambridge: Cambridge University Press, 2019), 3.

54 Ibid., 191, 164.

55 Ibid., 190–1.

56 Macdonald P. Jackson, 'One-Horse Races: Some Recent Studies', in *The New Oxford Shakespeare Authorship Companion*, ed. Gary Taylor and Gabriel Egan (Oxford: Oxford University Press, 2017), 48–59.

57 MacDonald P. Jackson, 'Material for an Edition of *Arden of Faversham*' (B.Litt. thesis, Oxford University, 1963).

58 Macdonald P. Jackson, *Determining the Shakespeare Canon: Arden of Faversham and A Lover's Complaint* (Oxford: Oxford University Press, 2014).

59 Jonathan Hope, *The Authorship of Shakespeare's Plays: A Socio-Linguistic Study* (Cambridge: Cambridge University Press, 1994); Arthur F. Kinney, 'Authoring *Arden of Faversham*', in *Shakespeare, Computers, and the Mystery of Authorship*, ed. Hugh Craig and Arthur F. Kinney (Cambridge: Cambridge University Press, 2009), 78–99; Marina Tarlinskaja, *Shakespeare and the Versification of English Drama, 1561–1642* (Farnham: Ashgate, 2014).

60 Will Sharpe, 'Authorship and Attribution', in *William Shakespeare and Others: Collaborative Plays*, ed. Jonathan Bate and Eric Rasmussen (New York: Palgrave Macmillan, 2013), 650.

61 Gary Taylor and Rory Loughnane, 'The Canon and Chronology of Shakespeare's Works', in *Companion*, ed. Taylor and Egan, 490.

62 Jack Elliott and Brett Greatley-Hirsch, '*Arden of Faversham*, Shakespearean Authorship, and "The Print of Many"' and MacDonald P. Jackson, 'Shakespeare, *Arden of Faversham*, and *A Lover's Complaint*: A Review of Reviews', in Taylor and Egan, *Companion*, 139–81 (quotation from 141) and 123–35.

63 Jackson, 'Gentle Shakespeare and the Authorship of *Arden of Faversham*', *The Shakespearean International Yearbook* 11 (2011): 35; Taylor, 'Introduction', *Arden of Faversham*, 490.

64 Brian Vickers, 'Authorship Candidates for *Arden of Faversham*: Kyd, Shakespeare, and Thomas Watson', *Studies in Philology* 118, no. 2 (2021): 308–41.

65 Darren Freebury-Jones, 'The Diminution of Thomas Kyd', *Journal of Early Modern Studies* 8 (2019): 251–77; Freebury-Jones, 'In Defence of Kyd: Evaluating the Claim for Shakespeare's Part Authorship of *Arden of Faversham*', *Authorship* 7, no. 2 (2018); Vickers, 'Verbal Repetition in *Arden of Faversham*: Shakespeare or Kyd?', *Notes and Queries* 65, no. 4 (2018): 498–502. Quotation from Freebury-Jones, 'Exploring Verbal Relations between *Arden of Faversham* and John Lyly's *Endymion*', *Renaissance and Reformation* 41, no. 4 (2018): 94.

66 Michael J. Hirrel, 'Thomas Watson, Playwright: Origins of Modern English Drama', in *Lost Plays in Shakespeare's England*, ed. David McInnis and Matthew Steggle (New York: Palgrave Macmillan, 2014), 201.

67 Gary Taylor, 'Shakespeare, *Arden of Faversham*, and Four Forgotten Playwrights', *Review of English Studies* 71, no. 302 (2020): 894; Vickers, 'Authorship Candidates'.

4

New directions

Susan of Faversham: Staging subordination in *Arden*

Emma Whipday

In staging the 'true crime' of the murder of a Kentish gentleman by his wife and her accomplices, *Arden of Faversham* explores early modern crises of political, religious and domestic authority.[1] Alice Arden is, as the title page of the quarto terms her, Arden's 'disloyall and wanton wyfe'.[2] She rebels against Arden's domestic authority: through her (open, though frequently denied) adultery; in inviting dangerous masterless men within her home and granting them the key to her husband's counting house; in hiring these men, and others, to commit her husband's murder; and finally, in striking the killing blow herself.[3] This murder is an act of 'petty treason', defined in the period as 'the [h]omicide of a master by a servant; of a husband by a wife; and of an ecclesiastical superior by his inferior'.[4] In rebelling against her husband and (by implication) her monarch, and in challenging the institution of marriage itself through her argument that 'Love is a god, and marriage is but words' (1.101), Alice is perhaps the most striking threat to household (and social) order in the world of the play, but she is by no means the only threat.⁵ Mosby is socially mobile, a 'botcher' (1.24) who has risen through patronage to wear silk and carry a sword, aping the status of gentleman; he seeks to cement this status in becoming, as Alice puts it, 'master' of Alice's 'house' (1.634), and plots to later kill Alice herself to ensure his own safety (8.43). Michael is a loyal servant to his mistress in agreeing to murder his master; he is therefore simultaneously an obedient household subject and a petty traitor, undermining hierarchies even as he upholds them. Furthermore, he threatens to prove a further danger to household hierarchies, in plotting to kill his elder brother for his land (1.171–4), and, in the immediate aftermath of Arden's murder, suggests to Susan that they kill their mistress with 'ratsbane' (14.298) to prevent her from betraying their involvement in the crime – an act that would make him a petty traitor twice over. The insubordination of Arden's household is situated by the play in the wider context of failed hospitality, neighbourhood quarrels and the contested distribution of formerly monastic land, exposing the fault lines both in horizontal neighbourly relationships and in the vertical authority of household and state. Yet among *Arden*'s murderers and accomplices, only one is consistently subordinated to both legitimate and illegitimate authority: Susan, a figure who has suffered relative critical neglect.

Introducing Susan: service and siblinghood

Susan is in fact a composite of two women involved in the murder and its aftermath: a servant in the Arden household, Elizabeth Stafford, who was (according to the Wardmote Book) present at the murder (though not an active participant in it), and Mosby's kinswoman Cicely Ponder, who was engaged to marry Arden's servant Michael and who helped to dispose of Arden's body.⁶ The fictional Susan of the play is both a maid in the Arden's household and sister to Mosby and becomes an accomplice after the fact by assisting her mistress in cleaning up Arden's blood and removing his body from the house. This conflation of the two female accomplices may have been a matter of theatrical necessity: the theatrical provenance of *Arden of Faversham* is unclear, but it seems likely that the company had just two boy actors able to play female roles. One of these boy actors was, presumably, exceptionally skilled, as Alice Arden is one of the largest and most prominent female roles on the early modern stage; indeed, Terri Bourus suggests that in giving so large a proportion of the play's lines to a single female role, the play is 'unique in the extant early modern repertoire', and she argues that the role was significant enough to have been performed by 'the young Richard Burbage'.[7] The role of Susan, in contrast, is minor, appropriate to the junior of two boy actors, and yet the theatrical conflation of the two accomplices to create this fictional figure is significant in its effect on the play's exploration of disrupted authority, as this discussion will explore.

Susan's displacement from the main plot, as the only accomplice not involved in the crime itself, reinforces her status as victim rather than perpetrator, a status that is linked to her obedience (and vulnerability) as a single woman subject to various competing household structures. As Amy Froide observes:

> Singlewomen were expected to remain in a dependent position in which they lived as daughters, or if their parents were deceased, as sisters, kin, or servants in another male's household.[8]

In this chapter, I suggest that the conflation of Elizabeth Stafford and Cicely Ponder allows the play to interrogate the competing pressures experienced by early modern female servants who, as single women, were simultaneously under the authority of the family they were born to; the household in which they served; and, potentially, their future husbands. As Iman Sheeha argues, *Arden of Faversham* is 'centrally concerned with the failure of the Ardens to be a responsible *master and mistress* to their domestic servants': Arden in failing to govern his household successfully, and Alice in perverting her role as household mistress by making her servants her accomplices.[9] This chapter suggests that Susan suffers the consequences of two further failures in authority: that in becoming an accomplice to murder, Susan is not only subordinated by her master and mistress but also by her brother and the men who seek to marry her. As Ros King has noted, conflating the two real women makes Susan 'the beloved of both Michael and the painter' (another would-be murderer, Clarke), which, as King puts it, 'has the effect of linking the murderers even more strongly together in both rivalry and obligation'; the murder becomes sexually motivated for Michael and Clarke, just as it is for Mosby and Alice, when Susan is constructed as the prize for which the murder is committed.[10]

Furthermore, Susan's positioning in relation to the authority structures of service, siblinghood and (projected) marriage enables the playwright to explore not only threats *against* early modern structures of authority but also the threats implicit within those structures.

Domestic conduct literature of the period was deeply invested in the ideal of the hierarchical household. Dudley Fenner, in his treatise 'The Order of the Household', writes that 'the household order hath 2. parts': 'the governours of the family' and 'those which are governed in the same'. He further specifies that 'for the most part, the chief of the familie are maried folke, and so in common, the governors of the house'.[11] Fenner's emphasis is upon both single hierarchical relationships and dual positions of submission and responsibility that a member of the household can inhabit – such as, as one of the governing 'maried folke', the housewife, who must be a governing mistress and mother but a submissive wife. In Susan's case, all her many roles involve submission; yet these loyalties can come into conflict, since she is represented as loyal to, and the property of, the two instigators of the plot against her master – Alice and Mosby. As an unmarried woman and a desirable match, Susan is vulnerable to the machinations of the household governors of both the family to whom she was born and the family she serves. Furthermore, the divisions between the 'maried folke' who should govern the latter household – her cuckolded master and her plotting mistress – complicate her household subordination: it is impossible for Susan to be simultaneously obedient to her brother, mistress and master.

Arden of Faversham offers a challenge to the domestic ideal of conduct literature, in uncoupling the relationship between domestic authority and state authority. As William Gouge writes:

> So we may say of inferiors that cannot be subject in a familie, they can hardly be brought to yeeld such subjection as they ought in Church or common-wealth. . . . As for children under the government of their parents, and servants in a familie, their whole calling is to be obedient to their parents and masters. . . .[12]

According to Gouge's formulation, obedient household subordinates were obedient state subjects; household rebels were traitors against the church and the commonwealth; and the entire purpose of those in subordinate positions was to obey the commands of those in authority. The failures of authority in *Arden* challenge Gouge's ideal that obedience in the household must imply obedience to church and commonwealth. In tracing Susan's fatal obedience to her brother, mistress and future husband(s), I argue that the play uses the invention of Susan to explore wider crises of authority in early modern England. I develop this argument through dramaturgical analysis of Susan in performance, to offer a four-dimensional close reading, both of her speech, silence and action onstage, and of her offstage construction by those in authority over her.

As the smaller and less significant of the two female roles in the play, Susan is likely to have been played by a junior apprentice. As Stern observes, apprentices were apprenticed to a sharer rather than the company and would be 'instructed' on their performance by that sharer; in more general terms, 'established actors instructed secondary actors'.[13] Susan's position as a servant, which was, as Sheeha argues, an 'apprenticeship' in 'huswifery', is therefore doubled by the position of the actor playing Susan as theatrical apprentice, whose own apprenticeship (and service) involves the performance of the servant role.[14]

In order to consider the 'part' that Susan plays, it is necessary to reconstruct the 'actor's part' (or 'cue-script'). Indeed, the two were interchangeable in the experience of the early modern actor, as Simon Palfrey and Tiffany Stern argue:

> 'Part' signified not just the character in a play. It stood for the written paper, often made into a roll, on which that part was transcribed, and the nature of the way in which the text was presented on that roll. It was the text an actor received, learned from, and in a very real sense owned.[15]

The part would contain an actor's lines, and a two- or three-word 'cue' (something that the amateur actor Flute in *Midsummer Night's Dream* famously misunderstands when he recites his part 'cues and all' [3.1.95]). In what follows, I reconstruct Susan's part and use it as a basis for an imaginative reconstruction of the onstage experience of the actor. Drawing on a practice as research workshop exploring whether the role of Susan can be performed unprepared and unrehearsed, I suggest that Susan's fatal obedience within the world of the play is doubled by the onstage subordination of the actor in performance.

'Susan is mine': Betrothing Susan

Susan's first entrance occurs in the play's lengthy first scene. Prior to this entrance, the boy actor playing this role must wait for his cue for 587 lines, during the course of which eight characters enter and exit. Susan is introduced some 440 lines before she appears onstage; when Michael promises Alice that he will kill his master, declaring 'he shall not live above a week' (1.145), Alice answers:

> On that condition, Michael, here is my hand:
> None shall have Mosby's sister but thyself. (1.146–7)

The joining of hands is characteristic of the marriage ceremony laid down in the Book of Common Prayer, which states 'the Minister receiving the woman at her fathers or friends hands, shall cause the man to take the woman by the right hand, and so either to give their troth to other'.[16] As Farah Karim-Cooper observes, the 'joining of hands was such an important part of a marriage, that Shakespeare's Beatrice suggests the phrase "take hands" is synonymous with nuptials'.[17] Alice's pledge to Michael is therefore a near-parody of marriage by private contract; Alice and Michael take hands, as the Book of Common Prayer requires, yet they do so not to seal their own vows, but rather to solemnize the exchange of Mosby's sister in marriage for the murder of Alice's husband. Alice has seemingly usurped the role of Susan in her own betrothal scene and has done so without even referring to her by name: Susan is here defined by Alice solely in relation to her familial position.

Alice's right to dispose of Susan appears to lie in Alice's dual relation to her. Alice is at once Susan's mistress, in a position of household authority over her, and the lover of Susan's brother, and therefore able (through her power over him) to usurp Mosby's authority as sibling. However, Alice's promise is challenged by the rival claim of her own lover: Mosby has promised his sister in marriage elsewhere, again in return for Arden's death, as Michael complains:

> I understand the painter here hard by
> Hath made report that he and Sue is sure? (148–9)

Michael's use of the nickname 'Sue' – the only such usage in the play – connotes a certain intimacy: a greater level of intimacy than that implied by Alice's once-removed references to Susan as 'Mosby's sister'. Yet Michael quickly reveals that he, like Alice, thinks of Susan primarily in terms of homosocial rivalry and personal gain. He plans to write a 'taunting' (1.157) letter to Clarke and agrees to kill his master because 'Susan, being a maid, / May beg me from the gallows of the shrieve' (1.165–6) – a hope that Alice quickly quashes – and fantasizes about killing his own brother for his inheritance, to make himself a more attractive match. Alice promises him that 'Susan's thine!' (1.160), reinforcing the sense that Susan is within her gift, and it is this promise that prompts Michael to agree to the murder.

When, later in the same scene, the painter Clarke promises to murder Arden through the device of a poisoned picture, he likewise constructs Susan in relation to the projected murder:

Provided, as you have given your word,
I may have Susan Mosby to my wife. (1.248–9)

Mosby engages in another parodic contract, declaring 'Clarke, here's my hand; my sister shall be thine' (1.260). Clarke answers:

Then, brother, to requite this courtesy,
You shall command my life, my skill, and all. (261–2)

Once the details of the murder have been agreed, the contract is confirmed by both Mosby and Alice, who join together in their disposal of Susan:

ALICE
    As I am a gentlewoman, Clarke, next day
    Thou and Susan shall be married.
MOSBY
    And I'll make her dowry more than I'll talk of, Clarke.
(1.285–7)

Mosby and Alice here assume dual responsibility for Susan. It is Mosby, as Susan's brother and the head of her familial household, who has the ability to discuss the precise terms of the dowry, yet it is the projected inheritance that Mosby shall gain through murdering Arden and marrying Alice that enables him to speak of the 'greater dowry' he will be able to provide.

Each of these parodic contracts is engaged in without the consent of Susan, highlighting her lack of agency in determining her own fate. This lack of agency is reinforced when Mosby uses his sister as a cover for his adultery later in the scene, telling Alice's husband:

> And, Arden, though I now frequent thy house,
> 'Tis for my sister's sake, her waiting-maid . . . (1.332–3)

Just as Susan's hand in marriage is bartered for murderous assistance without her knowledge, so Susan is unknowingly made the excuse for Mosby's transgressive presence. Yet Mosby eventually acknowledges the necessity of Susan's consent in the match he has made for her, asking Alice:

> How have you dealt and tempered with my sister –
> What, will she have my neighbour Clarke, or no? (1.539–40)

In reply, Alice asks, 'Think you that maids look not for fair words?' (1.542). This is the first glimpse the play provides of the possibility of Susan's autonomy – yet it is in reference to Alice's manipulation of this autonomy, as 'tempering' in this period was to 'control, direct, guide, rule, govern, overrule', as well as to 'bring into a suitable or desirable frame of mind; to dispose favourably, to persuade'.[18] Mosby is asking if Alice has used her position to 'temper' his sister, in imposing her domestic government – and her powers of persuasion – upon Susan.

Following the aforementioned parodic contracts, made in her absence, Clarke is at last dispatched to fetch the woman for whom they have been bartering:

> Go to her, Clarke – she's all alone within.
> Michael, my man, is clean out of her books. (1.543–4)

The assumption here is clear: as one man is out of favour, another will do. Alice acknowledges the necessity for Clarke's actions in the courtship – 'Let him woo himself!' (1.541), she instructs Mosby – but takes Susan's acceptance of this courtship for granted.

On Clarke's exit, the offstage Susan is placed, imaginatively, in a strikingly vulnerable situation: she is alone in the house where she is in service and approached by a man on the orders of her mistress. As Sheeha has observed, this is characteristic of the sexual vulnerability of servants to their household governors, though surviving court cases usually feature the master, not the mistress, in the position of sexual predator.[19] Susan has already been implicitly associated with sexual transgression by being made Mosby's excuse for adultery; here, Alice takes advantage of Susan's vulnerability by proxy, in inviting Clarke inside. The lines between Susan's own present-tense obedience to her mistress (and the brother with whom her mistress is in conference), and her future obedience to the man who will, if she is obedient to her mistress in the now of his approach, become her husband, have become blurred.

Some forty-three lines later, Susan herself finally enters – those few minutes of stage time in which Alice and Mosby are left alone to plot and wrangle presumably allowing long enough for Clarke to complete his 'wooing'. Susan's 'part' for this scene would look something like this:

———————————————————————— is amiss.

Here enters CLARKE *and* SUSAN.

———————————————————————— be the man?
It resteth in your grant. Some words are passed,
And haply we be grown unto a match
If you be willing that it shall be so. (1.587, 596–8)

The cue for her entrance – 'is amiss' – is spoken by her brother, but the actor playing Susan may not need to be alert to this cue, for he enters with the actor playing Clarke, whose position as Susan's future husband is visually affirmed by their joint entrance. It is Clarke who is first addressed when they appear; first Alice, and then Mosby, asks Clarke (rather than Susan) to report on the success of his wooing. In response to this, Susan's first act on stage is a silent one: Clarke declares 'Susan is mine!' (in a verbal echo of Alice's earlier 'Susan's thine'), to which Alice responds, 'You make her blush' (1.594). Alice completes Clarke's verse line here; just as Alice, in taking Michael's hand, usurps Susan's role in a parody of a marriage contract, so here, in joining metrically with Clarke, Alice reinforces the sense of a wooing by proxy even when Susan herself is present onstage. As I have argued elsewhere, the narration of a blush onstage is both a proprietary act (claiming authority over the body described) and a dramaturgical one; Alice at once narrates Susan's body in a sign of her power over her and meta-theatrically instructs the audience to imagine a blush on the (presumably blushless) actor's face.[20] Susan's first two onstage actions, then, are subordinated to the performances of others – she is accompanied onstage by Clarke, and her actions are described (and perhaps also, simultaneously, created) by Alice's blush-making observation.[21]

Susan's first line onstage is in response to a direct question from her brother: 'What, sister, is it Clarke must be the man?' (1.595). While he does not address her by name, the use of 'sister' has both a thematic and a dramaturgical function: it reminds the audience of the significance of the brother–sister relationship in providing Mosby with his (ambiguous) authority over Susan, and it informs the actor playing Susan that she is being asked a question, a dramaturgical 'cue' that accompanies the cue line. Susan's obedient answer to her brother is required for Mosby to confirm the match; her submission to his will supports his authority. Here, Gouge's prescription that a servant's 'whole calling is to be obedient to their . . . masters' is challenged by the familial authority that Mosby invokes, an authority that is reinforced by Susan's conception of herself as within her brother's 'grant', as Mosby confirms: 'You see my sister's yet at my dispose' (1.600). In her one line in this scene, Susan is wholly submissive; the 'tempering' that her brother imagined necessary has been proven to be redundant. Susan is then promised to Clarke on the condition that he poisons Arden; she does not comment on this and exits with the general '*Exeunt*'.

The experience of the actor in this scene is thus startlingly like that of the character: he is repeatedly discussed, but can only speak when directly addressed, and, beyond the blush narrated by someone else, there are no opportunities for individual action or volition, only reaction. Likewise, Susan is subordinated in this scene by gender, class, familial relation and service position, and this subordination produces her silence.

Having appeared onstage in the first scene, Susan does not enter again until the climactic murder scene. She is, however, yet again discussed in her absence. She is invoked repeatedly by Greene,

Black Will and Shakebag as the motive for Michael's complicity ('for her sake . . . the villain hath sworn the slaughter of his master' [3.126]; 'kill your master for his [Mosby's] sister's sake' [152]; 'gain his sister's love' [175]) – constructed at once as an object of desire and as defined in relation to her brother. She is also, in the following scene, discussed by her master. When Arden learns of Michael's designs on Susan through catching him with a love letter, he complains:

> Susan my maid, the painter and my man,
> A crew of harlots, all in love, forsooth. . . .
> Wilt thou be married to so base a trull?
> 'Tis Mosby's sister! Come I once at home,
> I'll rouse her from remaining in my house. (3.26–7, 30–2)

Susan is again defined in relation to her brother; she is threatened with homelessness because of Mosby's transgressions ("Tis Mosby's sister'). Yet Arden never does what he threatens; his assumption of household authority here, as throughout the play, is shown to be hollow. Neither Susan nor Michael remains 'his' maid or man; the latter will betray him to the conspirators Black Will and Shakebag, and both will attempt to clear the house of evidence in the aftermath of his murder. Arden's return home to supposedly 'rouse' Susan ends in the household he purports to govern conspiring together to bring about his death, and rather than ejecting Susan from the house, he first invites his murderous rival to supper and then unknowingly shelters two hired killers.

Susan knows neither of Michael's transgression, which so nearly leads to her dismissal, nor of the murderous plot in which she will shortly be implicated. She has witnessed the (unsuccessful) plan to poison Arden, but (to the audience's knowledge) is told nothing of the eventually successful plot. However, in the aftermath of the murder, her assistance in removing the evidence of the crime is taken for granted, and her complicity, like her betrothal, is decided without her knowledge. When planning the murder, Michael asks Alice, 'shall not Susan know it?' (14.167). Alice is confident that Susan will be loyal to her brother and mistress, at the expense of the loyalty due to her master, and answers: 'Yes, for she'll be as secret as ourselves' (14.168).

'Wash away this blood': Susan as accomplice

In the murder scene itself (scene fourteen), Susan finally becomes aware of what her mistress and future master have planned for her. The actor's 'part' for this scene looks something like this:

_____farewell too.

Exeunt [Black Will and Shakebag. Knocking]
[*Here enters*] SUSAN
Mistress, the guests are at the doors.
Hearken, they knock! What, shall I let them in?

_____away this blood.

The blood cleaveth to the ground and will not out.

_____the blood appears!

What's the reason, mistress, can you tell?

_____sit down too.

Peace, we have other matters now in hand.
I fear me, Michael, all will be bewrayed.

_____buy some ratsbane.

Why, Michael, wilt thou poison thyself?

_____fear she'll tell.

Tush, Michael, fear not her; she's wise enough.

_____counsel me.

Alas, I, counsel? Fear frights away my wits.

_____ filthy gore.

My brother, you and I shall rue this deed.

_____ to the fields.

Then they bear the body to the fields.

_____fear them not.

[*Here enter* SUSAN *and* MICHAEL.]
As we went it snowed all the way,
Which makes me fear our footsteps will be spied.

                 them again!

But it had done before we came back again.

                 this knife?

Ah, Michael, through this thy negligence
Thou hast betrayed and undone us all.

                 him too.

Exeunt. (14.254–6, 258–9, 261–2, 293–5, 298–301, 330–1, 333–4, 351–351 SD, 360–4, 388–90, 417)

An actor approaching this part might notice a few clues to Susan's role in the scene. She addresses at least two people directly ('Michael' and 'mistress'), both of whom are in positions of current or future authority over her. She also four times repeats the word 'fear' – in her fear that all will be discovered, in advising Michael not to fear 'her' (who may be assumed to be Alice, the only other female character), in describing herself as too frightened to 'counsel', and in her fear that her footsteps will be seen. That four of her eleven utterances in the scene focus on fear gives a sense of Susan's dominant emotion, and a clue to the potential delivery of these lines.[22] The actor might also note the emphasis on violence and its aftermath: Susan discusses evidence (bloodstains, snow-covered footprints and negligence involving a knife), potential madness or foolishness ('fear frights away my wits') and suicide ('wilt thou poison thyself?'). Susan's part also suggests that, unlike her courtship scene with Clarke, she is not here wholly responsive, nor is she silent; she initiates conversation, asking three separate questions (two of her mistress, one of Michael), and she is willing to contradict, rebuke and instruct the characters she addresses ('Hearken'; 'Peace'; 'Tush . . . fear not her'; 'My brother, you and I shall rue this deed'; 'But it had done'). Susan, then, is not negligible in this scene; here she has a voice and the power to use it.

Considering Susan's part in relation to the scene as a whole, we can see that Susan's entrance is cued by a verbal cue (Black Will's 'farewell too'), but there are two additional dramaturgical cues at the same moment: the exit of Black Will and Shakebag (presumably at the other door) and the knocking that prompts Susan's observation in her opening lines ('Hearken, they knock'). Susan's line on her entrance is addressed to her mistress; the actor therefore knows to whom it should be spoken. Her question – 'Shall I let them in?' – is the question of a servant, wishing to be told whether to admit guests, but it is also a question by an actor; if Alice answers in the affirmative, presumably he must exit and then re-enter with the actors playing the neighbours. The answer is negative, though by implication only; Alice instead addresses her lover. Only then does Alice turn to Susan, and give her an instruction which the actor could not have predicted from the 'part': 'And, Susan, fetch water and wash away this blood' (14.258).

'Wash away this blood' is a direct instruction, both from a mistress to a servant and from one actor to another.[23] As Susan Staub puts it, 'The murder becomes subsumed into the routines of the household'; Susan's involvement in cleaning up the bloody aftermath of the crime is here an element of her household work.[24] The surviving playtext does not clarify whether Susan enters and re-enters, or whether the water is already onstage to be 'fetched' (perhaps brought on when Michael is instructed to 'fetch me a cup of wine' earlier in the scene [203]). Either way, there is then a period of silence while Susan complies, for the next line is spoken by Susan herself: 'The blood cleaveth to the ground and will not out' (14.252). In that silence, Susan must both fetch the water and use it to attempt (and fail) to clean up the blood. As Catherine Richardson argues:

> The action is stark, with little dialogue and an intense and pressured focus on a parody of domestic routine. This silent work creates a space in which the aftermath of murder can be experienced in a symbolism which plays out from the indelibility of the physical stain.[25]

This period of silent household work is also, as Richardson and Tara Hamling suggest, 'a striking counterpart' to the game of tables that precedes the murder, and patterns 'leisure against work, male against female activities'.[26] After the hectic action of the murder scene – in which, after frantic asides between Black Will, Alice and Michael, Arden is first pulled to the ground with a towel, then hit with a pressing iron, then twice stabbed – this silence provides a pause, a moment of calm. But it also provides discomfort: discomfort for Susan, as she becomes gradually aware of the indelible nature of the blood which necessitates her failure in what Ariane Balizet terms a 'housekeeping problem'; and, presumably, discomfort for the actor, who, having heard his cue word, must understand that the silence that has fallen in the playhouse can only be broken when he has both fetched the water and demonstrably failed in the act of cleaning.[27] And yet, for the boy actor, this moment of difficulty also affords a moment of theatrical agency: this junior apprentice is ultimately in control of the duration of his cleaning attempt, choosing when this uncomfortable silence will be broken; the more experienced actors, like the audience, must wait on his pleasure.

Mosby then enters, and Alice complains to him, 'In vain we strive, for here his blood remains', implying that she and Susan continue to attempt to wash away the blood. Mosby responds:

Why, strew rushes on it, can you not?
This wench doth nothing! Fall unto the work. (14.267–8)

Here is another direct instruction, by a brother to a sister, which is also an instruction to the actor; 'Fall unto the work' is presumably addressed to Susan as the idle 'wench'. This line functions regardless of whether the boy actor playing Susan has responded to Alice's implied stage direction ('we strive'): if Susan does not, in fact, join with Alice in continuing to clean the blood, Mosby's words are a rebuke; if she is indeed 'striving', the line becomes a critique of her failed attempt – while instructing her to cease washing the bloodstain and instead hide it with rushes. Whatever the choices of the boy playing Susan, at this climactic moment Mosby engages with his sister only as a servant, concerned that she remove the evidence of his crime.

Susan presumably continues to clean a while longer, but, as a servant should, ceases this activity by the entrance of the first guests. She is then silent, with no actions required of her, until directly addressed by Michael:

Susan, shall thou and I wait on them? Or, and thou sayest the word, let us sit down too. (14.292–3)

His question is a symptom of the inversion of domestic order produced by Arden's death – when the two are accomplices to the murder of their master (and keep the secrets of their mistress), why should they continue in their roles as servants? But Susan silences him with her 'Tush', and the two discuss their predicament until interrupted by an instruction for Michael (but not Susan) from Mosby: the new domestic order is enforced, as Michael is ordered to bring his 'master' Mosby a cup of beer. Several of the guests then leave to fetch Arden, and Michael offers, in an aside to Alice, to 'rid the rest away', exiting with Bradshaw and Adam. It is at this point that Alice again turns to Susan:

> Go, Susan, and bid thy brother come. (14.328)

This is, again, a direct instruction, presumably addressed to both actor and character. But it is almost immediately contradicted:

> But wherefore should he come? Here is naught but fear.
> Stay, Susan, stay, and help to counsel me. (14.329–30)

If Susan has moved to exit, she must now turn back, a visible sign of her mistress's indecision. After Susan has responded to this with another statement of fear, there is another action, as described in the stage direction: '*Then they open the counting-house door, and look upon Arden*' (14.331 SD). The 'they' implies that Susan is involved in this action, but, as if to make doubly sure that Susan's attention is directed to the corpse, Alice also addresses her:

> See, Susan, where thy quondam master lies!
> Sweet Arden, smeared in blood and filthy gore. (14.332–3)

Susan is here a proxy for the audience; she, like us, is invited to view the corpse (presumably the body of the living actor who played Arden) in terms of both what it was (her master) and what it now is (grotesque evidence of Alice's crime). For those audience members who are not able to view the counting house, which may be located in the discovery space at the back of the stage, Alice's narration paints a gory picture. Alice's direct instructions to Susan continue; when Susan rebukes her ('My brother, you and I shall rue this deed', 14.334), Alice replies:

> Come, Susan, help to lift his body forth,
> And let our salt tears be his obsequies. (14.335–6)

Here, once again, Susan is being instructed to perform a grotesque version of her domestic duties as a servant (lifting her master's corpse), while at the same time being instructed in her role as an actor (to weep).

A few lines later, Mosby and Greene enter to plot the disposal of the corpse, but then Michael re-enters with the warning that the Watch are on their way. Susan is included in Alice's general instruction to those assembled (Mosby, Greene, Michael and Susan): 'convey the body to the fields' (14.354). She then re-enters on a cue from Alice ('fear them not'), to say:

> As we went it snowed all the way,
> Which makes me fear our footsteps will be spied. (14.361–2)

Here, Susan picks up on Alice's claim of fearlessness to reinforce her own anxiety about the discovery of the crime. Alice attempts to dispute this with a dismissive 'Peace, fool, the snow will cover them again!' (14.363), to which Susan responds, 'But it had done before we came back again' (14.364). In context, this line sits alongside the moments visible in Susan's part where she instructs or debates with the other characters: Susan is talking back, contradicting her mistress and refusing to be silenced by her.

Susan's line is followed by a knock – what was her initial cue to enter and speak is now a cue to fall silent. She has only one more speech in this scene: an aside to Michael. Here, for the first time, she initiates an aside:

> Ah, Michael, through this thy negligence
> Thou hast betrayed and undone us all. (14.389–90)

Here, she directly rebukes the man she was planning to marry, perhaps in recognition that, now, the marriage will never take place: the murder, which became the excuse for the engagement, has undone it.

Susan does not speak again in this scene; she is escorted offstage with the other murderers and accomplices, in silence. Her exit, like all of her actions up to this point, is narrated onstage; Franklin instructs the silent men of the Watch, 'Bring that villain, and Mosby's sister too' (14.415). Susan is again reduced to her identity as sister – and this identity is now to lead to her death.

As Oliver Morgan argues in his book *Turn-Taking in Shakespeare*, 'the speak-when-you're-spoken-to assumption is analytically useful in the study of dialogue'.[28] For the majority of her time onstage, Susan only speaks when spoken to, and is only spoken to by those in authority over her (mistress, brother or supposed future husband). This is due to Susan's subordinated household position, but it is also helpful to the actor playing Susan's role: when acting with a 'part' in a group scene, naming a character when addressing them offers a reminder to an inexperienced actor to respond to the speaker. Yet as the Arden household grows increasingly topsy-turvy in the aftermath of the crime, Susan is able to talk back to her fiancé and mistress, to speak without being spoken to, and to voice her disagreement with, and criticism of, them both: a moment of domestic insubordination that also grants the actor a moment of theatrical agency.

The extent to which the experiences of apprentice actors might map onto the experiences of their characters has been discussed by critics almost exclusively in terms of female impersonation. For example, Richard Madelaine observes of the boy actor playing the role of Katherine in *Taming of the Shrew*:

> Taming and training were often seen as synonymous in Shakespeare's day, and there is an analogous relationship between the taming of Kate – which involves training her to respond in ways that are perceived as 'feminine' – and the training of the apprentice actor who plays her. In these terms, what is interesting are the theatrical *training-functions* in the shrew's role, and in particular the training-functions of its *masculine* elements.[29]

I suggest Susan's role likewise involves 'training': not training in female impersonation, but rather, implied stage directions that enable both Susan to perform her role as a servant, and the boy actor to perform his role as Susan. In the examples I give above, Susan is repeatedly instructed in how she should move and behave in the scene: 'Susan, fetch water'; 'Go, Susan'; 'Stay, Susan'; 'Come, Susan'; 'See, Susan'; 'the wench does nothing'; 'our salt tears'. These instructions are simultaneously domestic and theatrical.

In a practice as research workshop at the 'Interconnections' conference at Newcastle University, I experimented with colleagues to explore the experience of the actor playing Susan in the murder scene.[30] It was not possible to replicate, with volunteer actors, the expertise of experienced early modern players, and so, to mimic the junior apprentice's level of comparative inexperience, I rehearsed the scene once with every actor except Susan. Susan was then given her 'part' at the workshop itself, and she was asked to speak her lines when cued and to behave only as the onstage characters instructed her.

Jennifer Richards, who volunteered to play the role of Susan, commented on the fact that she 'did not think' during the staging of the scene; with no prior preparation and no information beyond her lines, her role was entirely responsive. She moved when ordered to, followed Michael to the side of the stage when he addressed her in an aside, and responded whenever given either a personal instruction or an instruction that incorporated her as part of a group. The silence at the moment of 'washing' the blood became particularly tense in performance, as Jenny, intent on her task, took some moments to realize that her instruction had also been her cue: a moment of simultaneous tension within the imagined world of the play, and the theatrical world of the actors.

It was striking that this experiment 'worked' in performance: combined with the 'part', onstage instructions were sufficient to ensure the unrehearsed Susan was able to perform her role in the scene. This is not to suggest that the Elizabethan actor playing Susan would have been reliant entirely upon his part and onstage instructions; indeed, as Stern suggests, it is likely that an apprentice actor would have rehearsed with (and been 'instructed' by) his master. Rather, I suggest the play demonstrates a command of the dramaturgical potential of early modern theatre in constructing Susan's 'part' to cue both the imagined role and the theatrical performance. *Arden of Faversham* provides a theatrical framework within which the junior apprentice's relative inexperience can be safely situated, through personal address, implicit stage directions and onstage authority structures that mimic those in the world of the play, all of which would have enabled the theatrical reality to reinforce the theatrical illusion.

Concluding Susan: The maidservant's tragedy

Susan appears onstage once more after the murder scene: in the final scene, along with the other prisoners being led to 'speedy execution' (18.39). Her 'part' for this scene is as follows:

> _____too late.
> Ah, gentle brother, wherefore should I die?
> I knew not of it till the deed was done.
> _____too long.
> Seeing no hope on earth, in heaven is my hope. (18.18–20, 35–6)

Susan's 'part' here encapsulates her transition in the scene, from bemoaning her fate to accepting it. In both cases she is cued by her brother; in the first instance she replies to him directly, and he responds:

> For thee I mourn more than for myself,
> But let it suffice, I cannot save thee now. (18.21–2)

In the second, she follows her brother's final lines, in which he blames 'women' – presumably Alice – for his misfortunes (34–5). Michael likewise attempts to cast the blame on the women involved in the plot, telling Susan:

> An if your brother and my mistress had not promised me you in marriage, I had ne'er given consent to this foul deed. (18.23–5)

While Michael is clear that the agency lay with Mosby and Alice, he nonetheless emphasizes that Susan was the prize for which he consented to participate in the murder. Yet Michael, too, experiences an alteration over the course of this short scene; his next and final line is, 'Faith, I care not, seeing I die with Susan' (18.37). Susan, however, engages with neither his blame nor his romantic vision of lovers dying together; indeed, she is given no opportunity to respond to Michael's misogynistic attack, as the Mayor silences Michael's recriminations with an explicit 'Leave to accuse each other now' (26). When she has the chance to speak again, she focusses on her personal salvation; throughout the scene, she reinforces her identity as innocent sister and as hopeful Christian, ignoring the supposed husband from the future that will never come to pass.

Unlike Michael, Susan does not have moments of direct address to the audience, and her motivations are correspondingly opaque; while Michael is what Robert Weimann has influentially termed a *platea* character, able to involve the audience in his interior struggles and moral dilemmas, Susan inhabits only the *locus*, the imagined world of the play, and never the space of the theatre itself. She therefore lacks both social privilege (within the world of the play) and theatrical privilege (in her inability to address the audience).[31] She does speak several asides, but these are asides to other characters, not to the audience. And yet, in the short final scene, comprising only thirty-nine lines, eleven of these are by or about Susan; a strikingly high proportion for a character who at first glimpse may seem negligible. She appears in only three scenes and has twenty-one lines in total, and yet the play invites us to view her death as a tragedy, one that prompts even her murderous, woman-hating brother to grieve. Her obedient victimhood is presented to the audience by Mosby as a cause for mourning, granting the apprentice actor the opportunity to invite such mourning through his performance. Furthermore, Susan's insistence on herself as a tragic *sister* reinforces her status as a single, obedient woman, the foil to Alice's transgressive sexuality and violence. Her final line affirms the eventual outcome of Susan's tragic fate: she meditates on heaven.

Arden suggests the transgressive potential of female agency in early modern England; Alice is an outspoken and powerful protagonist who champions her own desires and challenges existing power structures. Yet the play also stages how the intersection between class and gender can render those in subordinate positions vulnerable to the machinations of others. Mosby's societal position is what renders Alice's adultery surprising to her husband, yet it is also the cause of Arden's murder – Mosby's desire to transform himself from 'botcher' to landowner and gentlemen fuels his transgressions. For Susan, the same societal position is very differently inflected: through her gender and dependent domestic and familial position as an obedient sister and servant, she is doubly subject – and doubly vulnerable – to those who would barter her hand in marriage to secure their own desires. In placing herself at her brother's disposal and showing herself loyal to her mistress even in the aftermath of murder, Susan's virtuous adherence to the hierarchical structures of the household will mean her death.

But Susan is, of course, imaginary. She is a composite of two historical women whose position in the play offers a reflection on, and interrogation of, the wider experiences of (unmarried) sisters and servants in early modern England. As this chapter has shown, Susan's obedience as a character is mapped onto the obedience required by Susan as a role: Susan is trained as both future housewife and current actor. The incorporation of murder into her domestic apprenticeship destabilizes the household order that her obedience should reinforce, offering Susan a limited opportunity for vocal agency, and the actor an opportunity to show the tragic potential of Susan's role. Susan's fatal obedience reinforces her individual victimhood, but it also suggests that when those in household authority transgress, domestic obedience can be as dangerous to the social order as domestic insubordination.

Notes

1 Thanks are due to the editors of this volume for their generous, thorough and supportive feedback and also to the speakers, chairs and attendees at the RSA 2021 panel on 'Women and Agency' and at the 2021 'All the World's a Stage' conference at Liverpool University, at which I presented early versions of this chapter, for their thought-provoking questions.

2 Anon, *The Lamentable and True Tragedie of M. Arden of Feveresham in Kent* (London, 1592), Ar.

3 On the significance of Black Will and Shakebag as 'masterless', see, for example, Michael Neill, '"This Gentle Gentleman": Social Change and the Language of Status in *Arden of Faversham*', *Medieval & Renaissance Drama in England* 10 (1998): 73–97.

4 Leon Radzinowicz, *A History of English Criminal Law* (London: Stevens, 1948), 628.

5 On the petty traitor, see for example Frances E. Dolan, 'Tracking the Petty Traitor across Genres', in *Broadside Ballads in Britain, 1500–1800*, ed. Patricia Fumerton and Anita Guerrini with the assistance of Kris McAbee (Farnham: Ashgate, 2010), 149–71.

6 *The Tragedy of Master Arden of Faversham*, ed. M. L. Wine (London: Methuen, 1973), 161.

7 Terri Bourus, '*Arden of Faversham*, Richard Burbage, and the Early Shakespeare Canon', in *Early Shakespeare, 1588–1594*, ed. Rory Loughnane and Andrew J. Power (Cambridge: Cambridge University Press, 2020), 206, 211.

8 Amy M. Froide, 'Marital Status as a Category of Difference: Singlewomen and Widows in Early Modern England', in *Singlewomen in the European Past, 1250–1800*, ed. Judith M. Bennett and Amy M. Froide (Philadelphia: University of Pennsylvania Press, 1999), 237.

9 Iman Sheeha, *Household Servants in Early Modern Domestic Tragedy* (Basingstoke: Routledge, 2020), 12.

10 Ros King, '*Arden of Faversham*: The Moral of History and the Thrill of Performance', in *The Oxford Handbook of Tudor Drama*, ed. Thomas Betteridge and Greg Walker (Oxford: Oxford University Press, 2012), 635.

11 Dudley Fenner, 'The Order of Household, Described Methodically out of the Word of God with the Contrary Abuses Found in the World', in *Certain Godly and Learned Treatises* (Edinburgh, 1592), 2, 32. See Catherine Richardson, 'Household Manuals', in *The Elizabethan Top Ten: Defining Print Popularity in Early Modern England*, ed. Andy Kesson and Emma Smith (Farnham: Ashgate, 2013), 169–78.

12 William Gouge, *Of Domesticall Duties: Eight Treatises* (London, 1622), 18–19.

13 Tiffany Stern, *Rehearsal from Shakespeare to Sheridan* (Oxford: Oxford University Press, 2000), 68. See also Scott McMillin, 'The Sharer and His Boy: Rehearsing Shakespeare's Women', in *From Script to Stage in Early Modern England*, ed. Peter Holland and Stephen Orgel (Basingstoke: Palgrave Macmillan, 2004), 231–45.

14 Sheeha, *Household Servants*, 47.

15 Simon Palfrey and Tiffany Stern, *Shakespeare in Parts* (Oxford: Oxford University Press, 2007), 1. See also Stern, *Making Shakespeare: From Stage to Page* (London: Routledge, 2004), 46–123.

16 Church of England, *The Booke of Common Prayer* (London, 1603), O8r.
17 Farah Karim-Cooper, *The Hand on the Shakespearean Stage: Gesture, Touch and the Spectacle of Dismemberment* (London: Bloomsbury, 2016), 53.
18 *OED*, 'temper', *v.*, 6, 7.
19 Sheeha, *Household Servants*, 50–1.
20 Emma Whipday, '"Thou Look'st Pale": Narrating Blanching and Blushing on the Early Modern Stage', in *Playing and Playgoing in Early Modern England: Actor, Audience and Performance*, ed. Simon Smith and Emma Whipday (Cambridge: Cambridge University Press, 2022), 37–56. See also Derek Dunne, 'Blushing on Cue: The Forensics of the Blush in Early Modern Drama', *Shakespeare Bulletin* 34, no. 2 (2016): 233–52.
21 'False feedback' that someone is blushing can itself prompt a blush; see Peter D. Drummond, 'Psychophysiology of the Blush', in *The Psychological Significance of the Blush*, ed. W. Ray Crozier and Peter J. de Jong (Cambridge: Cambridge University Press, 2013), 29.
22 On fear as a contagious emotion onstage, see Allison P. Hobgood, *Passionate Playgoing in Early Modern England* (Cambridge: Cambridge University Press, 2014), 34–63.
23 On boy actors performing domestic work, see Harry McCarthy, *Boy Actors in Early Modern England: Skill and Stagecraft in the Theatre* (Cambridge: Cambridge University Press, 2022), 63–4.
24 Susan C. Staub, 'Bloody Relations: Murderous Wives in the Street Literature of Seventeenth Century England', in *Domestic Arrangements in Early Modern England*, ed. Kari Boyd McBride (Pittsburgh: Duquesne University Press, 2002), 132; see also Catherine Richardson, *Domestic Life and Domestic Tragedy in Early Modern England: The Material Life of the Household* (Manchester: Manchester University Press, 2006), 135–6.
25 Richardson, *Domestic Life*, 124.
26 Tara Hamling and Catherine Richardson, *A Day at Home in Early Modern England: Material Culture and Domestic Life, 1500–1700* (New Haven: Yale University Press, 2017), 180–1.
27 Ariane M. Balizet, *Blood and Home in Early Modern Drama: Domestic Identity on the Renaissance Stage* (London: Routledge, 2014), 73; see also Emma Whipday, 'Everyday Murder and Household Work in Shakespeare's Domestic Tragedies', in *Staged Normality in Shakespeare's England*, ed. Rory Loughnane and Edel Semple (London: Palgrave, 2019), 215–36.

28 Oliver Morgan, *Turn-Taking in Shakespeare* (Oxford: Oxford University Press, 2019), 38.

29 Richard Madelaine, '"He speaks very shrewishly": Apprentice-training and *The Taming of the Shrew*', in *Gender and Power in Shrew-Taming Narratives, 1500–1700,* ed. David Wootton and Graham Holderness (Basingstoke: Palgrave Macmillan, 2010), 70–83 (emphases in original). On apprentice performances, see also Lucy Munro, *Shakespeare in the Theatre: The King's Men* (London: Bloomsbury, 2020), 32–42.

30 I am grateful to the performers in this scene for their performances and insights: Oskar Cox Jensen, James Harriman-Smith, Kirsten MacLeod, Jennifer Richards, Issy Tessier and Katheryn Thompson. I am also grateful to the Newcastle Humanities Research Institute for supporting the conference and to Barbara Gentili for inviting me to contribute this workshop.

31 See Robert Weimann, *Author's Pen and Actor's Voice: Playing and Writing in Shakespeare's Theatre*, ed. Helen Higbee and William N. West (Cambridge: Cambridge University Press, 2000), 180–215. See also Erika T. Lin, 'Performance Practice and Theatrical Privilege: Rethinking Weimann's Concepts of *Locus* and *Platea*', *New Theatre Quarterly* 22, no. 3 (2006): 283–98.

5

New directions

Mist opportunities: The play of the weather in *Arden of Faversham*

Chloe Kathleen Preedy

On 19 June 1590, the village of Stockbury, located some fourteen or so miles from Faversham in Kent, endured a severe hailstorm. According to an anonymous account published later that year, this 'mightie tempest' had a devastating impact, ruining 'great aboundance of corne and fruite' and shattering the windows of the parish church.[1] The contemporary report is especially alert to the economic consequences, advertising 'the impoverishing and undoing of divers men' and even calculating the cost to individuals: we learn that Master Potman lost a hundred pounds' worth of corn, and Goodman Edwardes 'all . . . he hath', while Goodman Allin's fifty-six acres and John Seede's twelve acres of wheat were left 'good for nothing'.[2] Such comprehensive destruction is characterized as a warning from God, with readers urged

> not onely to marke and behold with thy outwarde eye, the hailestones of unaccustomed bignesse, which hath beaten to

the ground and cleane spoiled the corne and fruite in the parish
... but also to print the remembraunce thereof in thy hart, and
bitterly lament the cause thereof, and with an unfained soule
aske mercy of him [God] for thy sinnes[.][3]

In particular, while God's 'great providence' is said to have protected the village's inhabitants from serious injury and 'so preserved' the adjacent parish of Hartlen 'that it received no harme', the pamphlet cautions against individual complacency, 'lest a worse thing happen unto thee'.[4]

For Alexandra Walsham, this 1590 pamphlet epitomizes the significance that environmental disturbances possessed for English Protestants.[5] Elizabethan authors were interested in the natural causes of extreme weather events, but most continued to interpret these prodigies as 'sermons inscribed by God in the sky': investigating the primary origins of meteorological phenomena was entirely compatible with speculation about their eschatological significance.[6] William Fulke's *Goodly Gallery* (1563), for instance, combines an emphasis on '*Natural Causes*' and scepticism about astrological models with a firm assertion of divine providence: the title-page quotes Psalm 148 on God's control of 'Fyre, Haile, Snowe, Ise, Wyndes, and stormes', while Fulke later credits the favourable operation of the winds to 'wonderfull and wyse providence'.[7] Fulke also indirectly provides a primary explanation for the storm that battered Stockbury twenty-seven years later, stating that hail results when 'hotte vapor[s] in the mydle region of the ayre' cool and thicken 'into a cloude whiche falling downe to the soden colde . . . is congeled into Ise'.[8] At the same time, Fulke's text implies that the hailstones that fell in June 1590 were not only of an 'unaccustomed bignesse' but noticeably untimely: hailstorms are said to occur most often '[i]n spryng and harvest tyme', 'seldome in sommer and wynter'.[9] For Fulke and his Protestant contemporaries, the challenge in such instances was to discern which unexpected natural phenomena possessed substantial import; to identify and disregard effects attributable to demonic deception, which God might permit in order to test the faithful; and to interpret heaven's coded messages without being misled by superstition or false assumptions.[10] Even homiletic texts acknowledge that printed reports cannot always be trusted, with the Stockbury author setting down the names of those who lost crops 'that all those that knowe the men or their dwelling place, may inquire whether this report be true or no'; yet the same reporter stresses that, 'if any should esteeme hereof as a matter of chance or fortune, or as a thing done by naturall course of the planet', they should recall the scriptural message that 'a sparrowe cannot light upon the ground without Gods permission'.[11]

The relationship between Kentish weather and divine will is important for the late Elizabethan tragedy *Arden of Faversham* (*c.* 1590), which was written within a year or so of the Stockbury hailstorm.[12] This play dramatizes the 1551 murder of the landholder Thomas Arden or Ardern. Expanding on Raphael Holinshed's detailed account in *The Chronicles of England, Scotland, and Ireland* (1577; 1587), the unidentified playwright foregrounds the numerous foiled attempts made on Arden's life before his wife Alice, her lover Mosby and their accomplices finally achieve their goal.[13] As Peter Lake and Michael Questier observe, this expanded sequence of failure at once invites and parodies providentialist readings, with the hired murderer Black Will concluding frustratedly after the sixth attempt that 'Doubtless he [Arden] is preserved by miracle' (14.31) – only to succeed on the seventh.[14] The comic effect and symbolic import of these episodes have been much discussed, but it is important to note that human actions are not the only factor in play.[15] Rather, *Arden* follows Holinshed's lead by simultaneously foregrounding the role of ambient influences, including Kent's topography and weather.[16] The religious significance of geography is implied from the start, when Arden's acquisition of 'the lands of the Abbey' registers the historical Reformation process whereby Henry VIII's government sold off seized monastic lands (1.5).[17] Other environmental factors are likewise represented in ways that intensify their presence. *Arden* contains numerous figurative and theatrically evocative references to the weather, with audience members prompted to imagine the ongoing impact of 'cold' air, 'clouds', 'sun' and 'mutable' 'wind[s]' upon the play's characters (4.107; 10.2; 12.46; 1.436). An actual February 1551 snowstorm recorded by Holinshed acquires particular significance in this context: where Holinshed notes the snow's role in preserving 'certaine footesteppes' between Arden's house and the field in which his body was discovered, *Arden*'s dialogue draws parallels between the offstage snowfall and the onstage action that emphasize the danger of ignoring the weather.[18] Moreover, the late Elizabethan tragedy features suggestive allusions to the London weather and an extended fog sequence that have no obvious precedent in contemporary chronicle sources: the latter may have been punningly inspired by Holinshed's report that Black Will's attempt to ambush Arden at the crossing to Sheppey failed when he 'mist the way', but none of the earlier extant accounts specifically mention a meteorological or symbolic fog.[19]

Both these meteorological additions have an interesting dramaturgical effect. Arden's friend Franklin's complaint that 'the air is very cold' in London operates primarily as a temporal cue to signal the onset of night (4.107). Yet this line is also a brief but telling reminder of the porous relationship between interior and exterior space, during an episode in which would-be intruders threaten Franklin's 'unlocked' house (4.101); Arden unknowingly foils this attempt on his life when he insists on checking the doors upon waking, but the draught noted by Franklin hints at Arden's continued vulnerability to betrayal from within. This attention to atmospheric conditions persists when Black Will and Shakebag transfer their efforts outdoors, seeking to ambush Arden as he travels to the Isle of Sheppey. The mist that now hinders their efforts to locate their target is especially pervasive in its effects. As this fog suffused the fictional and perhaps material environment of the staged play, early modern audiences would have encountered a performance aesthetic that is defined not by the storms that are so prominent elsewhere in Elizabethan drama, but by ephemeral and expansive vapours that might fill 'al the ayre' of an imagined Kentish landscape.[20] Yet this mist's symbolic import eludes the characters who debate its timely occurrence, even as contemporary habits of meteorological analysis might prompt playgoers to consider the interpretative stakes. Thus, during a period in which debates about divine providence often centred on the weather, *Arden of Faversham* confronted early audiences with a theatrical environment whose fogs and snowflakes might reflect and respond to ongoing debates about the value and import of viewing unusual atmospheric phenomena as 'extraordinary Preachers', or coded messages 'from Heaven'.[21]

'Did you ever see such a mist'?: Representing Kent

From a meteorological perspective, the mist that conceals Arden from Black Will and Shakebag in scene twelve represents a significant authorial intervention. As noted earlier, a fog is not mentioned in earlier accounts of the historical householder's murder, although it is possible that an oral tradition or lost source provided this detail.[22] *Arden*'s mist may alternatively have been inspired by Holinshed's reference to three consecutive occasions on which Black Will, 'lurking' to ambush Arden, at once 'lost his way' and 'mist . . . his purpose'.[23] Although the suggestive spelling used in the first and second editions of Holinshed's *Chronicles* is a standard Elizabethan variant, the play puns on the term 'mist' in a way that evokes the verb's weather-denoting counterpart: 'See how the sun hath cleared the foggy *mist*. / Now we have *missed* the mark of our intent' (12.46–7; my italics).[24] The aural pun is visually reinforced in Edward White's 1592 edition, which repeats the same 'mist' spelling: 'See how the Sunne hath cleard the foggy mist, / Now we have mist the marke of our intent.'[25] Shakebag's statement also importantly elides meteorological and symbolic content. At first glance, his description of the fog's dispersal prioritizes natural causes, echoing Elizabethan discourses that defined the 'mist, that goeth down toward the earth' as a product of 'vapor . . . lifted up into the ayre, by the heate of the sunne': according to Fulke, such 'grosse vapors' were 'usually a signe of fayre weather', as proves the case in *Arden*.[26] Yet Shakebag's image of the sun's rays dissipating 'foggy mist' also hints at this trope's potential to figure divine or monarchical influence, as in Shakespeare's Richard III's near-contemporary claim that the 'sun of York' has cleared 'the clouds that loured upon our house'.[27] Comparison with Fulke's criteria further suggests that the mist evoked in *Arden* is even more likely to suggest the second type of vapour Fulke mentions, which 'goeth up out of the water, or yᵉ earth as smoke', being 'seen in ryvers and moyst places'; this 'ascending' fog would enrich the theatrical evocation of marshy terrain, but its proclaimed dissipation is then more likely to register as either figurative or notably unexpected.[28] Such multiplicity complicates the significance that both the theatrical fog that preserves Arden and its subsequent dispersal by the sun might have possessed for Elizabethan playgoers. In the absence of more details about the fog's properties or a sustained character commentary on its effect, individual audience members might well have reached different conclusions about the expectedness and import of this theatrical mist's movements, as the play at once draws attention to the narrative significance of the changing weather and omits a firm didactic or meteorological explanation from the accompanying dialogue.

From a dramatic perspective, *Arden*'s mist is in part a practical response to the staging challenge posed by Holinshed's claim that Black Will twice 'lost his way' in Kent.[29] As Alan Dessen suggests, the theatrical suggestion of fog immediately enables the 'comic-inept' sequence in which the actors playing Will and Shakebag hesitantly feel their way across the stage, missing the entering Ferryman and probably each other as they attempt to locate a target, Arden, who has already left.[30] As well as condensing Will's extended travels in the Faversham area into a dramatically effective vignette, the implied vapours operate as a specific locational cue, evoking both the narrow strip of sea that separates the Isle of Sheppey from the mainland and the marshy environs of Faversham.[31] The Kentish landscape was perhaps not quite as notoriously waterlogged as that of the south-easterly Fenlands, but its 'Aire' was, as the chorographer William Lambarde rather grudgingly admits, considered 'somewhat thicke' 'by reason that the Countrye is on sundry partes bordered wyth water'.[32] Lambarde adds that Kent's coastline is distinctly damp, with areas such as Romney Marsh 'famous throughout the Realme' for their fertile 'soile' and notoriously 'unholsome Aire'.[33] Faversham, which lies around thirty miles north of Romney, would have been exposed to similar risks by its low-lying situation and proximity to the Swale channel. Later chorographers such as John Speed and William Camden followed Lambarde's lead, cautioning readers that 'the [Kentish] aire is somewhat thicke, and somewhere foggie, by reason of vapours' 'arising from the Sea, and Rivers that environ the same': Speed also included three more marshes in his 1612 index of Kent, while Camden reported that 'a great part thereof is very moist'.[34]

Speed and Camden's assessments postdate *Arden*'s composition and publication, but such environmental features might have been familiar to those involved in the play's original production. *Arden* is tentatively associated with Pembroke's Men, a company known for touring.[35] Kent was a favoured destination for Elizabethan players travelling outside London: James H. Forse notes that the Queen's Men performed eighteen times in the county during 1589, and Essex's Men seven times in the same year.[36] Four of these performances took place in the town of Faversham, with payment records suggesting that the Queen's and Essex's Men played there together on at least one occasion.[37] Sussex's, Strange's and the Admiral's Men also earned fees for performing in Kent during Elizabeth's reign, suggesting that at least some of the players who first presented *Arden* would have been familiar with the landscape it depicts.[38] Pembroke's Men were themselves touring south-east England by 1593, performing at Rye in July; M. L. Wine's speculation that *Arden* was one of the plays they took on tour is intriguing, if unproven.[39] *Arden* is certainly attentive to the environmental challenges that those travelling through Kent might encounter. On the one hand, the play's geographically specific journeys involve culturally familiar routes evocative of commerce and trade, perhaps hinting at the players' own hopes for a profitable visit.[40] On the other hand, the tragedy simultaneously registers the risks associated with traversing such a damp, 'foggie' county.[41] Building on Holinshed's account, the playwright hints that the local climate conspires with its watery topography to render the very ground treacherous to outsiders such as Black Will and Shakebag, with the Ferryman responding to the latter's fall *'into a ditch'* by observing that: 'You are well enough served, to go without a guide such weather as this' (12.22 SD; 12.28–9). The mist's implied formation within a play that is elsewhere so concerned with stewardship and the commodification of land thus intriguingly extends *Arden*'s already precise attention to topographical features by hinting at the local atmosphere's constraining influence on regional travel. Moreover, while the landowner Arden here benefits from weather that unexpectedly endangers those hired to ambush him, his later death at their hands and the tragedy's wider emphasis on financially motivated violence suggest an environment in which, as Lambarde noted of Kent's marshes, the 'lowe groundes' are at best a source of *'Wealth without healthe'*.[42]

'Mystical' 'mist[s]': A journey to hell?

As Catherine Richardson observes, *Arden*'s fictional geography relates prospectively providential interventions closely to the landscape from which they are generated.[43] The causal connection between the mist which preserves Arden from attack and the watery vapours arising from the Swale channel is entirely compatible with a potential symbolic function, especially during a period when writers often conflated medical and spiritual threats. Ensuring that 'neither horse nor man could be discerned' (12.52), the fog's darkening influence over the fictive sky hints at a more liminal human presence within the environment while prompting playgoers to consider the moral status of the characters who must navigate its effects. Black Will's opening remark that he finds himself 'almost in hell's mouth' (12.2) is especially evocative, as is his ill-fated suggestion to Shakebag that they 'go on like a couple of blind pilgrims' (12.21–2). It seems likely that Shakebag's subsequent fall into a muddy ditch would have been staged using a trapdoor where one was available, with the inherited architectural symbolism that associated the area below the stage with the underworld visually augmenting Will's prior verbal allusion: Thomas Dekker's 1606 reference to '*Hell* being under everie one of their *Stages*' suggests the performative resonance of that spatialized identification for early audiences.[44]

There is a good chance that such vertical action was complemented in performance by the production of smoky fumes that would have materially implied Black Will and Shakebag's proximity to hell. We cannot be certain how the episode was staged, and Alan Dessen cautions that explicit directions calling for a mist are rare in printed commercial plays from this period.[45] However, the play's dialogue implies a meteorological effect that is experienced as smoke. Arden jokes with the Ferryman about making 'more chimney room' (11.10); the Ferryman implies that the mist makes his eyes water, while he and his companions look as if their house was 'afire' (11.14–15); Arden exits complaining that he is 'almost stifled with this fog' (11.32); and Black Will, entering a few lines later, announces that he 'cannot see my way for smoke' (12.3). The episode does not *require* the onstage production of smoke, but it seems likely that such an effect was anticipated and perhaps used to simulate mist during at least some performances; various contemporary plays call for much more ambitious pyrotechnical effects, although the risks of using fire were probably harder to mitigate while on tour.[46] The perceptible presence of fumes would have intensified Will's comparison between the fictional Kentish landscape and 'hell's mouth' (12.2): the 'smootie' emissions from 'seacole fiers' were described by contemporaries as 'hellishe', while comparably sulphurous effects were traditionally associated with stage devils and ghosts.[47] The player presenting Shakebag might have already fired a gunpowder-powered weapon onstage, with the character's announcement in scene nine that he will 'discharge my pistol at the sky' implying both a transgressive assault on the fictive heavens and the material production of a 'stinking' odour long associated with Satan and hell (9.135).[48] Within the subsequent mist episode, the play utilizes smoke imagery and perhaps actual fumes to further suggest a theatrical atmosphere that is increasingly aligned with hell; at the very least, dialogue cues prompt playgoers to envisage a dark mist that resembles smoke in its visual and olfactory impact. Whether Arden's journey by ferry possesses the same ominous connotations as Black Will and Shakebag's experience of these fumes remains ambiguous, however. Thomas Kyd's depiction of 'churlish Charon' as 'the ferryman of hell' in his influential *Spanish Tragedy* (c. 1587) suggests that playgoers might well have interpreted *Arden*'s Ferryman in allegorical terms, especially when he meets the would-be murderers after Black Will's claim to be 'almost in hell's mouth' (12.2), while alternatively or concurrently recognizing the Ferryman's occupation as a locational cue for the Kentish coast.[49] Indeed, the murderers, their prospective victim(s) and the boatman all move through a liminal environment that is at once mundane and allegorical, as two potential interpretative frameworks temporarily converge under the influence of the smoky mist. More ominously, early playgoers would here have encountered an episode in which Arden's preservation is aligned with encroaching fumes redolent of hell, thus raising familiar questions that focus not so much on the theatrical relationship between natural and supernatural causation, but rather on whether this timely mist is the product of divine or demonic influence over the tragedy's natural environment. Indeed, the episode's overt comedy could have reinforced this impression, recalling the physical humour and clownish ineptitude associated with stage devils and the servants they torment in near-contemporary plays such as *Doctor Faustus* (c. 1588) and *Friar Bacon and Friar Bungay* (c. 1589).[50]

Hinting at providential influence while withholding a secure interpretative framework could have challenging implications. The fog that shadows this episode might itself suggest the risk of misconstruing atmospheric phenomena: early modern authors regularly associate fog and mist with confusion, deception or perceived misbelief, with John Rainolds, for instance, blaming a real-life matricide's lack of remorse on the 'foggie mists of Hell'.[51] Arden's early exchange with Franklin and the Ferryman registers a similar connection, as he likens the gathering 'mist' to 'a good companion's smoky brain, / That was half-drowned with new ale overnight' (11.7–8). Black Will, too, punningly conflates meteorological experience with alcohol consumption, remarking that the money Alice gives him to purchase 'good cheer' at the Fleur-de-Lis tavern 'will serve the turn / In case we fall into a second fog' (12.62, 66–7). Such vaporous imagery recalls that used by early modern physicians to discuss conditions said to cause 'fearefull fancies': Timothy Bright likens melancholy to a 'spleneticke fogge' that the 'brayne hath plentifully drunke of', while Robert Burton approvingly cites Levinus Lemnius's 1561 explanation that the 'ill smokes and vapors' 'which trouble the Imagination' 'ascend up to the Brain' *as smoak out of a chimny*'.[52] Arden's opening lines additionally echo those contemporary authors who used atmospheric analogies to denounce the 'foggy mists of superstition', implying that only the drunk or hungover playgoer will believe that 'This mist, my friend, is mystical' (11.6).[53] Yet Arden is himself a far from reliable interpreter. His earlier debates with Alice and Franklin about the prophetic import of dreams suggest that he is at once too prone to credit and too quick to dismiss the 'nightly fantasies' of 'troubled' minds (6.38, 6.34): a judgement implicitly reinforced by the audience's awareness that Alice and Michael have, respectively, misrepresented and invented the dreams that Arden evaluates (1.64–79; 4.85–107). Meanwhile, Arden's own post-nightmare prayer that 'God frame it to the best' is as wilfully oblivious to the foreboding implications and his interpretative responsibilities as his later acceptance of Alice's claim that he has been 'witched' into suspecting Mosby without cause (6.36; 13.103). Such subtly comedic exchanges implicitly connect the vapours of theatrical fog with the fumes that are said to cloud Arden's mind, exposing the common failings within his domestic and environmental relationships even as Alice misrepresents their nature.

Arden's flippant dismissal of the theatrical mist's 'mystical' import specifically anticipates his misplaced trust in Alice, with Dessen proposing that Arden's 'fall' is foreshadowed by the fog episode's emphasis on faulty perception.[54] In this regard, it is intriguing that the play expands the methods considered by Arden's murderers to mention a device that directly targets 'his sight' (1.230): where Alice hopes that 'some airy spirit' might carry her husband into the sea (1.93), Mosby's first instinct is to commission a poisoned portrait, that Arden might 'perish' 'gazing' on his wife's 'counterfeit' (1.232–3). Although this scheme is never attempted, Mosby's emphasis on the body's vulnerability to atmospheric influences is echoed in the later parallelization of an externally manifesting fog with Arden's confused judgements. Moreover, the theatrical mist's loaded significance leaves audience members similarly adrift, forced to individually confront the uncertain providential status of this meteorological occurrence. That disorientating effect is augmented by Franklin's repeated questioning of the Ferryman, whose supposed 'opinion of this mist' amounts to convoluted jokes about female inconstancy (11.11). The notion of a 'curst wife' who drives her husband 'out at doors' resonates tangentially with Arden's domestic troubles (11.12–14), but misleadingly so: Alice has long since discarded vague wishes that her husband might 'take horse and away' in favour of scheming against his life (1.91), and it is Arden's eventual return to and isolation within his house that proves deadly.[55] Nor do the Ferryman's 'bold' jests with Franklin and Arden offer local insight into the mist's significance (11.34), even if his 'feet see better' than Shakebag's 'eyes' (12.6); his subsequent offer to carry letters for Black Will at once reinforces his familiarity with the Kentish landscape and his status as a rustic clown capable of 'knavery' (12.35–6, 11.35).[56]

As Peter Kirwan observes, the Ferryman's irreverent, sexualized humour and capacity to figure damnation anticipates the role of the Porter in Shakespeare's later *Macbeth* (c. 1606).[57] These characters' shared debt to the devil-porters of medieval drama would in *Arden*'s case have enhanced symbolic associations between the Kentish fog and hell, while simultaneously consolidating the Ferryman's status as a country clown.[58] Such pre-Reformation and rustic antecedents further suggest that the Ferryman's muddled 'opinion' of *Arden*'s theatrical mist would most likely have recalled contemporary attacks on 'superstitious' almanacs. London-based authors such as Thomas Nashe mocked the supposed credulity of 'simple' rural readers:

> [T]he Country Plowman [now] feareth a Calabrian floodde in the midst of a furrowe, and the sillie Sheephearde committing his wandering sheepe to the custodie of his wappe, in his field naps, dreameth of flying Dragons, which for feare least he should see to the losse of his sight, he falleth a sleepe, no star he seeth

in the night but seemeth a Comet, hee lighteth no sooner on a quagmyre, but he thinketh this is the foretold Earthquake[.]⁵⁹

Arden's prior allusion to 'mystical' weather may be significant in this regard, too, since a term that might simply denote spiritual matter was weaponized by some Elizabethan authors against the 'palpable and grosse errours' of 'Astrology' and Catholic exegesis: for instance, Henry Howard's *Defensative against the Poison of Supposed Prophesies* (1583) denounces a would-be 'Prophete' whose 'darke and misticall' 'answeres' fail to conceal his ignorance.⁶⁰ Early modern astrologers employed the same terminology to distinguish their 'correct' practice from that of '[m]isticall' false prophets, who 'pretend divers, and sundry misticall causes' for meteorological phenomena while promoting theories that exceed what 'humane reason shall probably persuade, or divine authoritie canonically inforce'.⁶¹

Arden's mist sequence is one of the play's more developed episodes of attempted murder, lasting around seventy lines. The Ferryman's exchange with Black Will further hints at its anticipated dramatic impact when he demands: 'Did you ever see such a mist as this?' (12.38). As noted earlier, it is possible that this line registered a smoky effect more commonly experienced in masques or comparably lavish events.⁶² Whether or not perceptible fumes complemented the discursive evocation of fog in performance, early audiences seem to have appreciated the meteorological addition; when a related ballad about Arden's murder was published in 1633, it devoted two stanzas to the 'mist and fog' that 'did arise' to stay the murderers, with probable reference to the dramatic moments that resonated with *Arden*'s early audiences.⁶³ What the theatrical mist's timely formation might *mean*, however, is less apparent. The sequence would have confronted playgoers with verbal and perhaps olfactory, gustatory and visual cues that evoke an allegorical framework redolent of damnation, only to complicate such inherited symbolism: *Arden*'s characters query and joke about the mist's ominous significance, but without truly reacting to it as anything other than purely natural weather. The fog might ostensibly serve a didactic purpose, warning Arden and his aggressors of the material and spiritual dangers they face, but this device's simultaneous capacity to figure misjudgement and the unreliable 'opinion[s]' of its flawed onstage interpreters destabilizes moralizing theatrical conventions that Elizabethan playgoers might have already considered old-fashioned. Overall, then, this tragedy's experience of weather seems to reflect an Elizabethan context in which, although English Protestants retained a providential understanding of the world, their concurrent determination to repudiate Catholic 'superstition' exacerbated the interpretative challenges confronted by those encountering an unusual weather event, who might already be wondering whether this atmospheric phenomenon was a coded message from God or a demonic trick designed to try their faith.[64] In that regard, *Arden*'s approach echoes contemporary anxieties about the evidential limits and uncertain theological status of meteorological interpretation, as, in a play 'naked' of 'glozing stuff', the 'simple truth' of the weather must be 'discerned' by playgoers who – like the hapless Shakebag – are forced to navigate 'without a guide' (Epilogue 14, 17–18; 12.52, 12.61).

'The print of many feet': Reading the snow

Similar questions about the role of the weather resurface in *Arden*'s closing scenes. Having at last succeeded in killing Arden, Alice's accomplices 'convey' his body 'to the fields' outside (14.354). Yet Alice's confident assertion that she need not fear 'judge and juries', since her 'house is clear' (14.359–60), is immediately compromised by her maid Susan's more astute understanding of their environmental exposure: 'As we went, it snowed all the way, / Which makes me fear our footsteps will be spied' (14.361–2). The latter's fears are realized fewer than forty lines later, when the arrival of the Mayor and Watch is followed by Franklin's entrance and announcement that:

> I fear me he [Arden] was murdered in this house
> And carried to the fields, for, from that place,
> Backwards and forwards, may you see
> The print of many feet within the snow. (14.397–400)

The subsequent discovery of bloodstains on the floor and the fresh blood 'gushing' from Arden's wounds seal the fate of the murderers, as first Alice and then Mosby confess their guilt (16.5). Moreover, as Lake and Questier stress, these 'pseudo-miraculous' revelations are well timed to ensure the capture and punishment of all those who had a hand in Arden's death, suggesting that this consequence of Arden's long-delayed death may indicate an overarching providential schema.[65]

Unlike the mist that conceals Arden earlier in the play, the snow that helps to reveal his murderers has a direct precedent in Holinshed's *Chronicles*. In fact, the snow arguably has greater narrative prominence in his account: it is the 'footings still before them in the snowe' that initially prompt Holinshed's Mayor to examine Arden's house, whereas his dramatic counterpart has already ordered a 'search' based on 'the Council's warrant' when Arden's body is discovered (14.375, 371).[66] Likewise, the footprints that Franklin encounters are presented as supplementary evidence, reinforcing his fears rather than guiding his discovery of the bloodstained hand towel and knife (14.388). In contrast, Arden's blood has a more significant evidentiary role in the play, with Alice's references to the continued bleeding of Arden's body hinting at a possible stage effect: Lucy Munro reminds us that Elizabethan companies probably used sheep's blood or paint to simulate characters' wounds, although dramatic episodes that require blood to be shed onstage are rarer and would have required careful management to protect the actors' costumes.[67] Even the simple coupling of 'bloodstained' clothing with verbal references to 'gushing' wounds could have been theatrically evocative (16.5), augmenting *Arden*'s dramaturgical centring of the deceased's corpse within these closing scenes.[68]

Where Arden's body is foregrounded, the snow is displaced into the offstage fictional space of Faversham's fields: its effects reported to rather than observed by the play's audiences. What emerges instead is an enhanced emphasis on the parallel sequences in which the traces of theatrical action are imprinted upon the fictive snow. Holinshed's account notes without elaboration that 'it began to snow' as the murderers carried Arden's body out of his house and does not mention when the snowfall ceased. As Wine observes, that omission represents a rare departure from the text of Stow's manuscript, on which Holinshed drew, since Stow both provided that detail and explicitly attributed the timing to divine oversight: 'they comynge in a gayne into ye howse thowght that ye snow woulde have coveryd theyr fotynge (but sodeynly by ye good provydence of god, who wuld not suffer so detestable a murther longe hydden) it stint snowynge'.⁶⁹ Stow's version is a likely additional source for *Arden*, since the play's dialogue conveys similar information about the snow's operations. Moreover, as Duncan Salkeld points out, Stow's exact term 'fotynge' appears in relation to Shakebag and Black Will's prior weather-related misadventures, when the latter character explains to Alice and Mosby how they made 'false footing' in the fog and became 'berayed' (12.59–60).⁷⁰ Mosby's description of Will and Shakebag's muddied appearance suggests an aural pun on the risk that their dirtied clothing could betray their attempted ambush, in the same way that the traces of 'fotynge' in the snow will later ensure the successful 'murther' does not remain 'longe hydden'; the latter connection emerges in *Arden* along the same lines as in Stow's account.⁷¹

When Susan mentions the altered weather, Alice impatiently dismisses her maid's concerns, declaring that the snow 'will cover' their footprints 'again' (14.363). Yet Susan's protest that 'it had done before we came back again' is interrupted by a knock at the door (14.365), at once acoustically underscoring the external threat and preventing a response. Susan's belated objection further emphasizes Alice's complacency, with the latter's disregard for her neighbours' presence mirrored in her restricted environmental awareness. Indeed, as Emma Whipday argues, Susan's role in this episode 'is not negligible'; in this moment of domestic upheaval, 'she has a voice and the power to use it'.⁷² By refusing to be immediately silenced by her mistress, Susan further highlights that the obtuseness displayed by *Arden*'s conspirators exceeds that detailed in Stow's manuscript: while Stow suggests that the historical murderers had returned to the house before the snow stopped falling and merely failed to anticipate a change in the weather, the play's conspirators are reported to be outside when that dangerous moment occurs – but still fail to comprehend the consequent risk of discovery. Franklin's description of 'many feet' moving 'Backwards and forwards' reinforces this impression that the murderers lack a full understanding of the snow-covered environment they have entered into, evoking a confused action in which too many murderers engage in superfluous movement without a clear sense of purpose or progression (14.399–400). Indeed, where Holinshed attributes the high number of footprints to an issue with the household keys, *Arden* offers no further explanation for these multiplying marks.

The visual image of prints in the snow closely anticipates Franklin's concluding announcement that the 'print' of Arden's body 'was seen / Two years and more' in the 'plot of ground' he took from Reede (Epilogue 10–13). The relationship between this epilogue and the play's main narrative has long been disputed by critics: for instance, Lena Cowen Orlin considered that this 'miraculous' detail was 'primarily an afterthought' in the prose histories and play alike, whereas Garrett A. Sullivan interprets Franklin's lines as offering 'a mystified conception of the land as a force offended by Arden's covetousness and social irresponsibility'.[73] By substituting Arden's lasting impression in the grass for the footprints that once marked the overlying snow, this trope suggests the importance of attending to the environment, but without specifying the weather's didactic import. Like other atmospheric phenomena, snow could readily be understood as one of the 'scourges' sent by God 'to chastise and punish the froward', and early modern writers analogically identified its frozen vapours with purity and even redemption.[74] Yet the promise of meteorologically guided correction is implicit at best in *Arden*: Alice's hasty repentance is prompted instead by the sight of her husband's blood, after she has previously dismissed Susan's weather report, while Arden never seems to regret the harsh actions that his friend Franklin registers in closing.[75] The dramatic text also lacks a direct providential framework of the type found in Stow's manuscript; and, where Stow at least emphasized the historical snow's 'greate' volume, there is no indication that its theatrical equivalent is especially prodigious. Nonetheless, the apt timing of the snowfall is still suggestive. This snow's expected presence in the fictional wintery environment may even underscore the murderers' careless disregard for its presence and influence. Alice's assumption that the falling snow represents safety rather than danger may have seemed wilfully ignorant to early modern playgoers at once familiar with providentialist accounts of extreme weather events and conscious of snow's potentially deadly effects.[76] Her co-conspirators Greene, Mosby and Michael likewise fail to respond appropriately to the external environment they find themselves moving through, overlooking the snow's capacity to reveal their recent actions in their haste to return to the house. Such behaviour in part mirrors the 'negligence' found in

Susan's failure to scrub Arden's blood from the floor or Michael's to properly dispose of the murder weapon (14.389). However, the murderers' apparent reluctance to even acknowledge the risk of environmental exposure seems pointed, especially since Michael's failure to throw the towel and knife into the outside well offers another instance in which external traces are suppressed or forgotten.

Catherine Richardson has demonstrated that *Arden* both suggests and frustrates a 'geography of relative threat', complicating the comparative risk playgoers might associate with outside and inside spaces.[77] That tension is echoed in the play's depiction of atmospheric phenomena. Murderers such as Shakebag and Black Will are exposed to the oversight of both 'marrow-prying neighbours' and the heavens (1.134), yet remain indifferent to the spiritual messages that might be extrapolated from their experiences. Even characters who are less obviously at fault in the play, such as Franklin and the Ferryman, seem uncertain of their ability to interpret transient environmental events: whereas the physical landscape and household objects implicated in Arden's death can be successfully 'discovered' by informed observers, the returning Franklin's immediate desire to substitute 'blood' evidence for the 'many' marks he has discovered in the snow and his closing emphasis on an annually renewed, unfading 'print' that marks the earth may hint that he has reservations about the weather's observable but ephemeral influence (14.400, 402; Epilogue 12). Franklin's closing emphasis on recurring 'print[s]' rather than their production also echoes the memorial concerns hinted at by contemporary commentators (14.400), with readers of the *Most True and Lamentable Report* for instance instructed to 'print the remembraunce' of an already past hailstorm firmly 'in thy hart'.[78] Moreover, for early modern playgoers this 'print' trope might have simultaneously evoked the confessional tensions that complicated post-Reformation responses to environmental phenomena, with the idea that the landscape might bear the lasting trace of human action appearing elsewhere in traditional, pre-Reformation tales of the type distrusted by godly reformers: for instance, a pathway in Wiltshire associated with St Thomas Becket was similarly said to remain always visible, whether the field it led through was sown, fallow or covered in snow.[79]

Conclusion: Domestic tragedy and divine providence

Arden's attention to the weather is shared by many early modern plays. Changing weather patterns and providentialist interpretations of the storms that wrecked successive Spanish armadas prompted dramatic attention to meteorological representation, and interest in what Anne Lawrence-Mathers characterizes as 'do-it-yourself prognostication' rose sharply in Elizabethan England.[80] The latter development was perhaps especially pertinent to plays such as *Arden* or *A Warning for Fair Women* (c. 1587), which draw inspiration from prose accounts of real-life murders. Contemporary 'murder pamphlets' often stress the role played by God and the elements in ensuring the exposure and apprehension of the guilty.[81] Although their dramatic counterparts did not always retain those framing commentaries, their narratives might still follow or acknowledge providential patterns.[82] In *A Warning for Fair Women*, for instance, the deathbed revelation of a murderer's identity inspires another character to recall how, 'once', 'a sprigge of fearne borne by the wind, / Into the roome where as the murtherer was' prompted his confession.[83] This passage characterizes the relationship between the domestic interior and external environment in terms reminiscent of *Arden*'s conclusion: although the snow that helps to reveal the murderers remains outside the protagonist's home, the footprints that temporarily mark its surface enable Franklin to reconstruct their movements.[84] Yet such providential narratives might also complicate the cultural significance of the domestic and exterior spaces they represent. As Emma Whipday points out, early modern authorities defined the home in terms of its physical boundaries, with the Elizabethan judge Robert Monson asserting that '[t]he first, and chiefe use of an house is to defend man from the extremity of the winde, and weather'.[85] Conversely, tragedies such as *Arden* and *A Warning* hint that within a providential universe it is both impossible and undesirable to occlude all elemental influences; indeed, *Arden*'s murderers are condemned in part by their failure to account for that permeable relationship, as signalled by the performative overlap between Susan's realization about the snow and the arrival of the investigating Faversham residents at the door of Arden's house.

The earlier mist sequence in *Arden* complements this emphasis in its attention to not only the external environment but also the extent to which humoral theories assumed the contiguity of elemental and internal processes. Here, the would-be murderers again neglect their surroundings, with Shakebag suffering a symbolically suggestive fall as a result. The same is true to a lesser extent of Arden, Franklin and the Ferryman, who navigate the landscape successfully but reach no firm conclusion about the fog's sudden formation; Black Will remains the only character to interpret the mist in explicitly moralized terms, and he does not apply that understanding to his own situation. To further complicate the interpretative experience of the play's early audiences, a 'thicke myst' so redolent of hell might well be expected to facilitate rather than impede Arden's murder: Holinshed describes a 1537 ambush that was assisted by fog, while the murderer in *A Warning for Fair Women* reflects that 'gloomie' 'aire' and 'darknesse best fittes my intent'.[86] In disrupting such narrative associations, *Arden* simultaneously unsettles the expectations that audience members might have brought to such episodes, as the fictional Kentish weather operates in ways that invite but never confirm a providentialist understanding of its dramatic influence. Yet if *Arden* hints that the process of meteorological interpretation can be confusing and contradictory, the tragedy's outcome implies that discounting the potential significance of environmental factors is even more foolish. Thus, in adapting Holinshed's account of Arden's 1551 murder for the stage, the Elizabethan dramatist recognized that this tale of domestic upheaval and commercial rivalry is also a story about the play of the weather, and, by extension, the value, import and performance of meteorological analysis.

Notes

1 *A Most True and Lamentable Report, of a Great Tempest of Haile Which Fell Upon a Village in Kent, Called Stockbery* (London, 1590), A2r, A3r.

2 *Most True*, A3r.

3 *Most True*, A2v.

4 *Most True*, A3v, A4r, A2v.

5 Alexandra Walsham, *The Reformation of the Landscape: Religion, Identity, and Memory in Early Modern Britain and Ireland* (Oxford: Oxford University Press, 2012), 339, 345.
6 Walsham, *Reformation*, 327, 339, 336; Alexandra Walsham, 'Sermons in the Sky: Apparitions in Early Modern Europe', *History Today* 51, no. 4 (2001): 58, 60.
7 William Fulke, *A Goodly Gallerye . . . to Behold the Naturall Causes of all Kynde of Meteors* (London, 1563), A1r, C3v.
8 Fulke, *Goodly*, G6v. Gwilym Jones discusses Fulke's debt to Pliny the Elder in *Shakespeare's Storms* (Manchester: Manchester University Press, 2015), 26–8.
9 *Most True*, A2v; Fulke, *Goodly*, G7r.
10 Walsham, *Reformation*, 336, 361.
11 *Most True*, A3v. Cf. Matthew 10.29–31; also Luke 12.6–7.
12 The exact composition date is uncertain, but the play was written between 1587 and 1592, most likely around 1590–1, and published in 1592. See M. L. Wine, 'Introduction', in *The Tragedy of Master Arden of Faversham*, ed. M. L. Wine (London: Methuen, 1973), xliii–xlv; Martin Wiggins with Catherine Richardson, *British Drama 1533–1642: A Catalogue* (Oxford: Oxford University Press, 2013), vol. III, 10, 13. *Arden*'s authorship is discussed by Jane Kingsley-Smith, '*Arden of Faversham*: The Critical Story', in this volume.
13 On potential sources, see Wine, 'Introduction', xxxv–xliii; Lena Cowen Orlin, 'Man's House as His Castle in *Arden of Feversham*', *Medieval & Renaissance Drama in England* 2 (1985): 70–1; and Emily O'Brien, '*The Tragedy of Master Arden of Faversham*, True Crime, and the Literary Marketplace of the 1580s', *Shakespeare Studies* 45 (2017): 113–20. The various accounts of the historical Ardern's murder circulating in early modern England are discussed by Lena Cowen Orlin in *Private Matters and Public Culture in Post-Reformation England* (Ithaca: Cornell University Press, 1994), esp. 15–84.
14 Peter Lake with Michael Questier, *The Antichrist's Lewd Hat: Protestants, Papists and Players in Post-Reformation England* (New Haven: Yale University Press, 2002), 38.
15 See Kingsley-Smith in this volume.
16 On the significance of place, see Garrett A. Sullivan, Jr., *The Drama of Landscape: Land, Property, and Social Relations on the Early Modern Stage* (Stanford: Stanford University Press, 1998), 31–56; and Catherine Richardson, *Domestic Life and Domestic Tragedy in Early*

Modern England: The Material Life of the Household (Manchester: Manchester University Press, 2006), esp. 105–14.

17 See Frank Whigham, *Seizures of the Will in Early Modern English Drama* (Cambridge: Cambridge University Press, 1996; 2009), 63; Orlin, 'Man's House', 57–60.

18 Raphael Holinshed, *The Firste [Laste] Volume of the Chronicles of England, Scotlande, and Irelande* (London, 1577), 4M6r. Wine suggests that the *Arden* playwright consulted the 1587 edition of Holinshed's *Chronicles*, which features marginal annotations, but the Arden narrative is otherwise 'precisely the same in both the first and second editions . . . except for the usual printing-house sophistications in spelling and punctuation' (xl–xli). Cf. Raphael Holinshed, *The first and second volumes of Chronicles* (London, 1587), 5K1v–5K3v.

19 Holinshed, *Firste [Laste]*, 4M5r. See *The Diary of Henry Machen*, ed. John Gough Nichols (London: Camden Society, 1848), 4; 'Appendix III: The Account of Thomas Arden's Murder from *The Wardmote Book of Faversham*, ff. 59–60', in *Tragedy*, 160–3; *A Breuiat Cronicle Contaynynge all the Kinges from Brute to This Daye* (Canterbury, 1552), N3v; John Stow, 'The History of a Most Horible Murder comytyd at ffeversham in Kent', Harley MS 542, in Wine, 'Introduction', xlii–xliii; 'A London Chronicle: Edward VI', in *Two London Chronicles From the Collections of John Stow*, ed. Charles Lethbridge Kingsford (London, 1910), 17–27, *British History Online*; John Stow, *A Summarie of Englyshe Chronicles* (London, 1565), Dd4v–Dd5r; Holinshed, *Firste [Laste]*, 4M4r–4M6v; John Stow, *The Chronicles of England from Brute vnto this present yeare of Christ* (London, 1580), Uuu1v.

20 Fulke, *Goodly*, F8r. I owe the idea of a meteorological performance aesthetic to Gwilym Jones's *Shakespeare's Storms*.

21 Anthony Anderson, *A Sermon Preached at Paules Crosse, the 23. of Aprill* (London, 1581), G1v.

22 Emily O'Brien suggests that the work titled *A Cruell Murder Donne in Kent*, which was entered into the Stationers' Register in 1577, may have been about Arden (114), while the lost play *Murderous Michael* (1579) perhaps dramatized the same event from the perspective of Arden's servant Michael (see Kingsley-Smith in this volume, 15).

23 Holinshed, *Firste [Laste]*, 4M5r-4M5v; cf. Holinshed, *First and second*, 5K2v.

24 See 'miss, *v.*1', *Oxford English Dictionary Online* (Oxford University Press, 2019).

25 *The Lamentable and True Tragedie of M. Arden of Feuersham* (London, 1592), G2v.
26 Fulke, *Goodly*, F8r.
27 William Shakespeare, *The Tragedy of King Richard III*, ed. John Jowett (Oxford: Oxford University Press, 2000), 1.1.2–3.
28 Fulke, *Goodly*, F7v–F8r.
29 Holinshed, *Firste [Laste]*, 4M5r–4M5v.
30 Alan C. Dessen, 'Mist and Fog on the Elizabethan and Jacobean Stage', in *Speaking Pictures: The Visual/Verbal Nexus of Dramatic Performance*, ed. Virginia Mason Vaughan, Fernando Cioni and Jacquelyn Bessell (Madison: Fairleigh Dickinson University Press, 2010), 113.
31 Faversham borders on the Oare Marshes, while the area covered by the North Kent Marshes today includes the Swale and Sheppey.
32 William Lambarde, *A Perambulation of Kent* (London, 1576), A4r. Julie Sanders argues in *The Cultural Geography of Early Modern Drama, 1620–1650* that Richard Brome's *The Demoiselle* (1637) invokes Kent's sunken Goodwin Sands to mock the futility of proposals to drain the Fens, suggesting that Kent's geography seemed even more shifting to contemporaries (Cambridge: Cambridge University Press, 2011), 55.
33 Lambarde, *Perambulation*, U3v–U4r.
34 John Speed, *The Theatre of the Empire of Great Britaine* (London, 1612), A4v, A3r; William Camden, *Britain, or A Chorographicall Description* (London, 1637), Dd4v.
35 Wine, 'Introduction', xlv–xlvi; Wiggins and Richardson, *Catalogue*, III, 13; Kath Bradley, '"Poor Wench Abused by thy Misgovernance": *Arden of Faversham* on Stage', this volume, xx; Scott McMillin and Sally-Beth MacLean, *The Queen's Men and Their Plays* (Cambridge: Cambridge University Press, 1998), 67.
36 McMillin and MacLean, *The Queen's Men and Their Plays*, 39; James H. Forse, 'Touring in Kent: Some Observations from Records Published to Date', *Early Theatre* 22, no. 2 (2019): 124.
37 Forse, 'Touring', 124; *Records of Plays and Players in Kent, 1450–1642*, ed. Giles Dawson, *Malone Society Collections* 7 (Oxford: Oxford University Press, 1965), 62, qtd. in Siobhan Keenan, *Travelling Players in Shakespeare's England* (Basingstoke: Palgrave Macmillan, 2002), 12.
38 Forse, 'Touring', 126. Scott McMillin's suggestion that Pembroke's Men emerged in the mid-1590s as an offshoot of Strange's Men is intriguing in this regard: 'Casting for Pembroke's Men: The *Henry VI* Quartos

and *The Taming of A Shrew'*, *Shakespeare Quarterly* 23, no. 2 (1972): 155–8. See also Roslyn L. Knutson, 'Pembroke's Men in 1592–3, Their Repertory and Touring Schedule', *Early Theatre* 4, no. 1 (2001): 130–1.
39 Knutson, 'Pembroke's Men', 134; Wine, 'Introduction', xlvii.
40 Richardson, *Domestic Life*, 106.
41 Camden, *Britain*, Dd4v.
42 Richardson, *Domestic Life*, 104–6; Lambarde, *Perambulation*, U3v. On the play's preoccupation with land ethics, see Sullivan, *Drama*, 31–56; Orlin, 'Man's House', 58–60.
43 Richardson, *Domestic Life*, 107.
44 Tiffany Stern, '"This Wide and Universal Theatre": The Theatre as Prop in Shakespeare's Metadrama', in *Shakespeare's Theatres and the Effects of Performance*, ed. Farah Karim-Cooper and Tiffany Stern (London: Bloomsbury, 2015), 17–19; Thomas Dekker, *Nevves from Hell* (London, 1606), B1v.
45 Dessen, 'Mist', 107.
46 See, for example, Philip Butterworth, *Theatre of Fire: Special Effects in Early English and Scottish Theatre* (London: Society for Theatre Research, 1998); Lawrence Manley, 'Playing with Fire: Immolation in the Repertory of Strange's Men', *Early Theatre* 4, no. 1 (2001): 115–29.
47 Hugh Plat, *A nevv, Cheape and Delicate Fire of Cole-Balles* (London, 1603), B4v; Jonathan Gil Harris, 'The Smell of *Macbeth*', *Shakespeare Quarterly* 58, no. 4 (2007): 466, 476–7.
48 Harris, 'Smell', 476.
49 Thomas Kyd, *The Spanish Tragedy*, ed. J. R. Mulryne and Andrew Gurr (London: Methuen Drama, 2009), 1.1.20, 27.
50 Cf. Christopher Marlowe, *Doctor Faustus, A-Text (1604)*, in *Doctor Faustus: A- and B-texts*, ed. David Bevington and Eric Rasmussen (Manchester: Manchester University Press, 1993), 103–98, 1.4 and 2.2; Robert Greene, *Friar Bacon and Friar Bungay*, in *English Renaissance Drama: A Norton Anthology*, ed. David Bevington et al. (New York and London: Norton, 2002), 129–81, 15.
51 Dessen, 'Mist', 107; John Rainolds, *The Triumphs of Gods Revenge Against the Crying and Execrable sinne of (Willfull and Premeditated) Murther* (London, 1635), Cc3v.
52 Timothy Bright, *A Treatise of Melancholie* (London, 1568), G4r, G2v; Robert Burton, *The Anatomy of Melancholy* (Oxford, 1621), V7v, R2v. See also Levinus Lemnius, *The Touchstone of Complexions*, trans. Thomas Newton (London, 1576), S5v.

53 Burton, *Anatomy*, Bbb2r.
54 Dessen, 'Mist', 114.
55 See Richardson, *Domestic Life*, 108–11.
56 As Alan Stewart explains in *Shakespeare's Letters*, the rustic stage carrier persona that Richard Tarleton created for the Queen's Men influenced subsequent depictions of dramatic messengers (Oxford: Oxford University Press, 2008), 132–5. Cf. William Shakespeare, *Titus Andronicus*, ed. Jonathan Bate (London: Arden Shakespeare, 2005), 4.3.77–111.
57 Peter Kirwan, private communication; William Shakespeare, *Macbeth*, ed. Sandra Clark and Pamela Mason (London: Arden Shakespeare, 2015), 2.3.
58 Shakespeare, *Macbeth*, 2.3.1–2n; Glynne Wickham, 'Hell-Castle and its Door-Keeper', *Shakespeare Survey* 19 (1967): 68–74.
59 Thomas Nashe, *The Anatomie of Absurditie* (London, 1589), B4r. See also Nashe's mock-prediction that 'Saturne retrograde in Gemini shewes that there shall this Winter fall such greate fogges and mistes', in *A vvonderfull, Strange and Miraculous Astrologicall Prognostication* (London, 1591), C1v.
60 Henry Howard, Earl of Northumberland, *A Defensatiue against the Poyson of Supposed Prophesies* (London, 1583), ¶1r, Cc2v. Cf. 'mystical', *adj.* 1–3, OED.
61 John Harvey, *A discoursiue probleme concerning prophesies* (London, 1588), B2v.
62 Dessen, 'Mist', 107.
63 *[The] complaint and lamentation of Mistresse Arden of [Fev]ersham in Kent* (London, 1633).
64 See, for instance, George Gifford's complaint that the 'common opinion, when there are any mighty windes and thunders with terrible lightninges, that the Devill is abroade and doth it', ignores God's overarching control: 'this wicked folly which possesseth the mindes of the ignorant sort, is a fruit of Poperie'. *A Discourse of the Subtill Practises of deuilles by vvitches and sorcerers* (London, 1587), D3v.
65 Lake and Questier, *Antichrist's*, 39.
66 Holinshed, *Firste [Laste]*, 5M6r.
67 Lucy Munro, '"They eat each others' arms": Stage Blood and Body Parts', in *Shakespeare's Theatres and the Effects of Performance*, ed. Farah Karim-Cooper and Tiffany Stern (London: Bloomsbury, 2013), 78–85. Cf. Holinshed, *Firste [Laste]*, 5M6r.

68 Cf. Kyd, *Spanish Tragedy*, 4.4.88–97.
69 Stow, 'History', qtd. in Wine, 'Introduction', xlii–xliii.
70 Duncan Salkeld, private communication.
71 Stow, 'History', qtd. in Wine, 'Introduction', xlii–xliii.
72 Emma Whipday, 'Susan of Faversham: Staging Subordination in *Arden*', this volume, 103.
73 Orlin, *Private*, 67–8; Sullivan, *Drama*, 55. See also Richardson, *Domestic Life*, 113–14; and Kingsley-Smith in this volume, 15–16, on the wider critical debate.
74 Pierre de La Primaudaye, *The Third Volume of the French Academie*, trans. Richard Dolman (London: George Bishop, 1601), O8v.
75 Psalm 51's image of being washed 'whiter than snow' (7) is for instance discussed by the Protestant theologian Théodore de Bèze in *Christian Meditations vpon Eight Psalmes*, trans. I. S. (London, 1582), E6r–E6v. See also William Shakespeare, *Hamlet (Q2)*, ed. Ann Thompson and Neil Taylor (London: Bloomsbury, 2016), 3.1.135–6, 3.3.45–6.
76 See, for instance, Konrad Lykosthenes, *The doome warning all men to the iudgemente*, trans. Stephan Batman (London, 1581), L4r.
77 Richardson, *Domestic Life*, 108.
78 *Most True*, A2v.
79 Walsham, *Reformation*, 45, 361–2.
80 Anne Lawrence-Mathers, *Medieval Meteorology: Forecasting the Weather from Aristotle to the Almanac* (Cambridge: Cambridge University Press, 2020), 173–93. On dramatic weather, see, for instance, Jones, *Shakespeare's Storms*; Todd A. Borlik, *Ecocriticism and Early Modern English Literature: Green Pastures* (London: Routledge, 2011), esp. 118–29; Sophie Chiari, *Shakespeare's Representation of Weather, Climate and Environment: The Early Modern 'Fated Sky'* (Edinburgh: Edinburgh University Press, 2019).
81 Lake and Questier, *Antichrist's*, 37, 31.
82 Ibid., 379, 37.
83 *A vvarning for Faire vvomen* (London, 1599), H2r.
84 Richardson, *Domestic Life*, 125–6.
85 John Manwood et al., *A Briefe Declaration . . . Concerning Private Dwelling Houses* (London, 1636), B1r; Emma Whipday, *Shakespeare's Domestic Tragedies: Violence in the Early Modern Home* (Cambridge: Cambridge University Press, 2019), 4–5.
86 *Warning*, E4v.

6

New directions

'What manner of man was he?' Will and the making of archival Blackness in *Arden of Faversham*

Brandi K. Adams

Many early modern English readers perusing the title page of the 1592 quarto of the anonymous play *The lamentable and True Tragedie of M. Arden of Feversham in Kent* (*Arden of Faversham*) would have recognized it as a theatrical adaptation of a sensational 'true crime' story summarized in great detail in Raphael Holinshed's *Chronicles of England, Scotland and Ireland* or in other shorter histories.[1] The printed playbook promises a retelling of the 'great mallice and discimulation of a wicked woman, the vnsatiable desire of filthie lust and the shamefull end of all murderers' (A1r), while reminding those readers familiar with the case about the individuals embroiled in a complicated domestic drama, including Arden, Mosby and Shakebag. The title page also reintroduces knowledgeable readers to Black Will ('Blackwill', A1r), one of two 'desperat ruffans' hired to kill Arden 'by the means of his disloyal and wanton wyfe, . . . for the loue she bare to one Mosbie'.² Of the characters named in the elaborate title page (Alice is not named initially), Will has an additional descriptor attached to him on the title page, in parts of the play itself and in Holinshed's *Chronicles*: he is called 'Black'.³ For early modern English readers, what might the word 'Black' have meant to them in this particular context? Was it a description of physical features or another means of distinguishing an individual from the larger community? Is it simply the name of a roguish ne'er-do-well contracted to kill a gentleman on behalf of his unhappy spouse?

In Catherine Richardson's edition of *Arden of Faversham*, Black Will is grouped with Shakebag and appropriately relegated to the position of 'low-status professional murderer' and 'stock rogue character', who represents certain expected 'typologies of comedy'.⁴ All of these characterizations are accurate as Black Will embodies everything an initially hapless, brash assassin-for-hire should; he swears endlessly, swaggers, initiates verbal and physical altercations and endures humiliating misadventures as he pursues Arden, including one in which he receives a wound to his head as a bookshop shutter falls upon him. In addition to his generically expected features, he shoulders an additional marker as other characters gesture to him and speak about him. While he is occasionally identified as Will, he is mostly identified as *Black Will* – a seemingly noteworthy sobriquet – throughout the course of the play.

These observations do not imply that Black Will ever appeared as a somatically marked character who donned blackface, nor do they necessarily mean that readers marked him as somatically black in their imaginations. At the same time, however, because of his name, he carries with him a tradition of early modern figurations of racialized blackness that Robert Hornback locates in characters associated with villainy and foolishness. As he appears in *Arden of Faversham* and in parts of the preceding history in Holinshed's *Chronicles*, Black Will is not only a strange admixture of the two but also, much like other traditionally Black (and blackface) characters, he is unmistakably associated with 'degradation, irrationality, prideful lack of self-knowledge, transgression, and related to all of these, folly'.⁵ In order to examine the role of Blackness in Black Will and *Arden of Faversham*, this chapter centres on scholarship focussed on early modern English race, race-making and racialization. It also begins to answer Peter Erickson's and Kim Hall's invitation for scholars to 'continue expanding and theorizing the archive of race, seeking out new texts, questions, and vocabulary'.[6] Recent publications address aspects of racialized whiteness in the play, in which blushing indicates levels of (white) 'maidenly bashfulness and virginity' in the case of Susan, and an absence of blushing which implicates Alice in the murder of her husband, but there are other elements of whiteness, blackness and otherness that still need to be explored.[7] This chapter begins by acknowledging the role of race in Holinshed's version of the domestic drama, which is perhaps the most widely recognized source for the play.

Holinshed (and all of the individuals responsible for charting this extensive history) shapes a narrative about English whiteness and fairness, fidelity in marriage and fears about racialized others which can disrupt both the English domestic sphere and the state at large. In his initial outline of the 'circumstances' surrounding the murder, Holinshed lionizes both Arden and his wife as the embodiment of English perfection.[8] He describes Arden as 'a manne of a tall and comelye personage' who was married to a woman who matched him physically. Holinshed recalls that Arden's wife was similarly 'yong, tall, and well fauoured of shape and countenaunce', and he implies that together they made an ideal couple. Her disgrace, at least according to Holinshed, begins with her accidentally becoming involved with Mosbie, whom he describes as a 'tailor by occupation, a blacke swart man, seruant to the lord North'.

Unlike the theatrical adaptation, Mosbie is reported to be 'blacke' and 'swart', which marks him both as a racialized other with dark skin and as evil, for 'swart' also functioned as a figurative marker of ill will.[9] Holinshed takes pains to describe the nature of Mosbie's relationship with Arden's wife in which he 'oftentimes [lay] in Ardens house: in somuch that within two yeares after, he obtained such favour at hir hands, that he laid with hir, or (as they terme it) kept hir, in abusing her bodie'.[10] Because she was enamoured with Mosbie, Arden's wife persisted in 'loathing hir husband, [and] wished and after practised the meanes how to hasten his end'. Holinshed implicitly criticizes Arden's wife's desire for a man other than her husband alongside her conscious decision to abandon her role as a gentleman's wife – despite the concessions Arden makes to 'winke at hir filthie disorder' of consorting with a Black man.¹¹ Some readers of both the printed playbook and its historical precedent might have remembered this detail about Mosbie, making his affair with Arden's wife more sensational. As Mosbie is also purported to be a 'seruant', his own status seems even more complex, particularly as Urvashi Chakravarty has shown that the term has multiple meanings and a complex relationship to several forms of service in England – which could have included enslavement.¹²

In the 1587 edition of *The Chronicles*, next to the description of Mosbie, there is a printed marginal note that reads 'Loue and lust'. The note aligns Arden, the tall and comely (presumably white) gentleman, with love, while simultaneously associating Mosbie, the Black, swarthy tailor and servant, with lust. This comparison then constructs an extended binary that persistently associates Arden with England, and with the triumphant tales of monarchy, government and English whiteness throughout the *Chronicles*. Conversely, Mosbie represents disorder and the destruction of Arden's wife and marriage, as well as the persistent threats and potential contagion of Black and other nonwhite men. This binary also carries with it a 'trope of blackness' that Kim F. Hall identifies as having a 'broad arsenal of effects in the early modern period', including sustaining a racial hierarchy in which 'blackness and black men serve to heighten the whiteness of Europeans'.¹³ After drawing the parallel between Mosbie and lust, the marginal notes then focus upon 'blacke Will', terming him a 'terrible cruell ruffian with a sword', hired to kill Arden. As they follow Holinshed's narrative of the multiple attempts Black Will makes on Arden's life, they editorialize and highlight his transgressions. They identify Black Will as 'a notorious murthering ruffian', 'most heinous and wicked', a 'knave' and someone who 'maketh no conscience of bloudshed and murther'.¹⁴ Within the text, Black Will is closely aligned with Arden's wife and tangentially with Mosbie in their collective desire to murder Arden and dismantle the establishment of white English patriarchal manhood. Holinshed and his sources strongly suggest that Mosbie and Black Will introduce dangerous instability into the private and public lives of English gentlemen, whether by entering the home and dismantling marriages, or by murdering: not by passion or revenge but for pay.

If, as Ian W. Archer, Felicity Heal and Paulina Kewes suggest, '[t]he Chronicles were indeed a storehouse of examples which could be turned to debate the nature of the polity, the role of counsel, and the dangers of tyranny', it seems appropriate that any adaptation of the stories in it, including the tale of the murder of Arden of Faversham, should be examined closely on these terms.[15] In addition, given the way that the resultant play steadfastly prioritizes a white, Protestant Englishman as the apex of an organized state even as it details his murder, it is also necessary, I suggest, to consider the 1592 text's treatment of Black Will, a character who represents a disruption and an inversion of the established understanding of polity as it is represented in the *Chronicles*, especially as Mosbie's 'black', 'swart' appearance seems to disappear somewhere between the historical tale and its theatrical adaptation. In the play, Black Will destabilizes what I will call white polity: the political and social structures of governance that exist with conceptions of white Englishness as parts of expected social norms. As the central 'ruffian' of the 'true crime' play, Black Will may not be somatically Black, but he is discursively so. This discursive blackness becomes particularly evident as the polity of the play prioritizes 'land [that is] positioned variously in relationship to intersecting feudal, religious and familial discourses', while offering a strategic exploration of the 'social forces policing [public and private] spaces', along with 'surveillance through indiscriminate hospitality'.[16] Black Will works outside of the bounds of white polity in multiple ways – through his cheerful flouting of laws, his brash conduct, his vociferous love of money and his unexpected lyrically articulate moments. Black Will's name and ambiguous presence also disrupt those norms as he may or may not represent racial difference. Yet, his name and identity still have an effect on how other characters address him, and at times, how he addresses himself, despite his not being explicitly identified as 'blacke' or 'swart' as Mosbie is in the *Chronicles*.

Although he may not be explicitly racialized, Black Will embodies tropes of blackness and racial otherness that exist beyond what Ian Smith calls 'the politics of skin color', but which nevertheless divulge truths about the inherent structures of race and racial formation in early modern England.[17] Along with Smith, Ayanna Thompson urges an examination of race beyond somatic markers: 'Resisting a simplistic notion of race in definitive and finite terms, one can see how constructions of race vacillate to suit the political, social, and cultural moment. Thus, one must begin to think about the multiple ways race can be signified in performance, not limiting oneself to color alone.'[18] By extension, it is important to discern how constructions of race transfer from performance to the printed page, in elements such as speech prefixes and stage directions. This includes less obvious cues in the text that establish discursive spaces that mimic white structures of power. In what follows, I read *Arden of Faversham* alongside a transhistorical archive which contains multiple histories that complicate the relationship between names and race. The unstable relationship between onomastics and early modern people living in England allows us to reconsider what it means to be named Black Will both within this archive and outside of it in more readily available histories and plays. I also conduct a close reading of sections of the play where Black Will disrupts white polity in an articulation of difference, and finally, I examine a second drama in which a character named Black Will appears: Samuel Rowley's *When You See Me, You Know Me* (1605).

Black Wills in the English archives

In the National Archives Kew database, a short public record lists an entry for an enslaved person conveyed to the north of England in the mid-nineteenth century. It reads 'Slaves: "Black Will," a slave brought to Liverpool in 1848'.[19] Because the entry is not digitized, it is not immediately evident what information is available about this person. However, what may be surmised without the particulars of the record is this: he (for I assume it was a *he*) was a Black, enslaved individual who may have been forcibly brought to England, a country that declared slavery unlawful in 1807 by effectively ending the practice thus:

> all manner of dealing, either by way of purchase, sale, barter, or transfer, or by means of any other contract or agreement whatever, relating to any Slaves ... for the purpose of such Slaves or Persons being removed or transported either immediately or by transhipment at Sea or otherwise, directly or indirectly from Africa or from any Island, Country, Territory, or Place whatever ... is hereby in like manner utterly abolished, prohibited, and declared to be unlawful.[20]

Nevertheless, in 1848, for whatever reason, Black Will arrived or was transported into England with a name that also functioned as a somatic description. To read his name literally as a part of the discursive spaces of both the bureaucratic offices of nineteenth-century England and the National Archives, it almost appears redundant – a statement of the manifestly obvious. As an enslaved man, Black Will likely would have been conspicuously visible and recognizable as a person whose ancestry originated from the western parts of the African continent. However, in a subtler reading of his name, it remains possible that Black Will did not necessarily resemble other enslaved people, and that this appellation ensured that his identity was resolutely attached to theirs. For at this time in the history of slavery, as Marisa Fuentes, Jennifer Morgan, Saidiya Hartman and others have outlined in great detail, countless white men engaged in violent, forcible relations with enslaved Black African women, resulting in the birth of children who may not have been immediately visibly connected to their mothers, particularly by people in positions of power.[21] Because of this stark reality, Black Will's name may have been used both to call attention to the fact of his blackness and to provide justification for his enslavement while reifying his political, social and legal status within and outside of England's ostensibly abolitionist borders.

The traces of Black Will as an enslaved person in the archives reflect the frustratingly incomplete history of Black people that Saidiya Hartman describes as 'one of failure, precisely because these accounts have never been able to install themselves as history, but rather are insurgent, disruptive narratives that are marginalized and derailed before they ever gain a footing'.[22] Black Will's inchoate archival record also joins countless others in what Imtiaz Habib designates as the 'palimpsests of human presence, the outlines or substances of whose narratives no ancillary light can sharpen, and who must therefore be read as the models of their own meaning' as he writes about early modern Black people inhumed in English archives.[23] As Habib and others have shown, someone called Black Will is only one representative of the confusion surrounding names, of the persistent instability of archives as well as the electrifying possibilities for the recovery of important histories of difference. By 1848, Black Will was certainly not the first person by his name to enter England as an enslaved person, nor is he the first person with that name listed in the National Archives UK database. However, through the work of archivists and the creators of this database, the Black Will who entered England in 1848 is able to be listed transhistorically alongside other 'Black Wills' from concurrent and earlier periods, some of whom have material aspects of their lives readily available for examination. The questions surrounding the man called Black Will of 1848 provide an aperture through which to consider the histories and possible identities of men who appear earlier in English archives who share his name. What exactly does it mean to be called Black Will? An examination of these men and their shared identities provides insight into the ways in which the name Black Will could articulate perceived racial difference over time. It may also demonstrate how descriptive names reflect cultural histories of white racial formation that either completely ignore or hyperfixate on any kind of bodily difference. The history of race, particularly critical race, is neither teleological nor does it have an explicit linear relationship to time or space; later historical occurrences can provide insight about earlier histories while providing frameworks to examine and elucidate the past. In other words, the Black Will of 1848 creates a post-history through which to consider the lives of other earlier men – both fictive and real – with the same name.

Another Black Will is listed in the National Archives database as having been a 'krooman' (crewman) on the HMS Griffin in 1833-4, 'during which time the said ship was employed in the Western Coast of Africa'. This Black Will is listed as assistant surgeon Alexander Bryson's case number 14, a man who was 'taken ill at sea; [with] disease or hurt, rheumatismus; taken ill, 26 March 1834; sent 13 May 1834 to Ascension Hospital'.[24] After this medical note, his record has no further description or resolution concerning his prognosis. His connection to or distance from the continent that his ship sailed near remains unmentioned. He is a Black Will who may or may not have had a surname, and whose name may have had additional meaning on the ship. Fourteen years after the medical records of the HMS Griffin were recorded, and one year before the enslaved Black Will (1848) was brought to Liverpool, a different person with the name Black Will (1847) was listed among the sick in another medical journal, that of the HMS Rapid, again while the ship was 'employed on the West Coast of Africa'. This time, Black Will was 'aged 19, Krooman; sick or hurt, scorbutus [scurvy]; put on sick list 2 January 1847, discharged 16 January 1847 to duty'.[25] Unlike the earlier Black Will (1833/4), this story of illness is positively resolved, as Black Will (1847) became well enough to return to his work on the ship. In the same folio record as Black Will's medical report, John Short is described as 'a black boy; sick or hurt, elephantiasis, he was sent to this ship from the Heroine for a passage to Sierra Leone'.[26] The record continues to list Short's extensive treatment. As Black Will and John Short are listed together in adjoining records of illness, what possibly connects them further is a blackness that is onomastic in Will's case, and observed or described in John's.[27] In theory, the man and the boy share a descriptive signifier, although it is unknowable if Edward Heath viewed them or their possibly shared blackness in the same way. This attempt to determine the identities of the pair serving on the ship is further complicated by the histories of the slightly later and earlier Black Wills who are perhaps more visible in historical archives, but who nevertheless remain steeped in archival ambiguities and silences.

Over 250 years before the previously mentioned Black Wills appear, a sixteenth-century Black Will, the alias of William Rydley (also Ridley), is listed in the Northumberland archives. He was charged with murder on 23 November 1591: 'Presentment: William Rydley, alias black will f. of Hetherton, yeoman; at Burtley, murdered George Atchyson with a sword worth 10s., giving him a fatal wound on the right side of his head five inches long and five inches deep so that he died instantly.'[28] Unlike the other individuals named Black Will on record (1833, 1847 and 1848), Rydley is instantaneously identified with a surname. But although he has family with whom he may be loosely connected, his identity could nevertheless be considered as fluid as the others. Rydley reappears in archival records in June 1597, six years after his initial mention in the Border Papers. He is the subject of questions directed at Ralph Eure, 3rd Baron Eure, at the behest of William Cecil Lord Burghley. In his capacity as Warden of the Middle March, Eure reluctantly accounted for Black Will and other fugitives and criminals who seem to have taken shelter in Scotland. Before ultimately losing his position, Eure identifies Black Will Rydley as hiding under the protection of Nicholas Weldon: 'William Ridley called "Black Will", the like, and we find though a fugitive, he returned and took a dwelling in Tindale under charge of the said lord warden and keeper.'[29] After this report of his whereabouts, Black Will/William Rydley fades into the records as he shares a rather common name with other men also called William Rydley who bought land, sued family members and who owed taxes to the crown. Black Will Rydley's Blackness seems to have been a mantle that could be at least partially obfuscated by an extensive and active community with the same surname.

Thirty-eight years before Black Will/William Rydley 'murdered George Atchyson with a sword', the most notorious and perhaps historically recognizable Black Will (at least to early modernists who focus on England) appears in both the Calendar of State Papers and Raphael Holinshed's *Chronicles*. Listed also as a murderer, this Black Will plays a pivotal role in an overly complicated plot hatched by a 'mistres Arden' to end the life of her husband, Master Arden of Feversham.[30] Like the Black Will listed in the ship surgeon's records in 1847, the Black Will of Holinshed's *Chronicles* is also paired with an individual specifically identified as Black, and like John Short (and Holinshed's Mosbie) is specifically termed Black (as well as swart). This Black Will (1553) is transformed and fictionalized in a later sixteenth-century adaptation of the murder case. The anonymously authored play adaptation extends the report compiled by Holinshed and also provides space to consider Black Will beyond his role as a murderer for hire. Despite the shift in genre, this fictional version of Black Will (along with Holinshed's version) nevertheless shares similarities with the later archival incarnations of Black Wills and raises similar questions about racial formation and identity.

Black Will of Faversham

When Black Will moves from archives and chronicles to printed drama, the ambiguity and inchoateness of his identity remain. Strangely, the Black Will of *Arden of Faversham* (1592) shares traits with an archival Black Will (1591) as they are both convicted of murder and both flee the country, with varying results. Neither man is identified specifically as racially Black, nor are they described in the kinds of specific detail that Bradshaw offers when he recalls the appearance of Jack Fitten as

> A leane faced writhen knaue,
> Hauke nosde, and verye hollow eied,
> With mightye furrowes in his stormye browes,
> Long haire down his shoulders curled,

His Chinne was bare, but on his vpper lippe,
A mutchado, which he wound about his eare... (C3v)

The description of this 'knaue' is lyrical, but still provides enough detail for Black Will to be identified as the man as who stole Lord Cheiny's plate and who was 'in Newgate for stealing a horse' (C3v). Unlike Fitten, the Black Wills of the English archives collectively remain elusive, as the scant listing of their lives provides little grounding for a physical description. The same holds true for the Black Will of the play. However, the archives expand the possibilities for a reading of Black Will as Black – or at least not exactly white – as both ill and well, and as a well-connected fugitive and murderer. His name and its possible meanings are as expansive as the archive itself. However, what remains consistent are the ways that Black Will is clearly identified as *Black*, at least in the spaces of the archives, and particularly in the case of William Rydley. In both the Northumberland Archives and the Border Papers, his alias of 'Black Will' is used repeatedly as an identifier either alone or in conjunction with his full name. For Rydley, the name Black Will was an indelible part of his identity as he stood convicted for murder or fled to the Scottish countryside.

Black Will's difference in terms of blackness may remain equivocal in the play, yet his character becomes racialized in the ways that others designate him through description or interaction. While he does not fit precisely into a stereotype of the early modern English stage's version of a 'moor', he nevertheless functions as an example of the 'projections of imaginations that capitalize on the assumptions, fantasies, fears and anxieties of England's pale-complexioned audiences' that Virginia Mason Vaughan identifies.[31] How people speak about him is as important as what he says in the play. Black Will is initially described in terms of his actions similarly to the marginal comments in Holinshed's *Chronicles* (1587) as Bradshaw introduces Black Will to Greene:

For such a slaue, so vile a roge as he
Lyues not againe vppon the earth,
Black-will is his name I tell you M. Gréene,
At Bulloine he and I were fellow souldiers,
Where he plaid such prankes,
As all the Campe feared him for his villany:

> I warrant you he beares so bad a minde,
> That for a croune heele murther any man. (C3r)

Before he names Black Will, Bradshaw spends two lines depicting him as a 'slaue' and 'vile roge' who shares no similarities with any form of humanity on earth. With the terms slave and vile rogue, Bradshaw creates the structures for future connections made between blackness and fitness for enslavement. As he recalls his former connection to Black Will, Bradshaw initially distances himself from his former 'fellow' soldier. In creating a history of Will for Greene, Bradshaw draws out his separation by characterizing Black Will's mind as 'bad' and then divulges that his erstwhile fellow will kill for hire. As he further detaches himself from their shared history, Bradshaw rejects reminiscences of the difference (racial or otherwise) that Black Will's presence invokes. He overtly criticizes the 'pranks', petty crimes and other infractions that Black Will committed during their encampment together. As Will approaches, Bradshaw also remarks upon the contaminating power of his presence as it extends to Shakebag (who is initially not identified by name), transforming him into a 'knave' tainted by association 'for bearing the other company' (C3r).

Conversely, Black Will reaffirms his connection to Bradshaw as he pointedly announces Bradshaw's change in class: 'No fellows now, because you are a gouldsmith, / And haue a lytle plate in your shoppe' (C3v). Even as Black Will goads him on, Bradshaw continually rejects their former relationship as fellows ('I Will, those dayes are past with me.') as Black Will insists that their association is continuous and rejoins: 'I but they be not past with me. / For I kepe that same honorable minde still'. Black Will invokes past honours, fellowship and kinship, while Bradshaw passively rebinds them together in a community of difference and inhumanity, a small acknowledging of his former life, as well as the power and usefulness of the criminal underworld. In order to extract information, Bradshaw maintains a form of intimacy and familiarity throughout the conversation – using the name Will, without the moniker – and indirectly requests help:

> Now I am going to London vpon hope,
> To finde the fellow, now Will I know
> Thou art acquainted with such companions. (C3v)

Bradshaw recognizes the immediate benefit that his previous intimate connection to Black Will provides to Greene. However, as forcefully as he attempts to distance himself, Black Will's contagion-like Blackness and his extended social networks entrap Bradshaw as he unknowingly conveys a letter detailing Alice's plans to murder Arden, making him an accessory to the crime. Will's historic connection to Blackness and his unchanging conduct prevent Bradshaw from successfully entering a new social sphere which would allow him to be permanently walled off from what he considers Black Will's inhumanity and difference.

As a character who is kept on edge because he cannot read Black Will or his motives, Michael, Arden's servant, laments his earlier decision to join Alice's scheme to kill Arden. As he laments his betrayal of Arden, he faults Black Will and Shakebag for pushing him to engage in behaviour outside of the expectations of white polity in the play. In his desire to reinscribe himself to Arden and the ethical world, Michael imputes the 'grim faced fellow pittiles Black Will' and Shakebag, 'stearne in bloody stratagem', with his impending demise. Michael attributes the darkness of death and repellant ugliness to Black Will and his physical facial features. Black Will represents Michael's fear as he contemplates mortality in his soliloquy and Michael can only conceive of Black Will as an object of terror and without pity as he graphically imagines his slow death at Black Will's and Shakebag's hands:

> Me thinks I see them with their bolstred haire,
> Staring and grinning in thy gentle face,
> And in their ruthles hands, their dagers drawne,
> Insulting ore there with a peck of oathes.
> Whilest thou submissiue pleading for reléese,
> Art mangled by their irefull instruments.
> Me thinks I heare them aske where Michaell is
> And pittiles black Will, cryes stab the slaue. (E1r)

Black Will further transforms into a ghoulish, otherworldly creature, his hair standing on end and continuously swearing, with Michael conjuring blackness as the grounding of Will's lack of empathy, much as the speaker of Shakespeare's sonnets defines the 'ill-will of the dark lady' in Carol Mejia LaPerle's analysis. LaPerle argues that the 'unkind kinlessness projected onto the dark mistress's ill-will is not separate from, but rather elemental to, the commodification of Black femininity'.[32] In Black Will's instance, Michael ascribes and employs racially encoded language to sublimate fear and disgust into the features of Black Will's face, turning it into the quintessence of hell: '[t]he wrincles in his fowle death threatning face / Gapes open wide, lyke graues to swallow men' (G4r). As he constructs a frightening anti-blazon in which the folds of Black Will's skin can create an opening to mimic graves, Michael calls forth Bradshaw's construction of Black Will as otherworldly, inhuman and unconnected to anything on earth. In his fright, Michael indirectly binds Black Will to representations of hell and the devil – which have a long association with blackness.[33]

Strangely, Michael ascribes most of the chilling aspects of murder to Black Will. He perversely compliments Shakebag for his academic, calculating approach to murder, for having strategy and a logic that Black Will lacks. While Black Will allegedly murders for sport, Shakebag is credited with aspects of whiteness – calm, lucid approaches to precarious situations. This placidity exists in the intimate spaces of his friendship with Black Will, in which Shakebag ignores the epithet 'Black' in conversation with his friend. In turn, Black Will resists the projections of inhumanity, monstrousness and death that Bradshaw and Michael attempt to force on to him. Instead, Black Will has agency to remove the mantle of 'Black(ness)' and distance himself from essentialist, fictive ideas associated with his blackness in the play. After Shakebag compares the impending darkness of the evening to Arden's being 'sent to euerlasting night', Black Will confesses in an uncharacteristic moment of softness that he wishes for the end of their task: 'would this thing were don / I am so heauy that I can scares go' (E2r). In that moment, he articulates a vulnerability to Shakebag that is unparalleled in other relationships in the play. Shakebag counters Black Will's discomfort by calling him names and encourages him to sleep while subtly acknowledging the 'fear' in Will's initial words. The conversational register that Shakebag uses for Will abruptly changes when he speaks about Black Will, particularly to characters outside of their social circle such as Greene. The intimacy and near-kinship disappears and is instead replaced with a mimicking of the language and bravado Black Will used when first vowing to undertake the murder. Boasting of their imminent success, Shakebag summons the rhetorical power of Black Will's name as he prematurely declares Arden's demise, 'as if he had beene condemned / By an act of parliament, if once Black Will and I / Sweare his death' (D1r).

Despite his close association with Black Will, Shakebag avoids subjecting Black Will to racialized language and concepts and himself escapes assignations of that language; yet as Will's counterpart, he comes to embody signs of whiteness. After Michael associates Shakebag with whiteness and rationality, he remains the calm counterpoint to Black Will's outbursts of bravado. Despite his suggesting that he 'cannot paint my valour out with words', Shakebag often delivers classically inflected blank verse lines as a riposte to Black Will's rougher pronouncements. He aligns himself with gentler verse and avoids the limelight into which Black Will is often thrust. As Arden escapes death with the help of Lord Cheyne, Shakebag expresses his disappointment in articulate terms, offering a stark contrast to Black Will. Displaying what Cheryl I. Harris identifies as the property of whiteness as a status, Shakebag represents literacy, forethought and order.[34] These are literary and artistic descriptors that, as Kim F. Hall explains, have been tied to binaries of light (as opposed to dark and blackness) for centuries.[35] As Black Will invokes violent imagery, Shakebag speaks four tightly metered lines that end in a couplet:

> *Wil* The Deuill break all your necks, at 4 myles end,
> Zounds I could kill my selfe for very anger.
> His Lordship chops me in, euen when
> My dagge was leaueld at his hart.
> I would his crowne were molten down his throat,
> *Sha.* Arden thou hast wondrous holye luck,
> Did euer man escape as thou hast done.
> VVell Ile discharge my pistoll at the skye,
> For by this bullet Arden might not die. (F3v)

As he remarks upon Arden's unusual ability to escape death, Shakebag invokes the heavens and rather neatly fires his pistol into the space that seems to be providing Arden with means to escape his fate. Throughout the play, Shakebag's words remain carefully calculated, a foil to the disordered, joyful hyperbole of Black Will, perhaps as a part of his tacit understanding of white polity and community, an understanding in which Alice revels and Black Will falters.

Whiteness, polity, Alice and Black Will

Shakebag maintains a firm grasp on the constraints of social and political whiteness, even as he plots the mechanics of Arden's murder with Black Will. This fastidious adherence to structures already in place stands in contrast to Alice Arden's political use of early modern English 'faireness' as protection for her machinations. She takes advantage of the stable political environment and order that both governs the town of Faversham that protects her and aligns her within the established structures of whiteness. Her actions prefigure Harris's description of whiteness as a property that provides her with material advantages (however fleetingly). Alice deploys Susan's physical whiteness ('fairness') in conjunction with her own as a resource to incite at least five individuals to participate in a murder.[36] She trades on this whiteness/fairness in order to enact her will and then eventually escape blame. She depends upon her own fairness to affect her accomplices, as she describes her woes to Greene in her early attempts to enlist his help with her crime. Greene opines, '[n]ow trust me mistres Ales, it greeueth me / So *faire* a creature should be so abused' (C3r, italics mine). Even though Greene's own motivations are monetary (as Arden took possession of land Greene believed to be his), he implicitly understands the rhetorical situation in which he is participating – that Alice's fairness is political and economic currency she spends in order to maintain a personal sense of order. Alice's displeasure and sadness in her domestic life contrasts sharply with expectations regarding her white femininity. Hall has persuasively argued that discourses such as that which surrounds Alice's fairness mark 'the site of crucial delineations of cultural difference' as well as 'the map upon which imperial desire and national identity are marked'.[37] In the play, she comprehends the power of her white racial fairness as she employs it not only to convince the men in the play to conspire to murder her husband but also to confuse Arden and Mosby about her relative loyalty to each of them.

When Mosby initially regrets his liaison with Alice, he openly challenges the discourse of her fairness. He curses Alice and laments the credit he spent in her name:

Nay if thou ban, let me breath curses forth,
And if you stand so nicely at your fame:

> Let me repent the credit I have lost,
> I have neglected matters of import,
> That would haue stated me aboue thy state:
> Forslowde aduantages, and spurnd at time. (E4v)

Alice's fairness kept him from 'matters of import', including his 'Mariage of an honest maide / Whose dowry would haue weyed down all that wealth / Whose beauty and demianor farr exceeded thee'. The marriage that he neglected for Alice would have changed his station, giving him a place that would be socially and politically superior to Alice, something which her fairness could not purchase. He returns to lamenting the loss he incurred in fiscal and credit terms by trading the 'honest maide' for Alice's uncertain, 'changing bad', fairness. He ascribes his relationship to bewitchment that requires 'excirsimes'. Invoking similar language to that which Michael uses in his description of Black Will, Mosby equates Alice with blackness. To him, she has become 'a rauen for a dowe', her fairness transformed into a black bird that portends death. To undo the spell he claims to have been under, he embarks on an incantation-like reversal of his feeling. Mosby dissociates her from whiteness and kindness: 'Thou art not faire, I vieud thee not till now, / Thou art not kinde, till now I knew the not'. In his rejection of her ostensible beauty, he also distances himself as she loses her value and whiteness, and he claims to divest his interest in her. But ultimately, her whiteness reasserts itself in the resolution of the quarrel, as Mosby's rejection of her fairness only lasts as long as their self-imposed conflict. In a clear understanding of her worth even as a married woman, Alice wagers her political capital on her fairness as a loyalty test. Because she and Mosby both understand the political capital associated with her fair complexion and her ability to leverage and use it within the space of the play, Mosby retracts his statements, acknowledges and reaffirms her whiteness and reestablishes her capital worth.

In addition to her understanding the currency of fairness, Alice manipulates white polity to engage in an open affair with Mosby and to plot murder. Her fairness and status as a gentleman's wife allows her to, for a time, circumvent the structures that punish unlawful, 'black' or 'dark' conduct. Although she cannot blush, as Emma Whipday notes, she can still conceal her plans behind her established identity and the ways she comports herself.[38] For Patricia Akhimie, conversations about conduct are another facet of racial and class difference in early modern England. Conduct functions as a 'way of evaluating the way other people do things' and also determines whether or not individuals have a capacity to improve in terms of their social standing. From the start of the play, Black Will is identified – and at times acknowledges himself – as the embodiment of such disorder and malevolence that he would easily choose to serve as 'warden of the company' of assassins if such an entity existed. Akhimie notes that, in some cases, there were people who were 'marked by a devastating lack: an inability to be better and even to know better – that is to know that they *should* be better'.[39] At times throughout the play, Alice teases the possibility of her redemption, or at least a tacit recognition of the erroneousness of her intent to murder her husband. Whatever destruction Alice (and to a certain extent even Mosby or Greene) enacts, Black Will exists in the world of the play as someone more violent, who can cause more harm. Importantly, he is identifiable by name, if not by somatic difference, as Black. Will and his Blackness serve to maintain the relative 'fairness' of Alice, even at her most villainous. His abstract, outsized – at times, even comedic – darkness complicates the narrative of her mariticide within the greater landscape of the play.

Alice also understands the currency of fairness and conduct in relation to Black Will. In order to ensure that Black Will fully commits to the plans to murder her husband, Alice announces that he is 'fair' (to her), and she will exchange her equally fair words for monetary compensation to ensure Arden's demise:

> Come blacke Will that in mine eies art faire,
> Next vnto Mosbie doe I honour thée,
> Instead of faire wordes and large promises,
> My hands shall play you goulden harmonie,
> Now like you this? say, will you doe it sirs? (N3v)

Alice understands that Black Will is not likely to be addressed in the way that she is, as his position in the community is separate from hers. Her fairness is not his; his understanding of polity is counter to hers because of his position as a 'cutter' for hire. However, she understands that the creation of a fair affect for Black Will will ensure that he understands and equates his new fairness with capital. She convinces him that she sees what everyone else cannot – that Black Will is, in fact, fair, and that his fairness has 'goulden harmonie' or economic value. Much like when the

Duke of Venice calls Othello 'more fair than black' (1.3.291) in Shakespeare's play, Alice endears herself to Black Will by assuring him the capital associated with whiteness in an economic system that she has engineered. She also metaphorically raises him to a position secondary to her lover to prove his necessity in the execution of their scheme and temporarily embraces Black Will's rejection of the secrecy that surrounds conspiracy and murder. From the beginning of *Arden of Faversham*, Black Will counters the silence about pay for his services:

> *Gre.* Well this it is, Arden of Feuershame,
> Hath highly wrongd me about the Abby land,
> That no reuendge but death will serue the turne:
> Will you two kill him, hoeres the Angels downe,
> And I will lay the platforme of his death:
> *Will.* Plat me no platformes giue me the money,
> And ile stab him as he stands pissing against a wall,
> but Ile kill him.
> *Sha.* Where is he? (C4v)

Unlike the quieter, more nebulous discussions surrounding the trade of Mosby's sister in exchange for Clarke's or Michael's participation in the murder, Black Will subverts expectations surrounding the act of murder and reduces Greene's plans into a scatological joke. Black Will's joyful pursuit of crime and death is an embrace of his difference and of the implicit connections that other characters make between him and death. For him – and perhaps even Shakebag to an extent – their lives, no matter how literary, are counter to the polity established in the play.

However, once they have committed the crime, they understand that they are in true transgression of the larger community and know that they must flee Faversham, particularly once Alice is apprehended by the Mayor. Once the murder takes place, Black Will's intimate friendship with Shakebag dissipates. Because of his privilege and his literacy, Shakebag is able to claim sanctuary. As he committed other crimes with joy, Black Will must exit the polity of England and go elsewhere:

> Shakebag I heare hath taken sanctuary,
> But I am so pursued with hues and cryes,

For petty robberies that I haue done,
That I can come vnto no Sanctuary. (J4r)

As the murder comes to light, Alice attempts to secure her fairness by denying knowledge of Black Will or the murder as she pretends her husband is not on the premises. She attempts to use her waning fairness and social power on the Mayor as she complains that demands to enter her home are excessive: 'I search and spare you not, through euery roome / Were my husband at home, you would not offer this' (I3r). She begins to embody the inverse blazon that Mosby sets up earlier in the play when he denies her fairness as he informs her 'It grieues me not to see how foull thou art' (E4v), although, at this point, he is implicated in the murder as well. Once Alice denies all knowledge of Black Will his blackness becomes reified once again, but in a frightening way as he attempts to flee England. As he seeks refuge out of the country in Flushing, Black Will carries with him an embodied blackness that stands in utter contrast with Alice Arden's fairness as articulated through the immediate and extended consequences of their collective crime. Black Will seeks refuge in Flushing as he 'run(s) full blanck at all adventures' and survives by covering his head with his buckler, perhaps as an attempt to pass for something he is not. The evocation of the white 'blanck' at the centre of a target separates the 'black' Will from the 'blanck' whiteness at which he aims, he carrying with him an embodied blackness that stands in utter contrast with Alice Arden's fairness'. Until his reported death, Black Will elides white polity that attempts to confine him throughout the entire play. Black Will's ebullient rejection of authority would occur again thirteen years later in 1605 with an incarnation of another Black Will.

Blacke Will redux

In 1605, in Samuel Rowley's *When You See Me, You Know Me*, an uncanny moment occurs about a third of the way into the text of the play. A character named Blacke Will appears and immediately rehearses both the petty and serious crimes of which he has had a part:

> So, how *I* am got within the Cittie, I am as safe as in a Sanctuarieat is a hard world, when *Blacke VVill,* for a venture of fiue pound,

must commit such pettie robberies at *Mile-ende,* but the plaine truth is, the Stewes from whence *I* had my quartaridgeas now growne too hote for me: theres some suspection of a murther lately done vpon two Marchants of the *Stilliard,* which indeede as farre as some fiue or sixe stabs comes too, I confesse *I* had a hand in. But mumbudget, all the Dogges in the towne must not barke at it. I must withdraw awhile till the heate bee ore, remooue my lodging, and liue vpon darke nights and mistie mornings. Now let me them see, the strongest watch in London intercept my passage.[40]

The cadence of his 'voice' is strangely familiar – an echo of the Black Will that appears in *Arden of Faversham* as he boisterously summarizes the 'fiue or six' times he stabbed 'two Marchants of Stilliard'. He has found respite in the city where he commits 'pettie robberies' at Mile End to survive. Unlike the Black Will of *Arden of Faversham*, this Black Will of 1605 seems artificially inserted into the play from another place and time. His familiar dismissal of cultural mores about crime and his verbal cadences are reminiscent of *Arden*'s Black Will, but he lacks temporal specificity. He materializes rather magically into the narrative of the play as a cheerful distraction to the coming scenes. Rowley's Black Will is the reverse of Black Will Slawter, who appears in *The True Tragedy of Richard III* (1594). Slawter embodies all of the violence of Black Will from Faversham, but without humour – aside from the moment King puns on his name: 'Slawter, I pray to God he come not to slaughter my brother and me, for from murther and slaughter, good lord deliuer vs' (F1r).[41] Like some of the Black Wills in the archives, he is identified by his full name with the qualification that the general public identifies him as 'blacke Will' specifically, which suggests that his appearance may have something to do with his name.

Catherine Richardson connects this reappearance of Black Will to a 1599 revival of *Arden of Faversham*, in which he functions as 'an epitome of lawless threat, but also maintain[s] the capacity for humour as part of his stage presence'.[42] In *When You See Me*, Black Will's verbal exchanges are not with a compatriot of his own standing such as Shakebag but with King Henry VIII. In his scene with Henry, Blacke Will fails to recognize the King and challenges him to a sword-fight, mirroring *Arden*'s Black Will as he lists his accomplishments and summons the rhetorical power of his name. He calls the King a 'slaue', assuring him that '*Blacke will* is knowne and feared though the seuenteene Provinces: there's not a sword and Buckler man in *England* nor *Europe,* but has had a taste of my manhood'.[43]

Although Blacke Will remains a criminal, he seems somewhat parodic, a happy and diverting interlocutor with the King who boasts about his notoriety in London. He unknowingly invites the king to become a fellow cutpurse and tries to impress him with his knowledge of the city's watchmen, who call him 'Good Maister *Blacke William*'.[44] In this strange comedic turn, Black Will's disdain of polity is still present, but his difference from the larger community is minimized. In Rowley's play he appears to be an ahistorical merry prankster who exists in a liminal space between fiction and biography, with his labyrinthine history and complex difference diluted. He is a Blacke Will without the English archives and a parodic version of the Black Will in *Arden of Faversham*, one who is unmarked by real difference. He is both Black Will and not – a recognizable figure, but one who is an adaptation of the original.

Whether he is to be found transhistorically in the archives, as part of a 'true crime' story in a chronicle, as a 'ruffan' with ambiguous origins, or even appearing as a remixed character in another play, Black Will both embodies and rejects expectations surrounding blackness. He reacts against white polity, particularly to those who would show him disdain. What remains fascinating is the incompleteness of answers about Black Will and who he is supposed to be in the archive, in *The Chronicles* or in the early modern English theatre. What premodern critical race studies contributes to the discussion about Black Will and his Blackness is a broad approach to perspectives of who any given Black Will could be and his relationship to the racialized world around him. In *Arden of Faversham* in particular, Black Will's Blackness is as multivalent as the text of the play and encourages readers to search for the discourses and realities of racial formation, the pervasive constructions of whiteness and the subtleties of a lively, jubilant, very *Black* Will.

Notes

1 Catherine Richardson, ed., *Arden of Faversham* (London: Bloomsbury, 2022). Richardson maps out the various ways the story

of Arden was shared in and around England, through various printed and manuscript histories.

2 *The Lamentable and True Tragedie of M. Arden of Feversham in Kent* (London 1592); all quotes come from this edition. I quote from this first edition to represent the various ways Black Will appears in the printed playbook.

3 Richardson notes that in a manuscript version of the case recorded by Henry Machyn in 1551, it is a Black *Tom* who receives capital punishment for the crime (3).

4 Ibid., 35.

5 Robert Hornback, *The English Clown Tradition from the Middle Ages to Shakespeare* (Cambridge: DS Brewer, 2013), 26.

6 Peter Erickson and Kim Hall, 'A New Scholarly Song', *Shakespeare Quarterly* 67, no. 1 (2016): 7.

7 Emma Whipday, '"Thou Look'st Pale": Narrating Blanching and Blushing on the Early Modern Stage', in *Playing and Playgoing in Early Modern England: Actor, Audience and Performance*, ed. Simon Smith and Emma Whipday (Cambridge: Cambridge University Press, 2022), 44–5.

8 Raphael Holinshed, *The First and Second Volumes of Chronicles Comprising 1 the Description and Historie of England, 2 the Description and Historie of Ireland, 3 the Description and Historie of Scotland* (London, 1587), 1062.

9 'swart, adj. and n.'. *OED Online*, June 2022. Thank you to Duncan Salkeld for pointing me to this moment in *The Chronicles*.

10 Holinshed, *Chronicles*, 1062.

11 Ibid.

12 Urvashi Chakravarty, *Fictions of Consent: Slavery, Servitude, and Free Service in Early Modern England* (Philadelphia: University of Pennsylvania Press, 2022), 1–10 and 14–88.

13 Kim F. Hall, *Things of Darkness: Economies of Race and Gender in Early Modern England* (Ithaca: Cornell University Press, 1995), 6.

14 *Chronicles*, 1063–4.

15 Ian W. Archer, Felicity Heal and Paulina Kewes, 'Prologue', in *The Oxford Handbook of Holinshed's Chronicles*, ed. Paulina Kewes, Ian W. Archer and Felicity Heal (Oxford: Oxford University Press, 2013), xxxiii.

16 Garrett A. Sullivan, '"Arden Lay Murdered in That Plot of Ground": Surveying, Land, and Arden of Faversham', *ELH* 61, no. 2 (1994):

232; Emma Whipday, '"Marrow Prying Neighbours": Staging Domestic Space and Neighbourhood Surveillance in *Arden of Faversham*', *Cahiers Élisabéthains* 88, no. 1 (2015): 96–7.

17 Ian Smith, *Race and Rhetoric in the Renaissance: Barbarian Errors* (New York: Palgrave MacMillan, 2009), 12.

18 Ayanna Thompson, *Performing Race and Torture on the Early Modern Stage* (New York: Routledge, 2008), 28.

19 'Slaves: "Black Will", a slave brought to Liverpool in 1848', 1848. The National Archives, HO 45/2238.

20 *British and Foreign State Papers, 1817–1818* (London: James Rigeway and Sons, 1837), 559.

21 Marisa J. Fuentes, *Dispossessed Lives: Enslaved Women, Violence, and the Archive* (Philadelphia: University of Pennsylvania Press, 2016); Jennifer L. Morgan, *Reckoning with Slavery : Gender, Kinship, and Capitalism in the Early Black Atlantic* (Durham: Duke University Press, 2021); Saidiya Hartman, 'Venus in Two Acts', *Small Axe* 12, no. 2 (2008): 1–14.

22 Hartman, 'Venus in Two Acts', 13.

23 Imtiaz Habib, *Black Lives in the English Archives, 1500–1677: Imprints of the Invisible* (Aldershot: Ashgate, 2008), 19.

24 Alexander Bryson, 'Journal of the HMS Griffin for 7 November 1833 to 6 November 1834', 1833–4. The National Archives, ADM 101/103/4B, ff. 14–15.

25 Edward Heath, 'Medical Journal of HMS Rapid, from 1 January to 31 December 1847', 1847. The National Archives, ADM 101/116/4B, f. 14.

26 Ibid.

27 See Habib, *Black Lives*, 12.

28 Northumberland Quarter Sessions, 23 November 1951. Northumberland Archives, QSI/1, f66r (355).

29 Ralph Eure, 'Eure to Burghley', 8 June 1957. *The Border Papers: Calendar of Letters and Papers Relating to the Affairs of the Borders of England and Scotland 1560–1603*, ed. Joseph Bain, Vol. 2: 1595–1603 (Edinburgh: H.M. General Register House, 1896), entry 652. SP 59/34 f.240.

30 Raphael Holinshed, *The First and second volumes of chronicles comprising 1 the description and historie of England, 2 the description and historie of Ireland, 3 the description and historie of Scotland* (London, 1577), 1391. He is not the only Black Will listed in *The*

Chronicles. In his rehearsal of Richard III's kingship, Holinshed lists William Slaughter, also called Black Will, as the protector of the two sons of Edward IV's sons until their untimely deaths. Slaughter is only mentioned in the 1577 edition of the Chronicles.

31 Virginia Mason Vaughan, *Performing Blackness on English Stages, 1500–1800* (Cambridge: Cambridge University Press, 2005), 5–6.
32 Carol Mejia LaPerle, 'The Racialized Affects of Ill-Will in the Dark Lady Sonnets', in *Race & Affect in Early Modern English Literature*, ed. Carol Mejia LaPerle (Tempe Arizona: ACMRS Press, 2022), 220.
33 See Hall, *Things of Darkness*, and Matthieu A. Chapman, 'The Appearance of Blacks on the Early Modern Stage: *Love's Labour's Lost*'s African Connections to Court', *Early Theatre* 17, no. 2 (2014): 77–94.
34 Cheryl I. Harris, 'Whiteness as Property', *Harvard Law Review* 106, no. 8 (1993): 1707–91.
35 Hall, *Things of Darkness*, 177–8.
36 Harris, 'Whiteness'.
37 Ibid., 178.
38 Whipday, 'Blush', 44–5.
39 Patricia Akhimie, *Shakespeare and the Cultivation of Difference: Race and Conduct in the Early Modern World* (New York: Routledge 2018), 5.
40 Samuel Rowley, *When you see me, you know me …* (London, 1605), D3r.
41 *The True Tragedie of Richard the third* (London, 1594).
42 Richardson, *Arden*, 17–18.
43 Ibid., D3v–D4r.
44 Ibid., D3v.

7

New directions

Crimson snow: *Arden of Faversham* as golden age detective story

Lisa Hopkins

The mystery of *Arden of Faversham*'s authorship is easily solved; it is an early work by Freeman Wills Crofts. Devotees of this 'master of the humdrum' will recognize several distinctive features of his style and technique.[1] As in *Antidote to Venom* and *The 12.30 from Croydon*, we see the murder of a rich male householder by someone who stands to gain financially from his death.[2] There is no suspense about the identity of the murderer; the interest lies rather in the cunningly charted shift of balance as the struggle to hang on to barely achieved economic stability begins to seem less important than the effect on the criminal's soul. This note of piety, rare in the first half of the twentieth century, when golden age detective fiction was being written, is echoed in the stern insistence that women are temptresses – sometimes inadvertently so, but always, like Eve, the root cause of guilt in men (lest we miss the point, *Antidote to Venom* gives a starring role to a snake). Again, as in

Antidote to Venom and *The 12.30 from Croydon*, and indeed in all Wills Crofts's work, events follow their inevitable trajectory as the guilt of the criminal is revealed and he is hanged (although the business of detection is truncated in *Arden* because the murder happens so close to the end). The play also includes some other classic tropes of detective fiction, most notably the footprints in the snow so beloved of Christmas crime stories, and its focus on the Arden household is firmly in line with the Latin origin of the word detection, *detegere*, to remove the roof: Emma Whipday notes that '*Arden of Faversham* offered its audience unprecedented access to the staged private spaces of an early modern home'.[3] One might even note that the uncertainty of the play's authorship echoes the mystery deliberately cultivated by the many writers of golden age detective fiction who adopted pseudonyms, with 'Nicholas Blake' veiling the identity of the poet laureate and 'Michael Innes' that of an Oxford don. This chapter will argue that considering *Arden of Faversham* as a golden age detective story invites us to notice its stress on material circumstances and helps us to see how it approaches the question implicit in all crime fiction, which is what is being detected – individual guilt, original sin, a flawed society or a combination of these?

Freeman Wills Crofts (1879–1957) was an Irish writer whose principal detective was Inspector Joseph French, whose deceptively obsequious manner to suspects causes him to be known to his colleagues at Scotland Yard as 'Soapy Joe'. Inspector French is a rather colourless character: he is not Belgian or a little old lady, he has no known hobbies or eccentricities and even Wills Crofts himself seems to have struggled to feel much interest in him, since in the foreword to *Inspector French's Greatest Case* he writes of his creation 'I have been wondering whether he has children', and later in the same book French tells an enquirer that he lost his eldest son in the war.[4] However under-characterized he may be, though, French is an impartial dealer of justice who always gets his man. Wills Crofts worked on the railways, and he believed implicitly in two things, trains and God. If there is a single moral to all his books, it is that crime is always punished and worldly success can never compensate for a troubled conscience.

To underline this message Wills Crofts draws on two Shakespeare plays, *Hamlet* and *Macbeth*, which he clearly considers serious works about the human soul.[5] Charles Swinburn in *The 12.30 from*

Croydon kills an old man for gain and is then led on to another murder to try to conceal his role in the first; George Surridge in *Antidote to Venom* 'screwed up his courage to the sticking point' (39), but like Macbeth he cannot sleep, and like Hamlet he wonders whether there is life after death (259) but dares not kill himself until he has cleared his conscience (260).[6] Shakespeare, it seems, provides a convenient measure for charting spiritual decay or spiritual growth.

This is not how most golden age detective writers use Shakespeare's contemporaries. A particularly interesting example of borrowing from early modern drama is the American writer John Dickson Carr, who presents a pertinent contrast to Wills Crofts in that the last of his Inspector Bencolin books, *The Four False Weapons*, begins with one character assuring another that what he is about to experience will be 'precisely the reverse of humdrum',[7] the term with which Wills Crofts has become synonymous. Carr incorporated echoes of early modern drama into the first four Inspector Bencolin stories in so low-key a way that they have never to my knowledge been previously detected.[8] His first book, *It Walks by Night*, has a madman who believes in werewolves, features a newly married woman whose toilette is interrupted when she sees in the mirror a man who wants to prevent her marriage and contains a scene in which another woman realizes that the hand touching her belongs to a dead man.[9] *Castle Skull*, which appeared a year later, has a body hanging in chains, characters called Hoffman and Jérôme, and someone known as the Duchess; there is also a case of impersonation.[10] Another book published in the same year as *Castle Skull*, *The Lost Gallows*, sees a vengeful father seeking to hang the two people who caused his son to hang himself,[11] and a year later *The Corpse in the Waxworks* features two women with dual identities, a character named Beatrice, and a man with a repellent facial disfigurement, and centres on a club whose members wear masks and sleep with people they can't identify.[12] Once the pattern is spotted, it will not take the reader long to see parallels with *The Duchess of Malfi*, *Hoffman*, *The Spanish Tragedy* and *The Changeling*, respectively.

John Dickson Carr stopped alluding to early modern drama in his later books and disowned the method: Douglas G. Greene declares that 'Carr understood the weakness of the Bencolin novels. Three years after the publication of *The Corpse in the Waxworks*, he said, "I used to believe that all the readers would find my stuff as dull as ditchwater unless I whooped up the grotesqueness everywhere, and turned all my characters into jumping-jacks".'[13] That is a fair summary not only of the Bencolin books but of the ways in which revenge tragedy is generally pressed into service in golden age detective fiction: it is there to ramp up the horror quotient. But horror was never what Freeman Wills Crofts was about; his interest is in temptation, to the extent that he arguably even tempts the reader when *The 12.30 from Croydon* offers us surprisingly detailed information on how to make a poisoned tablet that an elderly relative might unsuspectingly swallow.[14] He has no truck with the showy and spectacular crimes which caught the attention of many of his contemporaries and fed a mutual attraction between golden age detective fiction and Jacobean revenge tragedy, which flames into wild passion in the case of *The Duchess of Malfi*.[15]

Arden of Faversham is very unlike *The Duchess of Malfi*: not only is the heroine the killer rather than the victim but it is set at home rather than abroad, and in a bourgeois household rather than a ducal court. It is perhaps because *Arden of Faversham* shares the humdrum ethos which characterizes Wills Crofts's work that its inherent affinities with the detective story have largely escaped attention. I know of only three exceptions to this general neglect: in Patricia Wentworth's *Outrageous Fortune* the ship which is wrecked is the *Alice Arden*;[16] in Ruth Rendell's *A Sleeping Life* the books written by the victim Rhoda Comfrey include *Arden's Wife*;[17] and on the critical side, Esme Miskimmin notes, 'In *Arden of Faversham* . . . we see the murder of Arden and the apprehension of his killers through some textbook detection of footprints and bloodstains on the part of Franklin'.[18] The point of these allusions is Alice's guilt. In *Outrageous Fortune*, Susie Van Berg and Nesta Riddle are both bad wives, and calling the ship the *Alice Arden* underlines that. In *Sleeping Life*, the novels written by Rhoda Comfrey, which include *Her Grace of Amalfi* and *Killed with Kindness* as well as *Arden's Wife*, as well as her decision to live as a man, comment on the choices open to women in a way underlined by the book's references to the Women's Lib movement; but the killer is also a woman, the pale and innocent-seeming Polly Flinders. Women, it is clear, are complex creatures but generally bad news.

The title page of the 1592 quarto of *Arden of Faversham* would concur with that warning. It bills the play as

> The lamentable and true tragedie of M[aster] Arden of Feversham in Kent. Who was most wickedlye murdered, by the meanes of his disloyall and wanton wyfe, who for the love she bare to one Mosbie, hyred two desperat ruffins, Blackwill and Shakbag, to kill him. Wherin is shewed the great malice and discimulation of a wicked woman, the unsatiable desire of filthie lust and shamefull end of all murderers.[19]

This makes it quite clear that it is all Alice's fault. Black Will and Shakebag are hirelings and Mosby is mentioned only as a spur to Alice's actions, but the root cause of the crime is 'the great malice and discimulation of a wicked woman', and this is reiterated within the first few lines when Franklin says dismissively 'it is not strange / That women will be false and wavering' (1.2.19–20). However, authors of plays do not necessarily agree with the conclusions of their characters, and if the author of either *Outrageous Fortune* or *Sleeping Life* had been Freeman Wills Crofts, it is unlikely that the murderer would have been a woman; it would more probably have been a man motivated by desire for a woman, and there would also have been a pressing socioeconomic spur. Charles Swinburn in *The 12.30 from Croydon* is not an inherently bad man; he wants to save his business and to marry Una Mellor, and he is infuriated by rich Uncle Andrew's dogged refusal to believe in the slump of which everyone else in this northern manufacturing town is only too aware. Alice Arden is certainly eager to see her husband dead, but, if we look at the play with the lens supplied by Wills Crofts, we need to ask what other persons or factors share responsibility for the crime.

So if it is not in fact all Alice's fault, whose is it? One obvious candidate for the role of accessory before the fact is Ovid, because just as golden age detective fiction evokes early modern drama, so this particular early modern play has a 'mise-en-abyme' effect of its own in which another text lies behind the one that we see. This is also in line with another point of comparison between *Arden of Faversham* and detective fiction, their shared concern with their own literary status;[20] I have argued elsewhere that detective fiction tries to bolster its credentials by alluding to Shakespeare, and I suggest now that *Arden* attempts a similar strategy by alluding to both medieval and classical texts.[21] Arden reminds his wife,

> Sweet love, thou know'st that we two, Ovid-like,
> Have often chid the morning when it 'gan to peep,
> And often wished that dark Night's purblind steeds
> Would pull her by the purple mantle back
> And cast her in the ocean to her love. (1.59–63)

That is an interesting choice of reading matter for a good bourgeois household in small-town Kent; just as the barrister prosecuting Penguin Books in 1960 over the publication of *Lady Chatterley's Lover* exhorted every member of the jury to consider whether Lawrence's book was something he would wish his wife or his servants to read, so a young man from the Inns of Court who was attending a performance of *Arden of Faversham* in the 1590s might well have wondered whether Ovid was really the kind of thing he would wish his future wife to read. Although it was not until 1599 that Marlowe's translation of the Elegies was condemned to the flames, the most cursory perusal of Ovid's verse will leave nobody in any doubt that there are a lot of dirty bits. This is of course why he has been a staple of the curriculum at boys' schools – how else do you incentivize the learning of Latin – and it will certainly have been Arden who encountered him first and subsequently introduced Alice to him. He may be parading his fashionable classical learning here, but he is also inadvertently admitting to having introduced emotional dynamite into his household.

Arden seems to feel that thinking Ovidianly should have brought him and Alice closer together, but fidelity to one's marriage vows is not really the moral of Ovid, who would be more likely to authorize Alice's resolution that

> Love is a god, and marriage is but words,
> And therefore Mosby's title is the best.
> Tush, whether it be or no, he shall be mine
> In spite of him, of Hymen, and of rites. (1.100–4)

There is certainly a classical flavour to Alice's fantasies about Mosby:

> There is no nectar but in Mosby's lips.
> Had chaste Diana kissed him, she, like me
> Would grow lovesick, and from her watery bower
> Fling down Endymion and snatch him up.
> Then blame not me, that slay a silly man
> Not half so lovely as Endymion. (14.152–7)

Local author John Lyly had probably written his play *Endymion* around 1588, and it appeared in print in 1591, the year before *Arden of Faversham*. Alice hasn't quite got the point of the story, but she has noticed that classical texts are rich in stories of unfettered eroticism and she has also grasped that classical allusion is a prestige discourse; as a result she deploys it liberally, referring to 'raving Hercules' (1115) and 'Jove' (1.125), and takes it as authorizing her own behaviour. *Endymion*, like much of Lyly's work, flatters Elizabeth I; as with *Arden*'s sly introduction of what looks like an allusion to the death of the Earl of Leicester's wife Amy Robsart after falling (or being pushed) down a flight of stairs (15.8–9), there seems to be a sense that what is good enough for the queen is good enough for Alice.

Alice's use of a towel to kill her husband might possibly recall another classical story, that of how Clytemnestra gave a shirt, sewn up at the openings, to her husband Agamemnon to put on after his bath so that her lover Aegisthus could murder him. This is a parallel also implied by Alice's reference to 'the snakes of black Tisiphone' (14.148), since Tisiphone was one of the three Furies who would eventually pursue Orestes, son of Clytemnestra and Agamemnon, after he murdered his mother to avenge his father.[22] It is a particularly suggestive analogy because the series of killings in the house of Atreus produced the first known court case, which literally split the jury. Clytemnestra instigated the murder of Agamemnon because he had sacrificed their daughter Iphigenia at the behest of the goddess Artemis (or Diana, to give her the name by which Alice Arden would probably have known her); the death of Agamemnon then prompted their son Orestes to kill Clytemnestra and her lover Aegisthus. As dramatized by Aeschylus, Orestes is tried for the murder but the twelve jurors cannot reach an agreement: six feel that matricide is an unforgivable crime, but the other six take the view that it is excused by the fact that he was avenging his father. The goddess Athene claims a casting vote, which both acquits Orestes personally and establishes the principle that where a jury is split down the middle the presumption will always be for acquittal.[23] *Arden of Faversham*'s glance at this narrative lends the play a flavour of Raymond Postgate, whose 1940 crime story *Verdict of Twelve* explored how the members of a jury reach their individual and collective conclusion, but it may also have had a sharp topicality: Richard Bradshaw suggests that *Arden of Faversham* had an earlier incarnation as *A Cruel Murder Done in Kent*, a play which he thinks was put on 'to subtly ridicule Roger North and the Earl of Leicester' after the death of Amy Robsart.[24] Roger North and his brother Thomas, translator of Plutarch, were Alice Arden's stepbrothers; to suggest that the study of the classics undermines moral certainties incriminates them as well as her, and by implication slurs Leicester and even the queen. It begins to look as if Alice may not be the only guilty party, since those who promote works glamourizing passion and those who follow passion's dictates should arguably also be in the dock.

There is also the question of what Ovid replaced. Women of previous generations would not have heard of Ovid, but they might have had a Book of Hours to look at. Alice lacks this reflex piety; she speaks of burning her prayer book (8.116) and is inclined not so much to reverence objects which would once have been considered holy as to ask whether they might play any part in a murder plot: she and Mosby would like the painter to provide 'A crucifix empoisoned' (1.606). In this respect, another possible accessory before the fact is Henry VIII, whose reformation of the English church and dissolution of the monasteries had unsettled religious certainties and shaken faith. Black Will refers directly to Henry VIII when he says 'Why, Shakebag, I did serve the king at Boulogne' (9.24), something not likely to have been lost on local audiences and readers since the king had stayed a night in Faversham on his way to Boulogne in 1544. Although it is not mentioned in the play and might or might not have been known to the playwright, the historical Alice Arden had a direct personal connection with a notorious event of the late king's reign: her grandfather, Robert Brigandine, was the builder of Henry VIII's ill-fated ship the *Mary Rose*, named after his favourite sister Mary.[25] The *Mary Rose* sank on 19 July 1545 during the Battle of the Solent, when the English fought the French between Portsmouth and the Isle of Wight. Ironically enough, the Tudor princess whom the ship was named after had briefly been Queen of France during her marriage to Louis XII, at a time when France and England were allies; now Louis's successor Francis I was attempting to invade England with the nominal excuse of reversing the Reformation and restoring Catholicism.

The humiliating loss of the *Mary Rose* was a powerful emblem of the difficulties caused by Henry's break with Rome, and though nothing in the play glances directly at that particular episode, the effects of the Reformation are recalled in other ways, for the dissolution of the monasteries had significantly reshaped the appearance, ownership and uses of large tracts of land previously owned by the church. At the opening of the play, Franklin reminds Arden that

> My gracious Lord the Duke of Somerset
> Hath freely given to thee and to thy heirs,
> By letters patents from his majesty,
> All the lands of the Abbey of Faversham.
> Here are the deeds, sealed and subscribed with his name and
>   the King's.
> Read them, and leave this melancholy mood. (1.2–7)

The audience is thus informed that the play is set during the early years of Edward VI, at a point when his uncle the Duke of Somerset (Queen Jane Seymour's brother) is Protector of the Realm, and therefore at the height of the Protestant Reformation. Frank Whigham, observing that '*Arden of Faversham* is a history play', comments that '[it] seems to me a direct dramatic study of the fruits of the Dissolution';[26] indeed it actually contains the phrase 'sorrow for her dissolution', though Arden is referring to Alice rather than the abbey (4.8). Lena Cowen Orlin similarly argues that the story is repeatedly 'intersected . . . by the wide-ranging phenomena that followed from the English Reformation' and also notes that the historical Arden's house (still to be seen in Faversham and occasionally open to visitors), which 'incorporate[d] older abbey structures on the site', had panels which had originally been in the abbey (which also still survive) showing portrait medallions of King Stephen (1135–54), who had been buried there, and his queen Matilda.[27] The faint residual presence of Stephen in the town is the one respect in which *Arden of Faversham* does briefly come close to *The Duchess of Malfi*, for Stephen's tomb had been destroyed during the Reformation. In *The Duchess of Malfi*, as Antonio approaches the rendezvous which is to prove fatal to him, he and Delio pass through a ruined abbey which prompts Antonio to muse:

> I do love these ancient ruins:
> We never tread upon them but we set
> Our foot upon some reverend history.
> And questionless, here in this open court,
> Which now lies naked to the injuries
> Of stormy weather, some men lie interr'd
> Lov'd the church so well, and gave so largely to't,
> They thought it should have canopy'd their bones
> Till doomsday; but all things have their end:
> Churches and cities, which have diseases like to men,
> Must have like death that we have.
> Echo.   *Like death that we have.*[28]

In *Ancient funerall monuments*, John Weever makes a similar comment about King Stephen's burial in Faversham Abbey in 1154: 'His body rested here in quietnesse vntill the dissolution, when for the gaine of the lead wherein it was encoffined, it was taken vp and throwne into the next water. So vncertaine is man, yea greatest Princes, of any rest in this world, euen after buriall.'[29] The dissolution of the abbey may be good news for Arden in economic terms, but it has highlighted the extent to which 'man' is existentially 'uncertain'.

Even the economic benefit of the dissolution of the abbey is not completely certain. Mosby baits Arden about whether he really owns the lands which were once the abbey's:

> Master Arden, being at London yesternight,
> The Abbey lands whereof you are now possessed
> Were offered me on some occasion,
> By Greene, one of Sir Antony Aucher's men.
> I pray you, sir, tell me, are not the lands yours? (1.291–5)

Arden replies that they are, 'By letters patents from his majesty' (1.300). But letters patent do not stop the land itself remembering its earlier history and uses.

But this, above the rest, is to be noted:
Arden lay murdered in that plot of ground
Which he by force and violence held from Reede.
And in the grass his body's print was seen
Two years and more after the deed was done. (Epilogue 9–13)

A patch of land which was once owned by the Catholic church seems here to constitute itself voluntarily as the site of a small modern miracle of the kind which Protestant theology had consigned to history, since the official position of the new Church of England was that 'miracles are ceased'.[30]

The garden of Arden's house thus seems to range itself on the side of the ruined abbey, but there is a similar-but-different mechanism apparently underlying the ways in which the actual house operates. Iman Sheeha notes, 'Against all claims for ownership, the house chooses its master, aligning itself with Master Arden.'[31] As already noted, the real house inhabited by the Ardens contained relics from what was once the abbey and also had a nook behind the fireplace, which can still be seen and could potentially have been used as a place of concealment in times of religious uncertainty, and the house of the play does indeed seem possessed of a quasi-active agency as it retains the various pieces of physical evidence, which help to reveal the truth of Arden's murder. But the underlying logic here is different from what is going on in the garden: the house sides not with the abbey but with the person who profited from its despoliation, Arden. The impression of uncertainty is thus underlined; indeed Chloe Kathleen Preedy notes in this volume that even the weather could have ambiguous religious significance. There is in fact a remarkable affinity with the sceptical, apprehensive world of the 1930s in which so much golden age detective fiction was written and/or set, where no civilized person would dream of talking openly about God, and belief systems are definitely marked as residual rather than dominant.

If religious institutions such as Faversham Abbey have been toppled and religious certainties all called into doubt, where does that leave inhabitants of Faversham such as Alice and Mosby? An important point about Freeman Wills Crofts's books is that crime is never inevitable; George Surridge in *Antidote to Venom* might have led a blameless life if he had never met Nancy Weymore and if a venal lawyer had not filched the inheritance he expected from his aunt. In this sense, Wills Crofts's stories are implicitly non-Calvinist: everyone has a choice. This could also be said of *Arden of Faversham*, but the play is only uneasily Protestant in that it still feels the pull of Faversham Abbey, and it is also the product of a society in which, Sandra Clark argues, 'The notion of crime as an act defined and punishable by law did not exist as such and the term is rarely differentiated from sin'.[32] Again the lens offered by detective fiction is helpful here, because it can give us some perspective on the difference between sin and crime as we now understand it, and we might also consider some of the different ways in which sin itself might be conceptualized: should we be thinking of *original* sin, that is an inherited state of being always already fallen from grace which has been unalterable since Eve's decision to taste the apple, or should we be thinking of sin as a bad choice which may be redeemed by prayer, faith or absolution, whichever one's confessional preference may be? In other words, did Alice ever have a reasonable chance of avoiding temptation, and, if we recognize that she was tempted, can we reasonably blame her for falling? Alternatively, is Black Will right when, in a heady mixture of predestination and paganism, he declares that he was 'Marked in my birth-hour by the Destinies' (3.165) to kill Arden? *Arden of Faversham* is no *Doctor Faustus*, but it is invested in some of the same issues as Marlowe's tragedy and is not prepared to commit to whether it was 'The Lord of Heaven' or the rather more mundane Lord Cheyne who preserves Arden from one of the many assassination attempts (9.142–3).

The question of what spiritual choices people have might well seem to modern readers to be connected to what practical choices they have. The reason women tempt men to crime in golden age detective fiction is that it takes money to keep them in food and clothes, and there are very few ways they can earn money themselves other than working as a governess or a secretary. The economic possibilities for women in the sixteenth century were even more restricted; Alice could not have divorced Arden, nor could she have left him, and when she married him she forfeited any claim to her own fortune, which has become merely 'what you brought' (1.489). She could have hoped that he would die of natural causes, since widowhood was in economic terms the most desirable state for a woman in sixteenth-century England, but when he showed no signs of doing that it is not really surprising that she began to think about hastening his end.

This is why the final candidate for blame is society itself, and also why it is worth reading the play not only in the light of golden age detective fiction but also as a product of what Melissa Rohrer identifies as 'a significant trend in the theater of the 1590s of playwrights adapting true murder narratives from all manner of print genres: history chronicles, pamphlets, and broadside ballads'.[33] Sandra Clark notes that 'this was a time, in the post-Reformation period, when people believed themselves to be living in alarmingly disordered and sinful society', and this fear found expression in an arguably proto-sociological urge to record and understand as much as possible about notable crimes as soon as possible after they were committed.[34] Cheryl Birdseye argues that at least one of *Arden*'s discourses emerges directly from this true-crime context: 'Alice's testimonies demonstrate the playwright's experimentation with multiple petty-treason defences . . . *Arden of Faversham* offers audiences an opportunity to hear the voice of one of these petty-traitors'.[35] In this sense, the play anticipates the evolution of detective fiction into the still-popular 'true crime' docu-drama genre, a comparison implicitly instituted by Charles Nicholl when he opens his account of Elizabethan true crime plays by referring to *Crimewatch*.[36] Nicholl goes on to note:

> About a dozen [such narratives] are recorded in the years either side of 1600. A few made it into print: *Arden of Faversham* (1592), *A Warning for Fair Women* (1599), *A Yorkshire Tragedy* (1608), all of uncertain authorship. Others are known only by their titles, though their contents can be partly reconstructed when the title refers to a criminal case known from other sources.[37]

Although these plays told of what French historians of the *Annales* school would term 'petits récits' (little stories) and dealt with the personal and private, they were often treated as though they were grand narratives which focussed on the public and political. The anonymous *A Warning for Fair Women*, which tells the story of the murder of George Sanders, a respectable London citizen, by George Browne, who hoped to marry Sanders's wife Anne, was performed by the Lord Chamberlain's Men and appeared at the Globe in the same season as *Julius Caesar* and *Henry V*;[38] the murder of Arden, as has often been noted, was mentioned in Holinshed's *Chronicles*.

And yet the real fascination of these plays lies in the very triviality of the domestic scene in which they are set and which they chronicle. Nicholl sees this, declaring that 'the chief frisson of true crime is not suspense but recognition – the everyday landscapes where murder happens, the flowery wallpaper spattered with blood'.[39] This was an aspect of *Arden of Faversham* which was brought out very strongly in Polly Findlay's 2014 production for the Royal Shakespeare Company, in which the Ardens ran a business making cat ornaments for the home, and it also chimes with yet another aspect of golden age detective fiction, which is, as Jem Bloomfield astutely observes, obsessed with Jacobean furniture, particularly chairs.[40] This can help us notice how heavily invested *Arden of Faversham* is in the minutiae of domestic life, including the position and use of furniture: Catherine Richardson discusses how the play works to recreate 'the dynamics of a real parlour, a room crammed with the important and bulky furniture which signifies elite status',[41] and who gets to sit in the household's sole chair is an important marker of shifting power dynamics. Whereas no modern-day newspaper report of a crime is complete without telling us the murderer's age, and if she is a woman how many she is the mother of, Elizabethan crime narratives are far more interested in what the murderer has and in what the weapon cost, as in the account of how one of England's most promising playwrights met his end when 'the said Ingram, in defence of his life, with the dagger aforesaid to the value of twelve pence, gave the said Christopher then & there a mortal wound over his right eye of the depth of two inches & of the width of one inch'.[42] That the victim of this crime wrote *Doctor Faustus* becomes here less important than that the dagger that killed him cost twelve pence. There is a similar concern in evidence in *Arden of Faversham*. Where we would expect something like 'Mother-of-two Alice, 28', we are told only that Arden 'hoards up bags of gold / To make our children rich' (1.219–20) and that she considers herself in a position to reproach Mosby that she was 'too young to sound thy villainies' (18.17): there seem to be some children, but we have no idea how many, and Alice thinks of herself as young but we do not know how young. We do, however, know that her parlour contains a board for playing games on and a chair and that she has a supply of towels.

The same pragmatic concern with the workings of a household economy also informs Elizabethan crime drama's treatment of the aftermath of murder, particularly when it comes to the difficult question of disposing of the body. This is explored most extensively in the English scenes (as opposed to those set in Italy) of the play now known as *Two Lamentable Tragedies*, but which may once have been called *The Tragedy of Thomas Merry* and which Nicholl refers to as *Beech's Tragedy*. Nicholl observes that 'It correctly depicts the aftermath of murder – particularly a murder in a crowded urban setting – as a series of pressingly practical problems',[43] while Catherine Richardson notes that Yarington's 'notion of the English national identity of murder is that of a graphically pared down pragmatic language'.[44] How to get rid of the corpse is also a problem frequently explored in golden age detective fiction: *The 12.30 from Croydon* sees Charles Swinburne futilely trying to conceal the body of one of his victims in a lake, and *Antidote to Venom* offers a wry twist on the theme in that the body which must be satisfactorily accounted for is that of a snake. It too is deposited in water – in this case a water butt – which creates a suggestion of an attempt to cleanse and purify. The well into which Michael meant to throw the hand towel and the knife (14.392) and the snow in which the dead Thomas Arden lies might have had a similar whitening effect on the crimson of his blood, except that the plans of Alice, Mosby and their confederates are even more poorly laid than those of Wills Crofts's anti-heroes: they have no more idea of how to hide the body than they did of how to kill Arden, and all the snow actually does is show up the footprints which confirm their guilt. The material practicalities of murder are as much of a problem for the real murderers of Arden as for the murderers in detective fiction, and so too is the sense that water, which might have been put to cleansing or even salvific purposes, becomes instead a dangerously unstable medium which fails to dissolve human blood but does freeze enough to show human tracks.

This is not the only thing that *Arden of Faversham* shares with other true crime drama of the period, and also for that matter with golden age detective fiction. As in the novels of Agatha Christie, where everyone is guilty of something even if is not the thing which Poirot or Miss Marple is currently investigating, so Sandra Clark observes that 'No character in *Arden of Faversham* is without moral culpability or free of criminal responsibility'.[45] For this and other reasons, it is vital to collate and sieve all possible facts so that blame is correctly allotted, a process which if followed correctly ought to produce both social justice and narrative satisfaction. John Dickson Carr might have turned away from Jacobean drama in his later books, but he did not lose sight of the fundamental justification of all detective stories, which is to investigate the workings of justice. In *The Hollow Man*, Carr's series detective Dr Gideon Fell muses, 'What is justice? I've asked it at the end of nearly every case I've ever handled. I see faces rise, and sick souls and bad dreams'.[46] Elizabethan true crime dramas share Fell's anxiety and typically do their best to clarify both the precise degree of culpability of all the characters we have seen and also what ultimately became of them. *Arden of Faversham* does this too, but not quite with the same effect.

Superficially, *Arden of Faversham* adheres to the protocols of golden age detection, not least when it comes to the Big Reveal where the detective confirms not only where guilt lies but also how it has been detected. Catherine Richardson observes:

> Although Arden's body has been removed by the time the mayor and the watch enter, the line of footprints in the snow connects the spaces of murder and discovery, and the various objects which form relics from the site of the murder, the towel and the knife which were used to strangle and stab him, the rushes which stuck in his shoe from the floor of his parlour, and the blood which stained the floor where he sat, provide just enough traces to enable the truth to be discovered. These objects are placed together into an order which is productive of a coherent narrative – read in the right way, they generate a story, the one which the audience has just watched. The discovery of the clues is an immensely satisfying narrative scheme for an audience used to such a process of revelation.[47]

The 'immensely satisfying narrative scheme' which Richardson identifies in *Arden of Faversham* maps closely onto the protocols of golden age detective fiction, where Poirot assembles all the characters in the library and goes methodically through everything that has happened, or Freeman Wills Crofts's Inspector French finds himself invited to a small bachelor dinner party after the execution so he can explain how he detected the crime. The play even uses the language of detection when Michael imagines Black Will exclaiming, 'The peasant will detect the tragedy!' (4.80) and Mosby fears that Michael and the painter will 'fright me by detecting of [Arden's] end' (8.33).

However, nobody could suppose that justice is done in *Arden of Faversham*. As Bradshaw very reasonably points out, all he did was carry a letter, but he is nevertheless condemned to death, while the much more culpable painter escapes and is apparently never tracked down. In particular the conviction of Susan, who as Emma Whipday notes in this volume 'is consistently subordinated to both legitimate and illegitimate authority', is manifestly unsafe and would have been set aside by any competent modern court of appeal.[48] There is also something of an ambiguity about what befalls Black Will: yes, he was hanged in Flushing on a stage, but was it actually for the murder of Arden or for something completely different, of which he might or might not be guilty? One final notable point about Wills Crofts is that the victim is often not particularly attractive, but his death matters anyway. In fact all deaths matter: the reason often given by golden age detectives for their efforts to prevent and punish crime is that crime is pernicious not only for its effect on the victim but also – and arguably more so – for its effect on the soul of the perpetrator. What golden age crime very rarely shows is an innocent person suffering for a crime they did not commit, but Agatha Christie's *Ordeal by Innocence* opens after the execution of a young man who is subsequently proved guiltless and Patricia Wentworth's *The Case Is Closed* centres on the heroine's efforts to clear the name of her cousin's husband, who has been framed for a murder.[49] In *The Case Is Closed* the wife of the imprisoned man believes that he will simply give up and die. We do not hear much from Susan or from Rachel in *The Two Lamentable Tragedies* who is similarly entangled by the proven guilt of her brother, but we might well wonder about the effect of an innocent person of being falsely convicted, and whether they might not be led into that worst of sins (in a theological sense), despair. If that were to be the case, Susan and Rachel would both have been spiritually as well as physically killed by a flawed, sexist and partial judicial process.

Herein lies the most significant of the ways in which *Arden of Faversham* differs from other works from the pen of Freeman Wills Crofts. Golden age detective fiction shines light into dark corners, untangles knots and restores order. *Arden of Faversham* does not. It is true that the society it shows us is one in which crime is punished, but that does not make it just. The outcome of Orestes' trial for the murder of Clytemnestra and Aegisthus is decided by the direct intervention of the goddess Athene; in *Arden of Faversham* no divinity appears, and diplomatic relations between heaven and earth have been disrupted if not severed by the Reformation. George Surridge in *Antidote to Venom* repents, and we can therefore be reasonably confident that, within the logic of the narrative, he will go to the heaven in which Wills Crofts believed even if we personally do not; where do Alice and Susan go, and for that matter where does Arden go? The play has no answer to these questions, but that is of course one of the reasons why we continue to find it fascinating, and why devotees of golden age crime fiction will always enjoy it just as much as other products of the genre.

Notes

1 I take the term from Curtis Evans, *Masters of the 'Humdrum' Mystery: Cecil John Charles Street, Freeman Wills Crofts, Alfred Walter Stewart and the British Detective Novel, 1920–1961* (Jefferson, NC: McFarland and Company, 2012). The title of this chapter comes from Martin Edwards, ed., *Crimson Snow: Winter Mysteries* (London: The British Library, 2016).

2 Freeman Wills Crofts, *Antidote to Venom* [1938] (London: British Library, 2015); Freeman Wills Crofts, *The 12.20 from Croydon* [1934] (London: British Library, 2016).

3 Emma Whipday, '"Marrow Prying Neighbours": Staging Domestic Space and Neighbourhood Surveillance in *Arden of Faversham*', *Cahiers Élisabéthains* 88, no. 1 (2015): 95.

4 Freeman Wills Crofts, *Inspector French's Greatest Case* [1924] (London: HarperCollins, 2016), vii and 201.

5 See Lisa Hopkins, *Shakespearean Allusion in Crime Fiction* (Basingstoke: Palgrave Macmillan, 2016), 37.

6 Wills Croft, *Antidote to Venom*, 39, 259, 260.

7 John Dickson Carr, *The Four False Weapons* [1937] (New York: Collier Books, 1962), 12.

8 James E. Keirans, *The John Dickson Carr Companion* (Vancleave, MS: Ramble House, 2015) notes quotations from *Doctor Faustus* (279), *Hamlet* (282) and *Macbeth* (285) and has two pages of references to Shakespeare and his plays (307–9), but does not observe any of the borrowings I am about to propose.

9 John Dickson Carr, *It Walks by Night* [1930] (London: The British Library, 2019), 25, 33,151.
10 John Dickson Carr, *Castle Skull* [1931] (London: The British Library, 2020).
11 John Dickson Carr, *The Lost Gallows* [1931] (London: The British Library, 2020).
12 John Dickson Carr, *The Corpse in the Waxworks* [1932] (London: The British Library, 2021).
13 Douglas G. Greene, *John Dickson Carr: The Man who Explained Miracles* (Cincinnati: Crippen & Landru, 2019), 90.
14 Wills Crofts, *The 12.30 from Croydon*, 106–7.
15 See Lisa Hopkins, *Burial Plots in British Detective Fiction* (Basingstoke: Palgrave Macmillan, 2021), 93–118.
16 Patricia Wentworth, *Outrageous Fortune* [1933] (New York: Harper and Row, 1990).
17 Ruth Rendell, *A Sleeping Life* [1978] (London: Arrow, 2010).
18 Esme Miskimmin, 'The Act of Murder: Renaissance Tragedy and the Detective Novel', in *Reinventing the Renaissance: Shakespeare and his Contemporaries in Adaptation and Performance*, ed. Sarah Annes Brown, Robert I. Lublin and Lynsey McCulloch (Basingstoke: Palgrave, 2013), 288.
19 *Arden of Feversham* (London, 1592), STC (2nd ed.), 733.
20 See for instance Alexander Leggatt, '*Arden of Faversham*', *Shakespeare Survey* 36 (1983): 122.
21 Hopkins, *Shakespearean Allusion in Crime Fiction*; also see particularly Sarah Youngblood, 'Theme and Imagery in *Arden of Faversham*', *Studies in English Literature, 1500–1900* 3, no. 2 (1963): 212.
22 Catherine Belsey quotes John Rainolds in 1597 as referring to a woman who might serve her husband 'as Clytemnestra did Agamemnon, as Livia did Drusus, as Mrs Arden did her husband' (*The Subject of Tragedy* [1985] [London: Routledge, 1991], 141). Betty S. Travitsky comments that to see Alice as 'a bourgeois Clytemnestra' is 'traditional among critics of the play' ('Husband-Murder and Petty Treason in English Renaissance Tragedy', *Renaissance Drama* 21 [1991]): 178); Lena Cowen Orlin traces the first use of the phrase 'the bourgeois Clytemnestra' to John Addington Symonds and lists those who followed him (*Private Matters and Public Culture in Post-Reformation England* [Ithaca: Cornell University Press, 1994], 69, n.109). However, my point is that it may not be *the play* which is imitating Aeschylus so much as Alice herself.

23 Aeschylus, *The Eumenides*, in *The Oresteia*, trans. Robert Fagles (Harmondsworth: Penguin, 1977).

24 In Appendix 21 of Patricia Hyde, *Thomas Arden in Faversham: The Man Behind the Myth* (Faversham: The Faversham Society, 1996), 518. Leicester's biographer notes that 'Leicester's closest male friend, apart from his family, seems to have been Lord North, a contemporary who shared Leicester's interests and amusements'. Alan Haynes, *The White Bear: The Elizabethan Earl of Leicester* (London: Peter Owen, 1987), 122.

25 Hyde, *Thomas Arden*, 32–3.

26 Frank Whigham, *Seizures of the Will in Early Modern English Drama* (Cambridge: Cambridge University Press, 1996), 63. See also Richard Helgerson, 'Murder in Faversham: Holinshed's Impertinent History', in *The Historical Imagination in Early Modern Britain*, ed. Donald R. Kelley and David Harris Sacks (Cambridge: Cambridge University Press, 1997), 133–58.

27 Orlin, *Private Matters*, 16, 37, 39.

28 John Webster, *The Duchess of Malfi*, ed. John Russell Brown (Manchester: Manchester University Press, 1977), 5.3.9–19.

29 John Weever, *Ancient Funerall Monuments Within the vnited monarchie of Great Britaine* (London, 1631), 278.

30 William Shakespeare, *Henry V*, ed. T. W. Craik (London: Routledge, 1995), 1.1.67. As Craik notes, the phrase was proverbial.

31 Iman Sheeha, '"Looke in the place where he was wont to sit / See see his blood it is too manifest": Domestic Space and Patriarchal Authority in *The Tragedy of Master Arden of Faversham* (1592)', *Early Modern Literary Studies* 28 (2019): 14.

32 Sandra Clark, 'The Problem of Sin and Crime in Domestic Tragedy', *Early Modern Literary Studies* 28 (2019): 4.

33 Melissa Rohrer, '"Lamentable and True": Remediations of True Crime in Domestic Tragedies', *Early Modern Literary Studies* 28 (2019): 1.

34 Clark, 'The Problem', 1.

35 Cheryl Birdseye, '"Let death make amends for all my sins": (In)sincere Confessions in *Arden of Faversham*', *Early Modern Literary Studies* 28 (2019): 21.

36 Charles Nicholl, 'Fetch the Chopping Knife', *London Review of Books* 43, no. 21 (4 November 2021). Available online: https://www.lrb.co.uk/the-paper/v43/n21/charles-nicholl/fetch-the-chopping-knife (accessed 16 February 2022).

37 Ibid.
38 *A Warning for Fair Women*, ed. Gemma Leggott, *Early Modern Literary Studies* (2011), 6. Available online: https://extra.shu.ac.uk/emls/iemls/resources.html (accessed 16 February 2022). See also David Grote, *The Best Actors in the World: Shakespeare and His Acting Company* (Westport: Greenwood Press, 2002), 82.
39 Nicholl, 'Fetch the Chopping Knife'.
40 Jem Bloomfield, 'Mid-Century Jacobeans: Agatha Christie, Ngaio Marsh, P. D. James, and *The Duchess of Malfi*', *ELH* 87, no. 4 (2020): 1087.
41 Catherine Richardson, *Domestic Life and Domestic Tragedy in Early Modern England: The Material Life of the Household* (Manchester: Manchester University Press, 2006), 123.
42 Charles Nicholl, *The Reckoning*, 2nd ed. (London: Vintage, 2002), 19.
43 Nicholl, 'Fetch the Chopping Knife'. Emma Whipday's production of the play, titled *The Tragedy of Thomas Merry*, can be seen at: Two Lamentable Tragedies, 'Performance', *YouTube*, 26 March 2014. Available online: https://www.youtube.com/watch?v=qVpCYI6aM5s (accessed 16 February 2022).
44 Richardson, *Domestic Life*, 131.
45 Clark, 'The Problem', 9.
46 John Dickson Carr, *The Hollow Man* [1935] (London: Orion Books, 2013), 169.
47 Richardson, *Domestic Life*, 125.
48 Emma Whipday, 'Susan of Faversham: Staging Subordination in *Arden*', this volume, 92.
49 Patricia Wentworth, *The Case Is Closed* [1937] (London: Hodder and Stoughton, 2005).

8

Pedagogy

'Now I take you': Approaches to teaching *Arden of Faversham*

Kirsten N. Mendoza

As a domestic tragedy that recreates an actual crime, the localization of *Arden of Faversham* can belie the impressive range of issues that the play masterfully weaves together. This drama not only connects students to the historical specificities of sixteenth-century England but also opens up the opportunity to engage a classroom in deep reflection on methodological practices and the politics of knowledge creation. In *Teaching Social Justice through Shakespeare*, Wendy Beth Hyman and Hillary Eklund embolden teachers of early modern studies to adopt a justice-oriented pedagogy that 'reimagines early modern texts as potentially fundamental to collaborative meaning-making and liberatory action' in pursuit of 'equity and social change'(Hyman and Eklund 20–1). In taking up their call, this chapter presents teaching topics and approaches to *Arden* based on social justice pedagogy.

Through fostering difficult conversations on structural forms of inequality, discrimination and violence, teachers of *Arden* can help students interrogate multiple levels of overlapping power structures both within the play itself and without. After all, the strange artefacts of the past we have inherited are themselves shaped by power – by whose voices and versions of Arden's murder are privileged over others. It is a play that has the potential to invite interdisciplinary approaches and methods for making sense of this work, to engage students in a variety of ethical questions, to understand the characters' actions as a product of how will is itself circumscribed and engendered by entwining social, legal, religious and political pressures. In this way, *Arden* has the ability to make students acutely aware that their study of this play – that the work of the humanities – is less an analysis of one particular work but 'the cultivation of a way of looking at the world' (Hyman and Eklund 6).

The section 'The Arden web: Sources and early modern references' of this chapter focusses on the play as a retelling of a sensationalized murder. It introduces possible source materials that early modern playgoers may have been familiar with and highlights productive passages for comparing differing accounts of the historical Arden's murder. The section 'Plotting approaches to the play' of the chapter contains brief overviews of five possible approaches to the play that are particularly apt for generating critical discussions of power structures with students: (i) property, (ii) deviant will, (iii) justice, (iv) genre and (v) homicide in early modern England. When teaching this compelling and fun, provocative and thrilling play, one quickly recognizes that this work synthesizes a vast array of issues that alone makes it deserving of a prominent place in every early modern classroom today. With so many paths to take that draw in students with a diversity of interests, the question is not *if Arden* should be taught but what approaches should be plaited together in the limited time one has to get the deed done.

Hyman, Wendy Beth, and Hillary Eklund, 'Introduction: Making Meaning and Doing Justice with Early Modern Texts', in *Teaching Social Justice Through Shakespeare: Why Renaissance Literature Matters Now*, edited by Hillary Eklund and Wendy Beth Hyman, 1–23. Edinburgh: Edinburgh University Press, 2019.

The Arden web: Sources and early modern references

The early modern texts dealing with Thomas Arden's murder – distanced from us by time and culture – provide perfect case studies to help students distinguish between objective and more permanent *fact* and subjective, felt *truth*. Students may initially perceive sources on the Arden murder as documents bearing facts. A closer inspection of the differences between texts, however, reveals that their truths concerning the murder differ. In an era of fake news, alternative facts and the spread of disinformation, exercises based on close-reading comparisons help students critically evaluate sources, 'fostering the prudent discernment required for civic participation' (Hyman and Eklund 3). As a play that presents a real-life crime, *Arden* is well positioned to have students reflect on history as narrative, a mutable representation of the past. Through analyses of different sources and references to *Arden*, teachers can help students think about how power and privilege shape the narratives that persist and the 'truths' of a moment that have survived.

The historical Thomas Arden was a savvy social climber whose patronage by Edward, Lord North, brought Arden significant advancements. A powerful figure, North was appointed co-chancellor with Sir Richard Rich of the Court of Augmentations. In this position, North was in charge of determining land transactions, many of which were once church properties seized in the Dissolution of the Monasteries. North first employed Thomas Arden in the Court of Augmentations, and he proved a particularly gracious supporter of Arden by repeatedly helping his career. Thomas Arden eventually married Alice Mirfyn, the stepdaughter of North. North also appointed his son-in-law Arden as the King's Controller of the Customs of the Port of Faversham. Although North granted Sir Thomas Cheney a large portion of the Faversham Abbey lands as well as a nearby house, both the lands and the home were later conveniently sold to Arden.

However, North also had a special servant, one Mosby, who was having an affair with his stepdaughter Alice, Arden's wife. This convoluted web of greed, favour and desire that interweaved the Arden family with the North's household (and Mosby) is scathingly presented in Holinshed's *Chronicles*:

> And although (as it was said) Arden perceiued right well their mutuall familiaritie to be much greater than their honestie, yet bicause he would not offend hir, and so loose the benefit which he hoped to gaine at some of hir féends hands in bearing with hir lewdnesse, which he might haue lost if he should haue fallen

out with hir: he was contented to winke at hir filthie disorder, and both permitted, and also inuited Mosbie verie often to lodge in his house. And thus it continued a good space, before anie practise was begun by them against maister Arden. She at length inflamed in loue with Mosbie, and loathing hir husband, wished and after practised the meanes how to hasten his end. (Holinshed, vol. 6 1062)

According to Holinshed, the greed that overwhelmed Arden, which made him complicit in the affair and responsible for the misgovernment of his household, not only harmed his family and his authority as husband and master but also influenced his cruelty as a landlord. In addition to Greene and Read's wife (the mariner Reede in the play), whose plights are expanded upon in both the Holinshed source and the play, the *Chronicles* also state that Arden had managed to procure the Valentine fair to be located solely on his Abbey lands, thereby depriving the inhabitants of Faversham of the gain they had in previous years received. Although the play erases Lord North's explicit connections to Arden's family and fortune, it maintains a sense of the tensions caused by competing desires for patronage and favour since Mosby's master (North) is Lord Clifford in the play. Frank Whigham surmises that this alteration was a tactful deviation from source texts made to prevent the ire of the powerful North family members of the 1590s, Alice's prominent stepbrothers and half-sisters (Whigham 67): Roger, son of Edward and second Lord North and member of Gray's Inn; Thomas North, whose translation of Plutarch Shakespeare drew upon for *Titus Andronicus*; the wife of William Somerset, 3rd Earl of Worcester; and Mary, wife of Henry, 9th Lord Scrope of Bolton.

When I teach *Arden*, I invite students to investigate the artefacts about this case that so captivated English early modern commentators. The following list indicates sixteenth- and seventeenth-century materials on the Arden murder that can be incorporated in lesson plans. I typically wait until after students have studied the play since it helps for learners to have at least one narrative of the murder with which they are familiar as the basis for their comparisons. When students study these artefacts and make sense of these strange materials from the past, the differences in accounts help them to become aware that history is refracted through reiterative narrative models, narratives that are shaped by the person whose perspectives have been given the privilege of being written, printed and remembered. In our analysis of these texts, we spend time reflecting not only on what is said but also on what is left *unsaid*.

When students consider the potential biases that influence works on and references to Arden's murder, I ask them to note what details included in the play are conspicuously left out of the excerpts we study. For example, in both *The Complaint* and *The Unnatural Father*, Thomas Arden's rapacious cruelty as a landlord is completely absent. I have students think about how the circulation of these works may have influenced a playgoer or reader's perception of Thomas Arden. What aspects of the murder are repeated? What *sticks* in the discursive iterations of this crime? Furthermore, I have students think about *The Unnatural Father's* description of the murder as being 'fresh in memory' when the play was published seventy years after the crime was committed. How do such short references both provide 'proof' of the crime's enduring infamy and create a futurity in which Arden's murder can never be forgotten? Together, students practice the close-reading skills applied in their analysis of the play to these other artefacts with attention to how power, privilege and bias are always present in the retelling.

Whigham, Frank. *Seizures of the Will in Early Modern English Drama*. Cambridge: Cambridge University Press, 1996.

- Holinshed's *Chronicles* (1577, 1587): This lengthy, widely cited and generally accessible account of Thomas Arden's murder can be found in most scholarly editions of *Arden of Faversham*, including Catherine Richardson's 2022 Arden Early Modern Drama edition.
- *The complaint and lamentation of Mistresse Arden* (c. 1633): This ballad that imagines Alice Arden's scaffold confession is useful for considering the performance of penitence, the genre of scaffold confessions and the innocent depiction of Thomas Arden in comparison to his less flattering representations in other early modern texts.
- Excerpt from the Wardmote Book of Faversham: The official record of the murder: Alyce thesaid Morsby did not onely Carnally kepe in her owne house here in this towne[,] Butt also fedd her wt dilicate meates and sumptuous

app[ar]ell[.] All whiche things thesaid Thomas Ardern did well knowe and wilfully did p[er]mytt and suffred the same[,] By reason whereof she p[ro]cured her said housbands death.

- **Breviat Chronicle for 1551:** This yeare on S.[aint] Valentines daye at Feuersham in Kente, was commytted a shamefull mourther, for one Arden a gentilman, was by the consente of hys wyfe mourthered, wherefore she was brent at Cantorbury, and ther was one hanged in chaines for that mourther, and at Feuersham was. ii. [two] hanged in chaynes [one of them Arden's man-servant Michael Saunderson, who was hanged, drawn, and quartered], and a woman brent [Elizabeth Stafford, Alice Arden's day-servant], and in Smithfeld [in London] was hanged one Mosby and hys syster [Susan], for the same murther also.

- **The diary of Henry Machyn, a London merchant-tailor:** The xiiij day of Marche was hangyd, in Smyth-feld, on John Mosbe and ys syster, for the derth of a gentyll man of Feyversham, one M. Arden the custemer, and ys owne wyff was decaul ... and she was burnyd at Canturbery and her sarvand hangyd ther, and ij at Feyversham and on at Hospryng, and nodur in the he way to Canturbery, for the derth of M. Arden of Feyversham. [and at Flusshyng was bernyd Blake Tome for the sam deth of M. Arden.][1]

- **Stow's *Annals of England* (1592):** On Saint Valentines daie, at Feuersham in Kent, one *Arden* a gentleman was murthered by procurement of his owne wife, for the which fact, shee was the 14. of March brent at Canterburie : *Michaell* master *Ardens* man was hanged in chains at *Feuersham*, and a maiden brent: *Mosby* and his sister were hanged in Smithfield at London: *Greene* which had fled, came againe certaine yeeres after, and was hanged in chaines in the high way againste Feuersham, and *Blacke Will* the ruffian that was hired to do that acte, after his first escape, was apprehended, and brent on a scaffold at Flushing in Zeland.

- **Two lines from Thomas Heywood's *Troia Britannica* (1609):** At *Feuersham* was murdred by his Wife /*Arden*, by helpe of *Mosby* and *Blacke-Will*,

- John Taylor in *The Unnaturall Father* (1621, 1630): Arden of Feuersham, and Page of Plimmouth, both their Murders are fresh in memory, and the fearefull ends of their Wiues and their Ayders in those bloudy actions will neuer bee forgotten.

Plotting approaches to the play

On property

A consideration of property might seem an odd place to begin work with students, but the tensions that arise from Arden's possession of the Abbey Lands are necessary to help students understand how this play speaks to audiences in complex and contradictory ways. I begin discussions with students by having them think about the correlation today between staggeringly high rents and high rates of homelessness, such as in the San Francisco Bay Area. Many people have likely felt the pressures of high rent in their search for affordable housing. Such references help students to consider the views of Greene and Reede and to imagine, from their perspectives, how a potential early modern audience may have felt when hearing their pleas. With a simple poll, my previous students have generally admitted to feeling less moved by Greene than by Reede, in part because of Reede's supplications for the survival of his wife and children. This, of course, gives us an opportunity to talk about our cultivated biases, especially when we consider the vulnerability of children and how an emphasis on children often obscures the suffering of adults. As students become aware of their differing and highly individual responses to Arden as well as to Greene and Reede, they can develop a more critical reflection on how early modern audiences' responses may have been steered.

In Holinshed's *Chronicles*, Arden's violent murder is placed in relation to his pitiless greed and cruelty as a landlord. The play performed forty years later similarly draws upon the connections of Arden's death with his avarice and merciless control of land. In doing so, the drama resonates with the social and economic anxieties of the 1590s. In a popular eulogy to Henry Hastings, 3rd Earl of Huntingdon, the poem captures an ideal relation between lord – or landlord – and subject that romanticized a kind of feudalism ethic that was dying by the end of the Elizabethan period:

> His tenants that daily repaired to his house was fed with his bacon, his beef, & his souse. Their rents were not raised, their fines were but small, And many poore tenants paid nothing at all. No groves he enclosed, nor felled no wood, No pastures he paled to do himself good. To commons and country he lived a good friend, And gave to the needy what God did him send. (Quoted in Sullivan 232)

The model of a fatherly, compassionate and generous landlord was necessary prior to the sixteenth century because lords called upon their subjects to fight for them in battle. With the move towards standing armies as well as important changes in agricultural practices and political relations, this idealized feudal relationship slowly faded. According to Lawrence Stone, the 1590s would be the last decade in which land was understood as a means to gain military aid from loyal subjects. Around the time when *Arden* was first performed, the feudal relationship between landlord and tenant had gradually been replaced by a more calculated system in which economic gain took priority. During Elizabeth's reign, she issued several letters encouraging (or demanding) the wealthy to return to their land owing to a tendency for nobles, landed gentry and aristocrats to be more like absentee landlords failing to relieve the people who worked and resided in their territories.

These changes in social relations were intensified due to transformations in agricultural practices that altered engagements between landlords and tenants. The sixteenth century witnessed enclosures of land dedicated to specific crops or livestock. This proved disastrous for the many small tenant farmers who previously worked the land and suddenly found themselves unable to pay rent or who were no longer needed. Changes in farming practices made it far more enticing – from an economic standpoint – for landowners to be less generous. And, when the relation between landlord and tenant was based on economics rather than feudal loyalty, there existed even less incentive for landlords, like Arden, to be magnanimous. These social, agricultural and economic changes were tied to migration within England and an increase in poverty and vagabonds when plots of land were wrested from families and communities.

We witness Arden's cruelty as a landlord in scene one shortly after we see him onstage for the first time and again in scene thirteen, just before his murder. Even the epilogue refuses to have us forget the greed that caused the suffering of Reede and his family. Therefore, while a basic plot summary of *Arden* may initially lead students to intuit that sixteenth-century audiences likely sympathized fully with the victim of murder, a teacher's emphasis on land and property can help them understand that an early modern playgoer's emotional responses were likely more complicated than our students may have initially felt.

Amussen, S. D. 'Gender, Family and the Social Order, 1560–1725'. In *Order and Disorder in Early Modern England*, edited by Anthony Fletcher and John Stevenson, 196–217. Cambridge: Cambridge University Press, 1985.

Berg, Dianne. '"Tis Fearful Sleeping in a Serpent's Bed": *Arden of Faversham* and the Threat of the Petty Traitor'. In *Treason: Medieval and Early Modern Adultery, Betrayal, and Shame*, edited by Larissa Tracy, 340–55. Boston: Brill, 2019.

Burnett, Mark Thornton. *Masters and Servants in English Renaissance Drama and Culture: Authority and Obedience*. New York: St. Martin's Press, 1997.

Korda, Natasha. *Shakespeare's Domestic Economies: Gender and Property in Early Modern England*. Philadelphia: University of Pennsylvania Press, 2002.

Orlin, Lena Cowen. *Private Matters and Public Culture in Post-Reformation England*. Ithaca: Cornell University Press, 1994.

Smith, Steven R. 'The London Apprentices as Seventeenth-Century Adolescents'. *Past and Present* 61, no. 1 (1973): 149–61.

Stallybrass, Peter, and Allon White. *The Politics and Poetics of Transgression*. Ithaca: Cornell University Press, 1986.

Stone, Lawrence. *The Family, Sex and Marriage in England, 1500–1800*. London: Penguin, 1977.

Sullivan, Garrett A., Jr. '"Arden Lay Murdered in that Plot of Ground": Surveying, Land, and *Arden of Faversham*'. *ELH* 61, no. 2 (1994): 231–52.

On deviant, dangerous wills

Will, the faculty that represents volition and brings forth actions, suggests autonomy and demonstrates agency. As a 'dense and volatile theoretical concept', Kathryn Schwarz explains, will 'exemplifies the double and divided nature of agency . . . [that] has the power to sustain or disrupt order' (2). In *Arden,* rather than reify social structures, will threatens the stability of hierarchies. Since social justice pedagogy requires attention to the ways that justice and injustice are yoked to power struggles, it behoves us as teachers to make students aware of the wills of individuals within hegemonic structures that both forge subjects and simultaneously circumscribe them. In what follows, this section provides a brief overview of five categories of deviant will depicted in *Arden*: the wills of women, of servants and masters, of darker races and of masterless men. The short resources provide an overview of the negative stereotypes and discursive connotations associated with various identities in the Elizabethan period that influenced early modern understandings of the *Arden* characters and plot.

Schwarz, Kathryn. *What You Will: Gender, Contract, and Shakespearean Social Space* (Philadelphia: University of Pennsylvania Press, 2011).
Traub, Valerie. *Desire and Anxiety: Circulations of Sexuality in Shakespearean Drama.* (London: Routledge, 1992).

Of women

Holinshed's *Chronicles* introduces the love triangle of Alice, Arden and Mosby with a description of their physical attributes, demeanours and statuses:

> This Arden was a man of a tall and comelie personage, and matched in marriage with a gentlewoman, yoong, tall, and well fauoured of shape and countenance, who chancing to fall in familiaritie with one Mosbie a tailor by occupation, a blacke swart man, seruant to the lord North. (Holinshed, vol. 6, 1062)

The passage underscores the compatibility of Arden with his wife Alice, which serves as a foil to Alice's illicit attachment to Mosby, a lower-class man with a black complexion. The signifiers conveying that Alice and Mosby are ill-matched are repeated in other well-known early modern plays. For example, in Shakespeare's *Othello,* both Brabantio and Iago emphasize their racist perception that Othello and Desdemona are too unlike each other to be a proper match. Brabantio believes that his daughter's desires would have better fit the 'wealthy, curled darlings of [their] nation' (1.2.68). Similarly, Iago manipulates Roderigo into believing that 'very nature will instruct [Desdemona]' to find someone more alike in 'years, manners and beauties, all which the Moor is defective in' (2.1.231–2, 227–8). In *Titus*, Bassianus and Lavinia taunt Tamora, the captive-Goth-queen-turned-empress-of-Rome with her sexual preference for Aaron, 'her raven-coloured love' over Saturninus, her 'snow-white goodly steed' (*Titus* 2.2.83, 76). In both plays and Holinshed's *Chronicles*, erotic desire for a person of a darker race and of a different class is presented as an ill-match that transgresses property as well as social and natural order. Furthermore, as Lara Bovilsky has argued, desire for a Black man is presented in these works as evidence of white women's wayward wills (57). This is especially true when one considers the adulterous and murderous liaisons of Alice and Tamora. Even Desdemona's lawful marriage – her elopement without her father's consent – is viewed as treasonous (Iago later uses this to convince Othello of her propensity towards disloyalty as a daughter and wife). All three women – Alice, Tamora and Desdemona – are perceived as rebellious agents who challenge not only their fathers and husbands but also patriarchal authority in general.

In the matrimonial vows from the 1552 Book of Common Prayer, husbands vowed to 'loue her, comfort her, honour, and kepe her, in sickenes, and in health', while wives consented to 'obey hym and serue hym, loue, honor and kepe him, in sickenes and in health' (Church of England 152). Women's obedience as well as submission to their husbands was required according to the religious rite of marriage. Catherine Belsey argues that the 'horribleness' that makes the domestic crime of Arden's murder worthy of being part of English history is not actually the heinousness of the attack and its premeditation but rather 'Alice Arden's challenge to the institution of marriage' – her refusal to submit to hierarchal patriarchal structures that bridled the wills of women through the institution of marriage (84). Women and servants were legally bound to double standards, which dates to the 1352 statute of treasons, a statute that would last until 1828. Sir Edward Coke defines petty treason as 'when a servant slayeth his master, or a wife her husband, or when a man secular or religious slayeth his prelate to whom he oweth obedience' (Sir Edward Coke, Statutes 2:51–2). Husbands and masters who murdered their wives and servants would not be charged with petty treason, a crime with harsher punishments than felony murder in the period. In this way, the double standards that viewed murderous subordinates negatively were reified by law, which sent a clear message to the commonwealth that the murder of one's superiors was a severe and egregious crime that was at once private and public, a flagrant transgression that disrupted the familial, social, political and (perceived) natural order of early modern England.

Belsey, Catherine. 'Alice Arden's Crime'. *Renaissance Drama* 13 (1982): 83–102.
Bovilsky, Lara. *Barbarous Play: Race on the English Renaissance Stage.* Minneapolis: University of Minnesota Press, 2008.
Catty, Jocelyn. *Writing Rape, Writing Women in Early Modern England: Unbridled Speech.* New York: St. Martin's Press, 1999.
Church of England. *The boke of common prayer and administracion of the sacramentes, and other rites and ceremonies in the Churche of Englande.* London, 1552.
Dolan, Frances E. *Dangerous Familiars: Representations of Domestic Crime in England, 1550–1700.* Ithaca: Cornell University Press, 1994.
Donaldson, Ian. *The Rapes of Lucretia: A Myth and Its Transformations.* New York: The Clarendon Press, 1982.
Jed, Stephanie H. *Chaste Thinking: The Rape of Lucretia and the Birth of Humanism.* Bloomington: Indiana University Press, 1989.

Of servants and tyrannous masters

Just as a husband had the authority to discipline his wife, a master was lawfully allowed to beat ill-behaved servants within reasonable limits and was even socially encouraged to do so for the cultivation of moral households. Almost 60 per cent of fifteen- to twenty-four-year-olds laboured as servants in early modern England. For many of these youths, Ann Kussmaul notes, this was a 'transitional occupation, specific to their transitional status between childhood and adulthood' (3–4). As Frances Dolan emphasizes, servants 'blurred boundaries and confused categories', were 'dependent yet depended upon, familiar yet not wholly known or controlled, a class yet not one' (67).

Although statistically servants (like wives) were more likely to be abused than to harm their masters, broadsides sensationalized the trope of the murderous servant. In such pamphlets, Iman Sheeha explains, 'murderous servants . . . [either] decide, on their own initiative, to kill a master or a mistress for reasons such as resentment, anger, and greed [or they] kill in obedience to a master's or a mistress's command and in anticipation of some form of reward, whether financial or social' (23). Tempted by Alice with the prospect of marriage to Mosby's sister Susan, Michael certainly falls under the second category. His moving soliloquy in scene three reveals the duress of multiple allegiances. Torn between his master, his mistress and Mosby, Michael reveals the great difficulty in upholding all bonds at once and of being an agent in a position of subordination. As a subordinate whose survival depends on gaining the trust and approval of his superiors, Michael cannot please one without offending (or being complicit in the death of) the other. Furthermore, although he is a servant, Michael also has a will of his own; his hopes and desire are negotiated through his web of loyalties. The servant's position of trust and familiarity within the household combined with the knowledge that servants likely possess multiple, affective allegiances and their own ambitions mean that masters never fully know their subordinates whose wills are always – to a certain degree – open to suspicion.

Arden is a landowner whose unscrupulous withholding of property from others receives censure in the play. When Greene complains to Alice, he declares himself to be a gentleman degraded by Arden to beg for a means of living: 'Your husband doth me wrong / To wring me from the little land I have' (1.470–1). In addition to Arden's disrespect of lineage and of the honours due to a gentlemen, Arden is presented as unreasonably defensive of his property. Reede confronts Arden with having 'wrongfully . . . detained' the land from him, 'although the rent of it be very small' (8.13–15). In both cases, the play has Greene and Reede both assert their right to plots of land while emphasizing Arden's lack of compassion; this lack is not just cruel but *irrational*, since he does not stand to gain much by withholding the land from them. Like the tyrant dominated and ruled by insatiable lust, Arden's 'desire of wealth is endless in his mind, / And he is greedy-gaping still' (1.474–5).

The early moderns associated political tyranny with sexual transgressions and likened a monarch's (or master's) refusal to consider the wills of their subjects and their right to property as a figurative rape. Jean Bodin's *Six Bookes of a Commonweale*, for example, distinguishes a monarch from a tyrant through their differing approaches to authority and contrasting views on possession: the one of them 'accounteth his owne goods to be the goods of his people; the other reckoneth not only the goods, but even the bodies of his subjects also to be his owne' (*The Six Bookes of a Commonweale* [London, 1606], 212). Unlike the monarch whose possessions are understood by him to belong to his people, the tyrant understands his authority over subjects to mean that he possesses their goods as well. Through the metaphor of rape, Bodin further illustrates the grievous extent of a tyrant's immoral character that denies any circumscription to his power and violates the bounds of his subjects' rights to property, safety and life. According to this framework, then, someone who cannot control his urges, someone who is enslaved to his lusts, is – ultimately – proven to be unfit to rule.

The metaphor of rape as a means of emphasizing Arden's cruel avarice is most evident in the play's description of Arden's treatment of Reede. Bound for sea, not knowing whether or not he will return, Reede cannot move Arden to pity when he asks Arden to consider his wife and children, whose survival requires the plot of land which 'by force and violence' Arden held from him. This language of force resonates strongly with discourses on rape. The play thus undermines Arden's authority as a property owner when it represents him as a tyrant unfit to wield power over others since he is 'enslaved' by his desires.

The dual representation of Arden as a victim targeted by insubordinate subordinates and as a landowner who exploited his privilege and preyed upon those with less power than himself acknowledges that, while anxiety circulated regarding the vulnerability of those with authority, the early modern English were similarly well aware and critical of the abuses committed by those of higher statuses at the expense of disenfranchised members of the commonweal. The depiction of Arden as a greedy and cruel landlord will help students recognize a more complex and unideal (and, perhaps more 'real') victim while preparing them to engage with difficult conversations on justice within the play (see section 'On justice' of this chapter) as well as early modern homicide statistics (see section 'Homicide statistics in early modern England' of this chapter). Indeed, victims are rarely – if ever – able to fulfil the ideals of complete innocence unless their representations are carefully constructed. How did an early modern audience perceive a less-than-ideal victim of murder, a man who himself caused suffering (and perhaps indirectly the deaths of others)? How does the added element of Arden's cruelty impact students' perception of Arden's murder? What do student reactions tell us about what might have been an early modern response to an unideal Arden but also about our own current social prejudices on criminality, victimization and justice?

Akhimie, Patricia. *Shakespeare and the Cultivation of Difference: Race and Conduct in the Early Modern World*. New York: Routledge, 2018.
Bushnell, Rebecca W. *Tragedies of Tyrants: Political Thought and Theater in the English Renaissance*. Ithaca: Cornell University Press, 1990.
Dolan, Frances E. *Dangerous Familiars: Representations of Domestic Crime in England, 1550–1700*. Ithaca: Cornell University Press, 1994.
Kussmaul, Ann. *Servants in Husbandry in Early Modern England*. Cambridge: Cambridge University Press, 1981.
Sheeha, Iman. *Household Servants in Early Modern Domestic Tragedy*. New York: Routledge, 2020.

Of darker races

In my courses focussed on the early modern period, I always make a point to emphasize that Black men, women and children lived in England and were part of English communities. The undergraduate students with whom I have worked generally assume one of three things regarding African and Black people in England and Scotland in the sixteenth century: (1) they simply did not exist; (2) the few who were in England must have been enslaved or attached to foreign ambassadors; (3) if present, they existed in such isolated numbers that render the recognition of their presence 'wholly unnecessary'. In other words, English Tudor history is one without Black people in it; it is an exclusively (and, for some, romanticized) *white* history.

Elizabeth's reign marked a 'radical increase in the numbers of black people in England . . . [due to the] seafaring enterprises of merchants and mariners'. But, as Imtiaz Habib underscores, Black Tudors were part of England even before her accession in 1558 due to her grandfather's (Henry VII) and father's (Henry VIII) foreign initiatives as well as those of the Scottish James IV (Habib 65).

In other words, by the time Arden's murder had taken place and certainly during Elizabeth's reign, Black Tudors may have been second- or third-generation men, women and children born in the realm. 'The Africans that lived in towns and rural communities in early modern England', Onyeka Nubia points out, 'resided with Englishmen and women. Many of them would have considered themselves members of local communities, more than subjects of a nation state' (Nubia 31). As a play set in Faversham (rather than in Venice, Rome, Fez etc.) about a real sixteenth-century murder, *Arden* offers a particularly powerful opportunity for teachers to challenge misconceptions that deny the belonging of Black people within early modern English history.

The work of Imtiaz Habib has forced scholars, students, theatre practitioners and researchers to consider how the term 'Black' is used in these early modern artefacts as a designator of racial difference. Race, as Geraldine Heng defines it, is a term that recognizes the repeated patterns and tendencies to differentiate human beings into groups through selective external and perceived internal markers of difference (e.g. religious difference and sexuality could sometimes code the individual as being internally black) that are then essentialized and imagined to be innate and immutable attributes. As Barbara and Karen Fields have underscored, 'Race is not an element of human biology. . . . Race is not an idea but an ideology' (121). The recognition of race as an ideology, as Ruben Espinosa explains, means understanding how 'race, then, is mobilized at various historical moments, including our own, to sustain an imbalance of power and oppressive structures that always favour whiteness' (6). The double emphasis on Mosby's darker complexion in Holinshed's account not only others him by marking his difference from Alice and Arden; it also further associates him with the pejorative. His description as a 'blacke' man cannot be dissociated from his unlawful and transgressive desire to usurp Arden's place in his bed and at his table as master of the house. Mosby, however, is not the only character associated with darkness; Brandi K. Adams's chapter in this collection explores the meanings accrued by the murderer Black Will. As teachers, when we have our students consider the connections between Mosby's dark complexion and Black Will's internal darkness, we can help them to understand the workings of racist ideologies in early modern accounts of the Arden murder that shape racial privilege in favour of whiteness at the expense of blackness.

In *A true discourse of the late voyages of discouerie* (1578), George Best draws upon a racialized understanding of black skin as a somatic mark of eternal sin, a hereditary infection of the blood beginning with the sin of Noah's white son Cham. God punished Cham's disobedience by marking his son Chus and all his posterity with bodies both 'blacke & loathsome, that it might remaine a spectacle of disobedience to all the World' (31). In this account, blackness is passed down to Cham's descendants from one generation to another. And, as Patricia Akhimie points out, somatic markers perceived as hereditary and natural were also understood as 'endowed at birth. The power of racialist ideology then allowed that the meanings associated with somatic marks were also inherited, linking possessors of such marks as related by some biological or blood tie' (187). Like Cham, Mosby abhors his inferior status and covets Arden's wife, authority, and lands. In this way, the Holinshed account that underscores Mosby's black complexion does not simply mark him as physically different and the improper 'mate' of Alice. It relies on the symbolism of blackness to infuse Mosby's darker skin tone with meaning. Mosby's external body, then, serves as the confirmation of a hereditary predisposition to aspire to a position that according to class, blood and racial hierarchy did not belong to him.

Akhimie, Patricia. 'Bruised with Adversity: Reading Race in *The Comedy of Errors*'. In *The Oxford Handbook of Shakespeare and Embodiment: Gender, Sexuality, and Race*, edited by Valerie Traub, 186–96. Oxford: Oxford University Press, 2016.
Espinosa, Ruben. *Shakespeare on the Shades of Racism*. New York: Routledge, 2021.
Habib, Imtiaz. *Black Lives in the English Archives, 1500–1677: Imprints of the Invisible*. Aldershot: Ashgate, 2008.
Hall, Kim F. *Things of Darkness: Economies of Race and Gender in Early Modern England*. Ithaca: Cornell University Press, 1995.
Heng, Geraldine. *The Invention of Race in the European Middle Ages*. Cambridge: Cambridge University Press, 2018.
Kaufmann, Miranda. *Black Tudors: The Untold Story*. London: Oneworld, 2017.
Loomba, Ania. *Gender, Race, Renaissance Drama*. Manchester: Manchester University Press, 1989.

Nubia, Onyeka. *England's* Other *Countrymen: Black Tudor Society*. London: Zed Books, 2019.
Olusoga, David. *Black and British: A Forgotten History*. London: Macmillan, 2016.
Vaughan, Virginia Mason. *Performing Blackness on English Stages, 1500–1800*. Cambridge: Cambridge University Press, 2005.

Of masterless men

During the Elizabethan period, England was engaged in multiple wars against the Spanish and in Ireland and the Netherlands. 'At the peak, England had about eighteen thousand troops in Ireland. Another twelve thousand saw action in the Netherlands. At least forty thousand were mustered to face the Spanish Armada, with more serving in the navy' (Spooner 58). The need for a steady stream of new recruits to fill the posts left vacant due to high mortality rates among soldiers who died from injury, disease and starvation meant that those who may have been impressed to serve as soldiers included the 'unenthusiastic and ill-disciplined' (Thomas 229). As a consequence of these constant wars on many fronts, by the mid-1590s, England witnessed an unprecedented number of discharged, demobilized and maimed soldiers who returned home. Many of these men did not receive much pension and were either unpaid or underpaid, which then forged the connection between poverty and military service. Scarcity and inflation of the late sixteenth century further exacerbated tensions between townsfolk and former soldiers. Not only did the government place the onus on local parishes and municipal county officials to provide for disabled army soldiers but very little was done to reintegrate ex-soldiers, including able-bodied men, into economic work structures and society in general.

Former soldiers, a growing group of impoverished, masterless men without a place or purpose, were sometimes viewed by civilians with concern and contempt. Black Will's criminal deeds committed abroad and in England reinforce the anxieties surrounding ex-soldiers to which audiences of the late sixteenth century would have been attuned. The play has Bradshaw warn Greene that while he and Black Will served at Boulogne during the campaigns of Henry VIII, Will had committed 'such pranks' that even their fellow English soldiers 'feared him for his villainy' (2.9–10). It is worth mentioning that, in 1544, Henry VIII's *Statutes and ordynances for the warre* expressly attempted to curb war crimes committed by the English with the threat of death as punishment for the murder, robbery and rape of the Boulonnais' civilian population. The need for such regulations, as well as accounts of the hanging of English soldiers ordered by the dukes of Norfolk and Suffolk as punishment for looting, attests to the continued transgression of those statutes (Murphy 21). It also makes clear how war provided licence for such debauched violations. In the case of Black Will, his time in Boulogne is romanticized as he disconcertingly declares that his wicked deeds are 'not past with [him], for [he] keep[s] that same honourable mind still' (2.28–9). His atrocities committed abroad against the French return with him home to haunt the English.

Archer, Ian W. *The Pursuit of Stability: Social Relations in Elizabethan London*. Cambridge: Cambridge University Press, 1991.
Beier, A. L. *Masterless Men: The Vagrancy Problem in England, 1560–1640*. London: Methuen, 1985.
Griffiths, Paul. *Youth and Authority: Formative Experiences in England, 1560–1640*. Oxford: Clarendon Press, 1996.
Hitchcock, David. *Vagrancy in English Culture and Society, 1650–1760*. London: Bloomsbury, 2016.
Murphy, Neil. 'Violence, Colonization and Henry VIII's Conquest of France, 1544–1546'. *Past and Present* 233, no. 1 (2016): 13–51.
Spooner, Aaron. 'Shakespeare's Itinerant Soldiers and Foreign Wars: The Elizabethan Crisis of Debt in the Economy of Hal's England'. *Journal for Early Modern Cultural Studies* 12, no. 1 (2012): 49–84.
Thomas, Phillip. 'Military Mayhem in Elizabethan Chester: The Privy Council's Response to Vagrant Soldiers'. *Journal of the Society for Army Historical Research* 76, no. 308 (1998): 226–47.

On justice

Cruentation practices or corpse-touching – also known as the ordeal of the bier – were collective rituals that offered reassurance to the community that murder will out. In the medieval and early modern periods, the spontaneous bleeding of a victim's corpse as a result of being in the presence of the murderer or of being touched by the murderer was an important form of evidence used against suspected criminals. Michael Dalton's *The Countrey Justice* (1618), for example, affirms that a bleeding corpse was cause for suspicion, and James I describes that a 'dead carkasse . . . wil gush out of bloud, as if the bloud were crying to the heave[n] for reve[nge] of the murtherer' (Gaskill 227). Cruentation resulted from beliefs both supernatural and divine. But, though the miraculous message from the deceased was believed to come from God to enable authorities to enact earthly justice in bringing forth retribution upon the guilty, the practice itself was intensely psychological, an aspect that *Arden* displays to the fullest. 'Although the legal function of cruentation is to identify the killer', Lesel Dawson explains, 'literary texts also highlighted its profound emotional and psychological impact, in which the murderer reexperiences the act of wounding from the position of spectator' (153). Audiences first get a sense of how the interpretation of Arden's blood is read by Alice as a text that conveys her guilt. When Arden's blood gushes forth from the ground the more Alice attempts to remove it, she understands this miracle as a result of her insubordinate feelings, for she 'blush[es] not at [her] husband's death' (14.254, 256). Later, as Alice speaks her husband's name while set before her husband's lifeless body, blood gushes forth from the corpse to condemn her (16.4–6). While the spontaneous bleeding gives the Mayor a sense of certainty that the correct criminals have been apprehended, the audience of the play, of course, knows exactly who were the confederates in Arden's murder and, possibly, Alice's eventual punishment. Cruentation, then, allows *Arden's* Alice to voice guilt and to seek – or at least perform – a desire for repentance.

With its final line declaring that audiences will learn of 'the shamefull end of all murderers', the title page promises a neat conclusion wherein justice will ultimately be served. Indeed, to a certain degree, the drama does provide a sense that all those who shed blood by force will receive violent ends, for even Arden's death is infused with providential meaning as his murdered body's print remained on that 'plot of ground / Which he by force and violence held from Reede' (Epilogue 10–11). The play deviates from Holinshed's account which states that George Shakebag's fate was never known. Instead, the drama reports Shakebag was 'murdered in Southwark' after having taken sanctuary (Epilogue 3–4). Mercy, compassion and protection, it seems, are denied to those who show none to others. From servants to landowners, from masterless ruffians to illicit lovers, all seem to be held accountable for the abuses they enact. However, despite this purportedly tidy end, in which overlapping plots from multiple agents weave together and end up plaiting them all, the skein of justice depicted in *Arden* unravels with the swift execution of innocent Bradshaw, whose involvement in the murder – according to the play – was purely unintentional. Justice, therefore, exceeds its bounds when even the innocent are executed unjustly and meet the same shameful end of murderers. What makes this play so deliciously attractive, perhaps, is that despite the title page's attempts to reassure audiences as part of a homiletic tradition, the drama itself resists and frustrates precisely that reassurance.

Dawson, Lesel. '"In Every Wound there is a Bloody Tongue": Cruentation in Early Modern Literature and Psychology'. In *Blood Matters: Studies in European Literature and Thought, 1400–1700*, edited by Bonnie Lander Johnson and Eleanor Decamp, 151–66. Philadelphia: University of Pennsylvania Press, 2018.
Floyd-Wilson, Mary. *Occult Knowledge, Science, and Gender on the Shakespearean Stage*. Cambridge: Cambridge University Press, 2013.
Gaskill, Malcolm. *Crime and Mentalities in Early Modern England*. Cambridge: Cambridge University Press, 2000.
Gaskill, Malcolm. 'Reporting Murder: Fiction in the Archives in Early Modern England'. *Social History* 23, no. 1 (1998): 1–30.

Genre

As one of the earliest English domestic tragedies, *Arden* provides a useful example of the experimentation in genre that occurred in Renaissance stages of the 1590s. From a pedagogical perspective, the status of this play within the so-called 'Shakespeare Apocrypha' can help students think critically about the creation of knowledge. What questions do we ask? And, how do the questions themselves – the terms we select – shape the answer we find and the knowledge we create? *Arden* is primed for introducing these questions about research methods since the intense debates to (authoritatively) determine that Shakespeare is or is not the author, exemplifies how Shakespeare's name – a construction, itself, that holds a privileged position in the British (and Western) canon – actually circumscribes the imaginative possibilities of what we think could have been in the collaborative and experimental early modern theatre. Shakespeare, as we have inherited him today, is a symbol *par excellence* of one white man's exceptionalism and genius, a construction that requires the association of the canon exclusively with Shakespeare. Peter Kirwan calls for the 'critical retention of the "apocryphal" category as a discursive and fluid liminal space' (213) that recognizes the attachment of Shakespeare's name to the apocryphal works, like *Arden*, as derived from the influence of Shakespeare on the company as a loyal dramatist, actor and shareholder. Attributions might acknowledge 'his "ownership" of them insofar as they are commensurate with narratives of company ownership, genre experimentation, response and style' (113–14). Such an understanding of the interconnectedness of early modern plays resists the exclusionary politics of authorial canons that have limited the perception of the collaborative yet important role of authors in the workings of early modern theatre companies. Debates about attribution, then, can engage students on the politics of canons and how these structures have limited knowledge creation.

Though difficult to define, domestic tragedies in general deviate from the Aristotelian view of the tragic that pertains only to the lives of the nobility. Compellingly local and disconcertingly familiar, domestic tragedies – as Henry Hitch Adams defines them – focus on 'the common people' and are 'ordinarily set in the domestic scene, dealing with personal and family relationships rather than with affairs of state, and presented in a realistic fashion, and ending in a tragic or otherwise serious manner' (1–2). Lena Cowen Orlin offers a more expansive description of domestic tragedies as plays that speak to the anxieties and concerns of property owners, in which their house stands for a microcosm of kingly authority (a gentleman's rule over his family, servants and guests is like that of a king's rule over his subjects) that is undermined by those closest to the master, a definition that aptly describes the dynamics that drive the multiple and tangled plots within the play (82).

Expansive in its coverage of topics yet taut in its length and setting, *Arden* explores a variety of overlapping issues on property, power and desire within an English household, same-sex relations, community and space. The play explicitly illustrates how anxieties that surround questions about access, possession and the control of land can discursively (and easily) transmute to questions about the status of women as the property of men. Sexual transgressions in the play reverberate beyond the domestic space, and public concerns come to threaten Arden within his home. The adulterous triangle between Arden, Alice and Mosby is mirrored by the lower-class relationships of Michael, Susan and Clarke. Emma Whipday's chapter in this book describes Susan's position of submission and various loyalties that come into conflict in the plot against her master. 'Susan's . . . many roles involve submission', Emma Whipday argues, 'yet these loyalties can come into conflict, since she is represented as loyal to, and the property of, the two instigators of the plot against her master – Alice and Mosby' (Whipday 94). The courtship exchanges and potential access to Susan's person, again, unknown to Arden, undermine his authority and safety within his domain.

In most early modern dramas, tragedies belong to specific individuals as stated on the title page. The unfolding plot is dominated by the decisions, will and agency of the titular character. Although the 1592 title page declares the play to be 'The Lamentable and Trve Tragedie of M. Arden of Feversham in Kent', *Arden*, however, is driven by multiple plots and competing wills. Indeed, as Frances Dolan points out, this play about dangerous subordinates mimics the insubordination of its characters through the drama's refusal to be a tragedy that exclusively belongs to Arden (78). The term 'domestic tragedy' might at first deceptively convey limits on this extraordinary play when in reality it masterfully weaves together the concerns of family, of locality and of a nation, experimenting with and remaking genre conventions. And, just as the titles of 'master' and 'husband' convey a sense of authority that the play undermines, so, too, the title of the play belies the fact that the tragedy doesn't belong to Arden or to any single character at all.

Adams, Henry Hitch. *English Domestic Or, Homiletic Tragedy, 1575 to 1642*. New York: Columbia University Press, 1943.
Comensoli, Viviana. *Household Business: Domestic Plays of Early Modern England*. Toronto: University of Toronto Press, 1996.
Kirwan, Peter. *Shakespeare and the Idea of Apocrypha: Negotiating the Boundaries of the Dramatic Canon*. Cambridge: Cambridge University Press, 2015.
Lake, Peter. 'Deeds against Nature: Cheap Print, Protestantism and Murder in Early Modern England'. In *Culture and Politics in Early Modern England*, edited by Peter Lake and Kevin Sharpe, 257–83. Stanford: Stanford University Press, 1994.
Orlin, Lena Cowen. 'Man's House as His Castle in *Arden of Feversham*'. *Medieval & Renaissance Drama in England*, 2 (1985): 57–89.

Richardson, Catherine. *Domestic Life and Domestic Tragedy in Early Modern England: The Material Life of the Household*. Manchester: Manchester University Press, 2006.

Homicide statistics in early modern England

The play – filled with passion, wit and humour – sensationalizes the perceived threat of murderous subordinates, those who would commit atrocities against their superiors and even against God to get their will. Since *Arden* represents a 'true life crime' (and perhaps especially because this cultural artefact depicts a murder that actually took place in 1551), the drama has the potential to give contemporary students (as they did the early moderns) the misperception that masters and husbands in sixteenth- and seventeenth-century England faced constant threats to their lives from those they trusted most. A look at homicide statistics from the period, however, would suggest otherwise. At British History Online, students can browse the Middlesex Sessions records through the searchable database. Between 1590 and 1591, there were only eight murder cases (excluding infanticide and including attempted murder and cases of self-defence) that were heard by the Middlesex County Sessions. Approximately 24.7 per cent of all homicides in Essex in the years between 1560 and 1659 were domestic homicides involving family members, which includes servants and apprentices. Although there were surely unreported crimes, Duncan Salkeld importantly notes that 'the *perceived* threat of crime was at all times keenly felt' (194). Crime statistics are particularly beneficial for expanding a contemporary audience's understanding of violence in early modern England and can help students consider critically the differing representations of criminality in materials of the period. Through a comparison of these legal records with *Arden* as well as other early modern ephemera on the murder, students can wrestle with important questions about methodological practices – how we know what we know or *think* we know what we know based on cultural artefacts.

In the seventeenth century, it was common practice to enforce unwilling masters to accept apprentices as a means to provide for impoverished children in times of distress. Apprentices and servants sometimes suffered from ill-treatment, starvation, neglect and physical beatings. Historian J. A. Sharpe states, 'servants and apprentices ... were involved in homicide overwhelmingly as the victims of violence perpetrated by their employers' based on a study of persons accused of homicide at the Essex assizes between 1560 and 1709 (38). More importantly, although masters and mistresses during this period in Essex were accused of murder, very few were actually convicted and only one was hung for the crime. Sharpe suggests that since the 'act of correction' through corporal punishment – the moderate chastisement of a servant, apprentice and children – was not only legal but considered necessary for the production and maintenance of moral households, judges and juries may have worried that masters would be 'deterred from beating their charges by death sentences when correction ended in fatality' (38). Although *Arden* dramatizes the threat that servants posed to trusting and magnanimous masters, not only were servants and apprentices more likely to be the victims of domestic homicide but their deaths may have been viewed as unfortunate occurrences resulting from justifiable and necessary beatings they had deserved that, regrettably, went too far.

With servants and apprentices excluded, the children and stepchildren of the accused were the majority of homicide victims within the household. And wives were more likely to be the victims of spousal murder at a ratio of 2:1. Corresponding with 'a woman's place in the sixteenth and seventeenth centuries [being] firmly in the home', the Essex records reveal women were accused of just 7 per cent of homicides with non-familial victims as opposed to 42 per cent of homicides with family members as victims and 41 per cent with a servant or apprentice as victims (36–7). This data, Sharpe explains, indicates that while 'women were more likely to perpetrate domestic than non-domestic homicide, so they were more likely to be its victims' (37). Before introducing students to these statistics, I typically wait until after we have concluded the play and have discussed other artefacts on the case, like *The complaint and lamentation of Mistresse Arden*. Students have also found it generative to watch an episode introduction from the ongoing True Crime Network TV series *Deadly Wives*. As a learning community, we reflect together on the impression *Deadly Wives* gives of the dangers that lurk in our 'backyard', with happy families in picture-perfect homes. This exercise encourages students to take seriously their feelings as a means to generate questions about the sixteenth and seventeenth centuries when we compare and contrast their affective responses to ideas contained in *Deadly Wives* with the play, ballad and Holinshed's *Chronicles*. It is at this point that I introduce students to the fact that servants and women were more likely in the early modern period to be abused and murdered (a major crime that appeared rarely in court records) than to be murderers, and these connections between past and present open the opportunity for our community of learners to reckon with the long history of domestic and intimate partner violence.

Dolan, Frances E. 'Battered Women, Petty Traitors, and the Legacy of Coverture'. *Feminist Studies* 29, no. 2 (2009): 249–77.
Gowing, Laura. *Common Bodies: Women, Touch and Power in Seventeenth-Century England*. New Haven: Yale University Press, 2003.
Kane, Stuart A. 'Wives with Knives: Early Modern Murder Ballads and the Transgressive Commodity'. *Criticism* 38, no. 2 (1996): 219–37.
Middlesex County Records: Volume 1, 1550–1603, edited by John Cordy Jeaffreson. London, 1886. British History Online, http://www.british-history.ac.uk/middx/county-records/vol1.
Salkeld, Duncan. 'Crime'. In *The Ashgate Research Companion to Popular Culture in Early Modern England*, edited by Andrew Hadfield, Matthew Dimmock and Abigail Shinn, 193–206. Farnham: Ashgate, 2014.
Sharpe, J. A. 'Domestic Homicide in Early Modern England'. *The Historical Journal* 24, no. 1 (1981): 29–48.
Smith, Steven R. 'The London Apprentices as Seventeenth-Century Adolescents'. *Past and Present* 61, no. 1 (1973): 149–61.

Conclusion

Hundreds of years after the murder of Thomas Arden, this domestic tragedy continues to captivate the imagination of audiences. But we aren't simply seduced by this scintillating and volatile play's promise of its depiction of a true life crime. And, even though the cultural and historical specifics of early modern England may seem not only foreign but incomprehensible to some contemporary viewers, the fact is that domestic homicide and emotional abuse are not buried in the past but continue in our present; these are part of the fabric of our collective interpersonal experiences. For this reason, I introduce the play to students with a trigger warning designed to acknowledge the ubiquity of domestic violence (both physical and emotional) to prepare the classroom community for discomfort and to build an ethos of trust. Trigger warnings allow instructors to recognize that since students inevitably bring their experiential perspectives to bear on the topics they learn about, scenes that depict the trauma of domestic violence will necessarily impact people differently and, therefore, require some to be more vulnerable than others. By providing students with multiple ways into the play and strategies for analysing and joining the conversation, trigger warnings increase accessibility and open rather than obstruct learning. They serve as a means to acknowledge the existence of survivors in the classroom, provide students with an array of actionable ways to navigate/draw upon their psychosomatic responses to the content of the day and 'help to cultivate an environment of care and solidarity' (Mendoza 100).

The one thing that my students have found intimate and deeply relatable is the psychological and emotional dynamic between Alice and Mosby. Whenever I teach the play, students are drawn to the virtuoso, poetic quarrel scene as the two go from dissembling ill-intent to contemptibly casting blame on each other, from ridiculing one another where they know it would hurt the most (e.g. when Mosby 'slut-shames' Alice and when Alice taunts Mosby with his low-born status) ultimately to end in a lovers' reconcilement. '[N]eerer, and dearere any persons be', warns William Gouge in *Of Domestical Duties,* 'the more violent will that hatred be which is fastened on them' (352). It is in discussions of Alice and Mosby's intense attachment that students have used psychology research from other coursework as well as anecdotal reflections to inform their analysis of the play.

When we analyse the exchanges between Alice and Mosby, I also have students reflect on some emotional abuse statistics. Ridicule between lovers, which recurs in the romantic relationships in *Arden,* is both the most prevalent form of psychological abuse today and the kind of emotional abuse that has been reported to be the most negative for survivors. While signs of physical violence may sometimes heal, the consequences of ridicule persist even after survivors leave abusive relationships because this form of intimate partner violence attacks a victim's self-esteem (Follingstad et al. 113, 117). According to the National Intimate Partner and Sexual Violence Survey, 'an estimated 47% of men and women (in the

U.S.A.) will be victims of psychological aggression by an intimate partner in their lifetime' (2017 National Crime Victims' Rights Week Resource Guide). Despite the likelihood that college students will experience some kind of emotional abuse from an intimate partner, it is often difficult for those in abusive relationships to recognize psychological manipulation and violence let alone the long-term potential consequences of such damaging attachments.

There is something viscerally compelling about Alice and Mosby that may, even today, hit a little too close to home. While the vast majority of this chapter has focussed on the benefits of teaching *Arden* due to its ability to have students consider how power structures shaped the early modern period and (more abstractly) the politics of knowledge creation, I end by insisting that one potential benefit of *Arden* is that it opens the possibility for teachers to foster awareness and deep personal reflection on emotional abuse. Members of our learning communities – our students and ourselves – may see in the looking glass of Alice and Mosby unfamiliar-yet-familiar reflections of relationships that we have read about, have watched on TV and have seen among peers, friends and family members – reflections of relationships that we may ourselves have lived, and may in fact be living.

Follingstad, Diane, Larry L. Rutledge, Barbara J. Berg, Elizabeth S. Hause and Darlene S. Polek. 'The Role of Emotional Abuse in Physically Abusive Relationships'. *Journal of Family Violence* 5, no. 2 (1990): 107–120.

Mendoza, Kirsten N. 'Sexual Violence, Trigger Warnings, and the Early Modern Classroom'. In *Teaching Social Justice Through Shakespeare*, edited by Hillary Eklund and Wendy Beth Hyman, 97–105. Edinburgh: Edinburgh University Press, 2019.

Note

1 The bracketed portion was added to Henry Machyn's entry after it was originally written.

SELECT BIBLIOGRAPHY

All references to *Arden of Faversham* are taken from the Arden Early Modern Drama edition edited by Catherine Richardson, unless otherwise stated. Quotations from Shakespeare plays are taken from the Arden 3 editions, unless otherwise stated.

Editions of *Arden of Faversham*

Bate, Jonathan, and Eric Rasmussen, editors. *William Shakespeare and Others: Collaborative Plays*. Basingstoke: Palgrave Macmillan, 2013.
Findlay, Polly, and Zoé Swensen, editors. *Arden of Faversham*. London: Nick Hern Books, 2014.
Jacob, Edward, editor. *The Lamentable and True Tragedie of M. Arden, of Feversham, in Kent*. Faversham: J & J March, 1770.
Knight, Charles, editor. *The Pictorial Edition of Shakespeare*. London: Charles Knight & Co., 1838–41.
Richardson, Catherine, editor. *Arden of Faversham*. London: Bloomsbury, 2022.
Sturgess, Keith, editor. *Three Elizabethan Domestic Tragedies*. Harmondsworth: Penguin, 1969.
Taylor, Gary, John Jowett, Terri Bourus and Gabriel Egan, editors. *The New Oxford Shakespeare*. Oxford: Oxford University Press, 2016.
Tucker Brooke, C. F., editor. *The Shakespeare Apocrypha: Being a Collection of the Fourteen Plays Which Have Been Ascribed to Shakespeare*. Oxford: Clarendon Press, 1908.
Tyrrell, Henry, editor. *The Doubtful Plays of Shakspere*. London: John Tallis & Co., 1853.
White, Martin, editor. *Arden of Faversham*. London: New Mermaids, 1982.
White, Martin, editor. *Arden of Faversham*. New edition with introduction by Tom Lockwood. London: A & C Black, 2007.
Wiggins, Martin, editor. *A Woman Killed with Kindness and Other Domestic Plays*. Oxford: Oxford University Press, 2008.

Wine, Martin. L., editor. *The Tragedy of Master Arden of Faversham*. London: Methuen, 1973.

Selected Criticism

Adams, Henry Hitch. *English Domestic Or, Homiletic Tragedy, 1575 to 1642*. New York: Columbia University Press, 1943.
Adams, John Henry. 'Agentive Objects and Protestant Idolatry in *Arden of Faversham*'. *Studies in English Literature, 1500–1900* 57, no. 2 (2017): 231–51.
Akhimie, Patricia. 'Bruised with Adversity: Reading Race in *The Comedy of Errors*'. In *The Oxford Handbook of Shakespeare and Embodiment: Gender, Sexuality, and Race*, edited by Valerie Traub, 186–96. Oxford: Oxford University Press, 2016.
Akhimie, Patricia. *Shakespeare and the Cultivation of Difference: Race and Conduct in the Early Modern World*. New York: Routledge, 2018.
'A Lost Shakespeare Meet[s] Desperate Housewives 1950s Style'. *New Jersey Stage*, 30 June 2015. Available online: http://www.newjerseystage.com/articles/getarticle.php?ID=5508 (accessed 16 February 2022).
Amory, Mark. 'Botched Butchery'. *Spectator*, 10 April 1982.
Amussen, S. D. 'Gender, Family and the Social Order, 1560–1725'. In *Order and Disorder in Early Modern England*, edited by Anthony Fletcher and John Stevenson, 196–217. Cambridge: Cambridge University Press, 1985.
'An Elizabethan Tragedy'. *The Stage*, 4 September 1952.
Archer, Ian W. *The Pursuit of Stability: Social Relations in Elizabethan London*. Cambridge: Cambridge University Press, 1991.
Archer, Ian W., Felicity Heal and Paulina Kewes. 'Prologue'. In *The Oxford Handbook of Holinshed's Chronicles*, edited by Paulina Kewes, Ian W. Archer and Felicity Heal, xxix–xxxvii. Oxford: Oxford University Press, 2013.
'*Arden of Faversham*'. *The Stage*, 18 June 1953.
Bachman, Ronald D. 'Systematization: A Settlement Strategy'. In *Romania: A Country Study*, edited by Ronald D. Bachman. Washington: GPO for the Library of Congress, 1989. Available online: http://countrystudies.us/romania/39.htm (accessed 16 February 2022).
Balizet, Ariane M. *Blood and Home in Early Modern Drama: Domestic Identity on the Renaissance Stage*. London: Routledge, 2014.
Barber, John. 'Agutter's Star Quality'. *Daily Telegraph*, 1 April 1982.

Bars Closel, Régis Augustus. '*Utopia* and the Enclosing of Dramatic Landscapes'. *Renaissance and Reformation* 41, no. 3 (2018): 67–92.
Batali, Luminita. 'Vittorio Holtier, "The Tower and the Island, a Shakespearean Universe, an Attempt at Approach by Means of Centrality Archetypes"'. *Romanian Scene Designers*, 2005. Available online: http://www.romanian-scene-designers.org/Vittorio-Holtier-The-Tower-and-the-Island-a-Shakespearian-Universe-an-Attempt-at-Approach-by-Means-of-Centrality-Archetypes-s122_a4.htm (accessed 16 February 2022).
Beier, A. L. *Masterless Men: The Vagrancy Problem in England, 1560–1640*. London: Methuen, 1985.
Belsey, Catherine. 'Alice Arden's Crime'. *Renaissance Drama* 13 (1982): 83–102.
Belsey, Catherine. *The Subject of Tragedy* [1985]. London: Routledge, 1991.
Berg, Dianne. '"Tis Fearful Sleeping in a Serpent's Bed": *Arden of Faversham* and the Threat of the Petty Traitor'. In *Treason: Medieval and Early Modern Adultery, Betrayal, and Shame*, edited by Larissa Tracy, 340–55. Boston: Brill, 2019.
Billington, Michael. 'Arden of Faversham Review – Elizabethan Tragedy Goes Modern'. *The Guardian*, 7 May 2014.
Birdseye, Cheryl. '"Let death make amends for all my sins": (In)sincere Confessions in *Arden of Faversham*'. *Early Modern Literary Studies* 28 (2019).
Bloom, Gina. *Gaming the Stage: Playable Media and the Rise of English Commercial Theater*. Ann Arbor: University of Michigan Press, 2018.
Bloomfield, Jem. 'Mid-Century Jacobeans: Agatha Christie, Ngaio Marsh, P. D. James, and *The Duchess of Malfi*'. *ELH* 87, no. 4 (2020): 1079–104.
Borlik, Todd A. *Ecocriticism and Early Modern English Literature: Green Pastures*. London: Routledge, 2011.
Bourus, Terri. '*Arden of Faversham*, Richard Burbage, and the Early Shakespeare Canon'. In *Early Shakespeare, 1588–1594*, edited by Rory Loughnane and Andrew J. Power, 200–19. Cambridge: Cambridge University Press, 2020.
Bovilsky, Lara. *Barbarous Play: Race on the English Renaissance Stage*. Minneapolis: University of Minnesota Press, 2008.
Brown, David Sterling. '"Hood Feminism": Whiteness and Segregated (Premodern) Scholarly Discourse in the Post-Postracial Era'. *Literature Compass* 18, no. 10 (2021).
Burnett, Mark Thornton. *Masters and Servants in English Renaissance Drama and Culture: Authority and Obedience*. New York: St. Martin's Press, 1997.
Bushnell, Rebecca W. *Tragedies of Tyrants: Political Thought and Theater in the English Renaissance*. Ithaca: Cornell University Press, 1990.

Butterworth, Philip. *Theatre of Fire: Special Effects in Early English and Scottish Theatre*. London: Society for Theatre Research, 1998.

Catty, Jocelyn. *Writing Rape, Writing Women in Early Modern England: Unbridled Speech*. New York: St. Martin's Press, 1999.

Chakravarty, Urvashi. *Fictions of Consent: Slavery, Servitude, and Free Service in Early Modern England*. Philadelphia: University of Pennsylvania Press, 2022.

Chapman, Matthieu A. 'The Appearance of Blacks on the Early Modern Stage: *Love's Labour's Lost*'s African Connections to Court'. *Early Theatre* 17, no. 2 (2014): 77–94.

Chiari, Sophie. *Shakespeare's Representation of Weather, Climate and Environment: The Early Modern 'Fated Sky'*. Edinburgh: Edinburgh University Press, 2019.

Christensen, Ann C. *Separation Scenes: Domestic Drama in Early Modern England*. Lincoln: University of Nebraska Press, 2017.

Clark, Glenn. 'Hurried to Destruction: Reprobation in *Arden of Faversham* and *A Woman Killed with Kindness*'. *Renaissance and Reformation* 41, no. 4 (2018): 109–31.

Clark, Sandra. 'The Problem of Sin and Crime in Domestic Tragedy'. *Early Modern Literary Studies* 28 (2019).

Comensoli, Viviana. *Household Business: Domestic Plays of Early Modern England*. Toronto: University of Toronto Press, 1996.

Croggon, Alison. 'Arden v. Arden, The Hayloft Project – Review'. *The Guardian*, 24 November 2013. Available online: https://www.theguardian.com/stage/australia-culture-blog/2013/nov/25/arden-v-arden-hayloft-project-review (accessed 16 February 2022).

Daniel, Robert W., and Iman Sheeha. 'Introduction' to 'Door-bolts, Thresholds, and Peep-Holes: Liminality and Domestic Spaces in Early Modern England'. *Early Modern Literary Studies* 29 (2020).

Dawson, Lesel. '"In Every Wound there is a Bloody Tongue": Cruentation in Early Modern Literature and Psychology'. In *Blood Matters: Studies in European Literature and Thought, 1400–1700*, edited by Bonnie Lander Johnson and Eleanor Decamp, 151–66. Philadelphia: University of Pennsylvania Press, 2018.

Dessen, Alan C. 'Mist and Fog on the Elizabethan and Jacobean Stage'. In *Speaking Pictures: The Visual/Verbal Nexus of Dramatic Performance*, edited by Virginia Mason Vaughan, Fernando Cioni and Jacquelyn Bessell, 106–18. Madison: Fairleigh Dickinson University Press, 2010.

Dolan, Frances E. 'Battered Women, Petty Traitors, and the Legacy of Coverture'. *Feminist Studies* 29, no. 2 (2009): 249–77.

Dolan, Frances E. *Dangerous Familiars: Representations of Domestic Crime in England, 1550–1700*. Ithaca: Cornell University Press, 1994.

Dolan, Frances E. 'The Subordinate('s) Plot: Petty Treason and the Forms of Domestic Rebellion'. *Shakespeare Quarterly* 43, no. 3 (1992): 317–40.
Dolan, Frances E. 'Tracking the Petty Traitor across Genres'. In *Ballads and Broadsides in Britain, 1500–1800*, edited by Patricia Fumerton and Anita Guerrini with the assistance of Kris McAbee, 149–71. Farnham: Ashgate, 2010.
Donaldson, Ian. *The Rapes of Lucretia: A Myth and Its Transformations*. New York: The Clarendon Press, 1982.
Drummond, Peter D. 'Psychophysiology of the Blush'. In *The Psychological Significance of the Blush*, edited by W. Ray Crozier and Peter J. de Jong, 15–38. Cambridge: Cambridge University Press, 2013.
Dugan, Holly. '"As Dirty as Smithfield and as Stinking Every Whit": The Smell of the Hope Theatre'. In *Shakespeare's Theatres and the Effects of Performance*, edited by Farah Karim-Cooper and Tiffany Stern, 195–213. London: Bloomsbury, 2013.
Duncan, Sophie. *Shakespeare's Props: Memory and Cognition*. London: Routledge, 2019.
Dunne, Derek. 'Blushing on Cue: The Forensics of the Blush in Early Modern Drama'. *Shakespeare Bulletin* 34, no. 2 (2016): 233–52.
Durban, Kim. 'Research Topic'. *Alice Arden*, unpublished Masters thesis, University of Melbourne, 2000.
Elliott, Francesca. 'A Tale of Lovers with Murderous Intent'. *Flintshire Chronicle*, 25 February 2010.
Elliott, Jack, and Brett Greatley-Hirsch. '*Arden of Faversham*, Shakespearean Authorship, and "The Print of Many"'. In *The New Oxford Shakespeare Authorship Companion*, edited by Gary Taylor and Gabriel Egan, 139–81. Oxford: Oxford University Press, 2017.
Erickson, Peter, and Kim Hall. 'A New Scholarly Song'. *Shakespeare Quarterly* 67, no. 1 (2016): 1–13.
Espinosa, Ruben. *Shakespeare on the Shades of Racism*. New York: Routledge, 2021.
Evans, Curtis. *Masters of the 'Humdrum' Mystery: Cecil John Charles Street, Freeman Wills Crofts, Alfred Walter Stewart and the British Detective Novel, 1920–1961*. Jefferson: McFarland and Company, 2012.
Floyd-Wilson, Mary. '*Arden of Faversham*: Tragic Action at a Distance'. In *The Cambridge Companion to English Renaissance Tragedy*, edited by Emma Smith and Garrett A. Sullivan, 188–99. Cambridge: Cambridge University Press, 2010.
Floyd-Wilson, Mary. *Occult Knowledge, Science, and Gender on the Shakespearean Stage*. Cambridge: Cambridge University Press, 2013.
Follingstad, Diane, Larry L. Rutledge, Barbara J. Berg, Elizabeth S. Hause and Darlene S. Polek. 'The Role of Emotional Abuse in Physically

Abusive Relationships'. *Journal of Family Violence* 5, no. 2 (1990): 107–20.
Forse, James H. 'Touring in Kent: Some Observations from Records Published to Date'. *Early Theatre* 22, no. 2 (2019): 119–42.
Freebury-Jones, Darren. 'In Defence of Kyd: Evaluating the Claim for Shakespeare's Part Authorship of *Arden of Faversham*'. *Authorship* 7, no. 2 (2018).
Freebury-Jones, Darren. 'The Diminution of Thomas Kyd'. *Journal of Early Modern Studies* 8 (2019): 251–77.
Freebury-Jones, Darren. 'Exploring Verbal Relations between *Arden of Faversham* and John Lyly's *Endymion*'. *Renaissance and Reformation* 41, no. 4 (2018): 93–108.
Froide, Amy M. 'Marital Status as a Category of Difference: Singlewomen and Widows in Early Modern England'. In *Singlewomen in the European Past, 1250–1800*, edited by Judith M. Bennett and Amy M. Froide, 236–69. Philadelphia: University of Pennsylvania Press, 1999.
Fuentes, Marisa J. *Dispossessed Lives: Enslaved Women, Violence, and the Archive*. Philadelphia: University of Pennsylvania Press, 2016.
Gaskill, Malcolm. *Crime and Mentalities in Early Modern England*. Cambridge: Cambridge University Press, 2000.
Gaskill, Malcolm. 'Reporting Murder: Fiction in the Archives in Early Modern England'. *Social History* 23, no. 1 (1998): 1–30.
Gowing, Laura. *Common Bodies: Women, Touch and Power in Seventeenth-Century England*. New Haven: Yale University Press, 2003.
Green, Douglas. '*Arden of Faversham* (review)'. *Shakespeare Bulletin* 38, no. 2 (2020): 263–6.
Greene, Douglas G. *John Dickson Carr: The Man who Explained Miracles*. Cincinnati: Crippen & Landru, 2019.
Greg, W. W. 'Shakespeare and *Arden of Feversham*'. *Review of English Studies* 21, no. 82 (1945): 134–6.
Griffiths, Paul. *Youth and Authority: Formative Experiences in England, 1560–1640*. Oxford: Clarendon Press, 1996.
Grote, David. *The Best Actors in the World: Shakespeare and His Acting Company*. Westport: Greenwood Press, 2002.
Gruber, Elizabeth D. 'Nature on the Verge: Confronting "Bare Life" in *Arden of Faversham* and *King Lear*'. *Interdisciplinary Studies in Literature and Environment* 22, no. 1 (2015): 98–114.
Habib, Imtiaz. *Black Lives in the English Archives, 1500–1677: Imprints of the Invisible*. Aldershot: Ashgate, 2008.
Hall, Kim F. *Things of Darkness: Economies of Race and Gender in Early Modern England*. Ithaca: Cornell University Press, 1995.
Hallett, Victor. 'Arden of Faversham'. *Theatre in Wales*, 19 February 2010.

Hamling, Tara, and Catherine Richardson. *A Day at Home in Early Modern England: Material Culture and Domestic Life, 1500–1700*. New Haven: Yale University Press, 2017.
Harris, Cheryl I. 'Whiteness as Property'. *Harvard Law Review* 106, no. 8 (1993): 1707–91.
Harris, Jonathan Gil. 'The Smell of *Macbeth*'. *Shakespeare Quarterly* 58, no. 4 (2007): 465–86.
Hartman, Saidiya. 'Venus in Two Acts'. *Small Axe* 12, no. 2 (2008): 1–14.
Haynes, Alan. *The White Bear: The Elizabethan Earl of Leicester*. London: Peter Owen, 1987.
Hazlitt, William. *The Round Table and Characters of Shakespeare's Plays*. New York and London: J. M. Dent & Sons, 1936.
Helgerson, Richard. 'Murder in Faversham: Holinshed's Impertinent History'. In *The Historical Imagination in Early Modern Britain: History, Rhetoric, and Fiction, 1500–1800*, edited by Donald R. Kelley and David Harris Sacks, 133–58. Cambridge: Cambridge University Press, 1997.
Heng, Geraldine. *The Invention of Race in the European Middle Ages*. Cambridge: Cambridge University Press, 2018.
Hirrel, Michael J. 'Thomas Watson, Playwright: Origins of Modern English Drama'. In *Lost Plays in Shakespeare's England*, edited by David McInnis and Matthew Steggle, 187–207. New York: Palgrave Macmillan, 2014.
Hitchcock, David. *Vagrancy in English Culture and Society, 1650–1760*. London: Bloomsbury, 2016.
Hobgood, Allison P. *Passionate Playgoing in Early Modern England*. Cambridge: Cambridge University Press, 2014.
Hope, Jonathan. *The Authorship of Shakespeare's Plays: A Socio-Linguistic Study*. Cambridge: Cambridge University Press, 1994.
Hopkins, Lisa. *Burial Plots in British Detective Fiction*. Basingstoke: Palgrave Macmillan, 2021.
Hopkins, Lisa. *Shakespearean Allusion in Crime Fiction: DCI Shakespeare*. Basingstoke: Palgrave Macmillan, 2016.
Hornback, Robert. *The English Clown Tradition from the Middle Ages to Shakespeare*. Cambridge: DS Brewer, 2013.
Hyde, Patricia. *Thomas Arden in Faversham: The Man Behind the Myth*. Faversham: The Faversham Society, 1996.
Hyman, Wendy Beth, and Hillary Eklund, 'Introduction: Making Meaning and Doing Justice with Early Modern Texts'. In *Teaching Social Justice Through Shakespeare: Why Renaissance Literature Matters Now*, edited by Hillary Eklund and Wendy Beth Hyman, 1–23. Edinburgh: Edinburgh University Press, 2019.
'IUPUI Hoosier Bard presents *Arden of Fevershame*: Shakespeare's Clever Spin on a Real-Life Crime'. *IUPUI Newsroom Press Release*,

25 March 2014. Available online: http://archive.news.iupui.edu/releases/2014/03/shakespeare-arden-play.shtml (accessed 16 February 2022).

Jackson, MacDonald P. *Determining the Shakespeare Canon: Arden of Faversham and A Lover's Complaint*. Oxford: Oxford University Press, 2014.

Jackson, MacDonald P. 'Gentle Shakespeare and the Authorship of *Arden of Faversham*'. *The Shakespearean International Yearbook* 11 (2011): 25–40.

Jackson, MacDonald P. 'Material for an Edition of *Arden of Faversham*'. B.Litt. thesis, Oxford University, 1963.

Jackson, MacDonald P. 'One-Horse Races: Some Recent Studies'. In *The New Oxford Shakespeare Authorship Companion*, edited by Gary Taylor and Gabriel Egan, 48–59. Oxford: Oxford University Press, 2017.

Jackson, MacDonald P. 'Review of *Arden of Faversham*, Little Theatre, Auckland, University Theatre Workshop'. *Research Opportunities in Renaissance Drama* 28 (1984): 127.

Jackson, MacDonald P. 'Shakespeare and the Quarrel Scene in *Arden of Faversham*'. *Shakespeare Quarterly* 57, no. 3 (2006): 249–93.

Jackson, MacDonald P. 'Shakespeare, *Arden of Faversham*, and *A Lover's Complaint*: A Review of Reviews'. In *The New Oxford Shakespeare Authorship Companion*, edited by Gary Taylor and Gabriel Egan, 123–34. Oxford: Oxford University Press, 2017.

Jackson, MacDonald P. 'Shakespearean Features of the Poetic Style of *Arden of Faversham*'. *Archiv fur das Studium der Reveren Spracher and Literaturen* 230 (1993): 279–304.

Jed, Stephanie H. *Chaste Thinking: The Rape of Lucretia and the Birth of Humanism*. Bloomington: Indiana University Press, 1989.

Jones, Gwilym. *Shakespeare's Storms*. Manchester: Manchester University Press, 2015.

Kane, Stuart A. 'Wives with Knives: Early Modern Murder Ballads and the Transgressive Commodity'. *Criticism* 38, no. 2 (1996): 219–37.

Karim-Cooper, Farah. *The Hand on the Shakespearean Stage: Gesture, Touch and the Spectacle of Dismemberment*. London: Bloomsbury, 2016.

Kaufmann, Miranda. *Black Tudors: The Untold Story*. London: Oneworld, 2017.

Keenan, Siobhan. *Travelling Players in Shakespeare's England*. Basingstoke: Palgrave Macmillan, 2002.

Keirans, James E. *The John Dickson Carr Companion*. Vancleave, MS: Ramble House, 2015.

King, Ros. '*Arden of Faversham*: The Moral of History and the Thrill of Performance'. In *The Oxford Handbook of Tudor Drama*, edited by Thomas Betteridge and Greg Walker, 635–52. Oxford: Oxford University Press, 2012.

Kinney, Arthur F. 'Authoring *Arden of Faversham*'. In *Shakespeare, Computers, and the Mystery of Authorship*, edited by Hugh Craig and Arthur F. Kinney, 78–99. Cambridge: Cambridge University Press, 2009.

Kirwan, Peter. 'Arden of Faversham @ The Emlyn Williams Theatre, Theatr Clwyd'. *The Bardathon*, 20 February 2010. Available online: http://blogs.nottingham.ac.uk/bardathon/2010/02/20/arden-of-faversham-the-emlyn-williams-theatre-theatr-clwyd/ (accessed 16 February 2022).

Kirwan, Peter. 'Arden of Faversham (Em-Lou Productions) @ The Rose Theatre Bankside'. *The Bardathon*, 23 June 2010. Available online: http://blogs.nottingham.ac.uk/bardathon/2010/06/23/arden-of-faversham-emlou-productions-the-rose-theatre-bankside/ (accessed 16 February 2022).

Kirwan, Peter, editor. 'From Script to Stage'. In *William Shakespeare and Others: Collaborative Plays*, edited by Jonathan Bate and Eric Rasmussen, 748–84. Basingstoke: Palgrave Macmillan, 2013.

Kirwan, Peter. *Shakespeare and the Idea of Apocrypha: Negotiating the Boundaries of the Dramatic Canon*. Cambridge: Cambridge University Press, 2015.

Knutson, Roslyn L. 'Pembroke's Men in 1592–3, Their Repertory and Touring Schedule'. *Early Theatre* 4, no. 1 (2001): 129–38.

Knutson, Roslyn L. 'Shakespeare's Repertory'. In *A Companion to Shakespeare*, edited by David Scott Kastan, 346–61. New York: John Wiley, 1999.

Korda, Natasha. *Shakespeare's Domestic Economies: Gender and Property in Early Modern England*. Philadelphia: University of Pennsylvania Press, 2002.

Kussmaul, Ann. *Servants in Husbandry in Early Modern England*. Cambridge: Cambridge University Press, 1981.

Lake, Peter. 'Deeds Against Nature: Cheap Print, Protestantism and Murder in Early Modern England'. In *Culture and Politics in Early Modern England*, edited by Peter Lake and Kevin Sharpe, 257–83. Stanford: Stanford University Press, 1994.

Lake, Peter, with Michael Questier. *The Antichrist's Lewd Hat: Protestants, Papists and Players in Post-Reformation England*. New Haven: Yale University Press, 2002.

LaPerle, Carol Mejia. 'The Racialized Affects of Ill-Will in the Dark Lady Sonnets'. In *Race & Affect in Early Modern English Literature*, edited by Carol Mejia LaPerle, 205–21. Tempe: ACMRS Press, 2022.

LaPerle, Carol Mejia. 'Rhetorical Situationality: Alice Arden's Kairotic Effect'. *Women's Studies* 39, no. 3 (2010): 175–93.

Lawrence-Mathers, Anne. *Medieval Meteorology: Forecasting the Weather from Aristotle to the Almanac*. Cambridge: Cambridge University Press, 2020.
Leggatt, Alexander. 'Arden of Faversham'. *Shakespeare Survey* 36 (1983): 121–34.
Letts, Quentin. 'Rough Justice of a 16th Century Sort: Quentin Letts Reviews *Arden of Faversham*'. *Daily Mail*, 6 May 2014.
L. G. S. 'Café la Mama'. *Stage and Television Today*, 28 May 1970.
Lin, Erika T. 'Performance Practice and Theatrical Privilege: Rethinking Weimann's Concepts of *Locus* and *Platea*'. *New Theatre Quarterly* 22, no. 3 (2006): 283–98.
Loomba, Ania. *Gender, Race, Renaissance Drama*. Manchester: Manchester University Press, 1989.
Loughnane, Rory, and Andrew J. Power, editors. *Early Shakespeare, 1588–1594*. Cambridge: Cambridge University Press, 2020.
Mack, Gerhard. 'Räuber Hotzenplots: Terry Hands Inszeniert in Zürich *Arden von Faversham*'. *taz*, 13 February 1992.
Madelaine, Richard. '"He speaks very shrewishly": Apprentice-Training and *The Taming of the Shrew*'. In *Gender and Power in Shrew-Taming Narratives, 1500–1700*, edited by David Wootton and Graham Holderness, 70–83. Basingstoke: Palgrave Macmillan, 2010.
Manley, Lawrence. 'Playing with Fire: Immolation in the Repertory of Strange's Men'. *Early Theatre* 4, no. 1 (2001): 115–29.
Martin, Randall. 'Arden Winketh at his Wife's Lewdness, & Why!': A Patrilineal Crisis in *Arden of Faversham*'. *Early Theatre* 4, no. 1 (2001): 13–33.
McAdam, Ian. 'Protestant Manliness in *Arden of Faversham*'. *Texas Studies in Literature and Language* 45, no. 1 (2003): 42–72.
McIlvenna, Una. 'The Power of Music: The Significance of Contrafactum in Execution Ballads'. *Past & Present* 229, no. 1 (2015): 47–89.
McMillin, Scott. 'Casting for Pembroke's Men: The *Henry VI* Quartos and *The Taming of A Shrew*'. *Shakespeare Quarterly* 23, no. 2 (1972): 141–59.
McMillin, Scott. 'The Sharer and His Boy: Rehearsing Shakespeare's Women'. In *From Script to Stage in Early Modern England*, edited by Peter Holland and Stephen Orgel, 231–45. Basingstoke: Palgrave Macmillan, 2004.
McMillin, Scott, and Sally-Beth MacLean. *The Queen's Men and Their Plays*. Cambridge: Cambridge University Press, 1998.
Mendoza, Kirsten N. 'Sexual Violence, Trigger Warnings, and the Early Modern Classroom'. In *Teaching Social Justice Through Shakespeare*, edited by Hillary Eklund and Wendy Beth Hyman, 97–105. Edinburgh: Edinburgh University Press, 2019.

Minton, Eric. 'Shakespeare or Not, This is a Good One'. *Shakespeareances.com*, 14 April 2015. Available online: http://www.shakespeareances.com/willpower/onstage/Arden_Faversham-01-BST15.html (accessed 16 February 2022).

Miskimmin, Esme. 'The Act of Murder: Renaissance Tragedy and the Detective Novel'. In *Reinventing the Renaissance: Shakespeare and his Contemporaries in Adaptation and Performance*, edited by Sarah Annes Brown, Robert I. Lublin and Lynsey McCulloch, 286–300. Basingstoke: Palgrave, 2013.

Morgan, Jennifer L. *Reckoning with Slavery: Gender, Kinship, and Capitalism in the Early Black Atlantic*. Durham: Duke University Press, 2021.

Morgan, Oliver. *Turn-Taking in Shakespeare*. Oxford: Oxford University Press, 2019.

Munro, Lucy. *Shakespeare in the Theatre: The King's Men*. London: Bloomsbury, 2020.

Munro, Lucy. '"*They eat each others' arms*": Stage Blood and Body Parts'. In *Shakespeare's Theatres and the Effects of Performance*, edited by Farah Karim-Cooper and Tiffany Stern, 73–93. London: Bloomsbury, 2013.

Murphy, Neil. 'Violence, Colonization and Henry VIII's Conquest of France, 1544–1546'. *Past and Present* 233, no. 1 (2016): 13–51.

Neill, Michael. "This Gentle Gentleman': Social Change and the Language of Status in *Arden of Faversham*'. *Medieval & Renaissance Drama in England* 10 (1998): 73–97.

Nicholl, Charles. 'Fetch the Chopping Knife'. *London Review of Books* 43, no. 21 (4 November 2021). Available online: https://www.lrb.co.uk/the-paper/v43/n21/charles-nicholl/fetch-the-chopping-knife (accessed 16 February 2022).

Nicholl, Charles. *The Reckoning*, 2nd ed. London: Vintage, 2002.

Nubia, Onyeka. *England's Other Countrymen: Black Tudor Society*. London: Zed Books, 2019.

O'Brien, Emily. '*The Tragedy of Master Arden of Faversham*, True Crime, and the Literary Marketplace of the 1580s'. *Shakespeare Studies* 45 (2017): 113–20.

Olusoga, David. *Black and British: A Forgotten History*. London: Macmillan, 2016.

Orlin, Lena Cowen. 'Man's House as His Castle in *Arden of Feversham*'. *Medieval & Renaissance Drama in England* 2 (1985): 57–89.

Orlin, Lena Cowen. *Private Matters and Public Culture in Post-Reformation England*. Ithaca: Cornell University Press, 1994.

Orth, Maureen. 'A Made-for-Tabloid Murder'. *Vanity Fair*, 1 August 2003. Available online: https://www.vanityfair.com/culture/2003/08/laci200308 (accessed 25 March 2022).

Palfrey, Simon, and Tiffany Stern. *Shakespeare in Parts*. Oxford: Oxford University Press, 2007.
Peter, John. 'Review'. *Sunday Times*, 8 November 1970.
Porter, Eric. 'Dorothy Tutin Brings off a Taxing Role'. *Daily Telegraph*, 7 November 1970.
Price, Eoin. 'Review of *Arden of Faversham* (directed by Polly Findlay for the Royal Shakespeare Company) at the Swan Theatre, Stratford-upon-Avon, 11 August 2014'. *Shakespeare* 11, no. 3 (2015): 319–21.
Radzinowicz, Leon. *A History of English Criminal Law*. London: Stevens, 1948.
Richardson, Catherine. *Domestic Life and Domestic Tragedy in Early Modern England: The Material Life of the Household*. Manchester: Manchester University Press, 2006.
Richardson, Catherine. 'Household Manuals'. In *The Elizabethan Top Ten: Defining Print Popularity in Early Modern England*, edited by Andy Kesson and Emma Smith, 169–78. Farnham: Ashgate, 2013.
Richardson, Catherine. '"Scene of the Murder": Arden of Faversham and Local Performance Cultures'. *Early Modern Literary Studies* 28 (2019).
Rohrer, Melissa. '"Lamentable and True": Remediations of True Crime in Domestic Tragedies'. *Early Modern Literary Studies* 28 (2019).
Salkeld, Duncan. 'Crime'. In *The Ashgate Research Companion to Popular Culture in Early Modern England*, edited by Andrew Hadfield, Matthew Dimmock and Abigail Shinn, 193–206. Farnham: Ashgate, 2014.
Salkeld, Duncan. 'Shakespeare in *Arden*: Pragmatic Markers and Parallels'. *Shakespeare Survey* 76 (2023): forthcoming.
Sanders, Julie. *The Cultural Geography of Early Modern Drama, 1620–1650*. Cambridge: Cambridge University Press, 2011.
Schafer, Elizabeth. 'Troublesome Histories: Performance and Early Modern Drama'. In *The Cambridge Companion to Shakespeare and Contemporary Dramatists*, edited by Ton Hoenselaars, 244–68. Cambridge: Cambridge University Press, 2012.
Schlegel, A. W. *A Course of Lectures on Dramatic Art and Literature*, translated by John Black. London: Henry G. Bohn, 1846.
Schutzman, Julie R. 'Alice Arden's Freedom and the Suspended Moment of *Arden of Faversham*'. *Studies in English Literature, 1500–1900* 36, no. 2 (1996): 289–314.
Schwarz, Kathryn. *What You Will: Gender, Contract, and Shakespearean Social Space*. Philadelphia: University of Pennsylvania Press, 2011.
Sharpe, J. A. 'Domestic Homicide in Early Modern England'. *The Historical Journal* 24, no. 1 (1981): 29–48.
Sharpe, Will. 'Authorship and Attribution'. In *William Shakespeare and Others: Collaborative Plays*, edited by Jonathan Bate and Eric Rasmussen, 641–745. Basingstoke: Palgrave Macmillan, 2013.

Sheeha, Iman. *Household Servants in Early Modern Domestic Tragedy*. New York: Routledge, 2020.
Sheeha, Iman. '"Looke in the place where he was wont to sit / See see his blood it is too manifest": Domestic Space and Patriarchal Authority in *The Tragedy of Master Arden of Faversham* (1592)'. *Early Modern Literary Studies* 28 (2019).
Shuttleworth, Ian. '*Arden of Faversham*, Arden's House, Faversham, Kent'. *Financial Times*, undated. Available online: http://www.cix.co.uk/~shutters/reviews/00139.htm (accessed 23 March 2022).
Shuttleworth, Ian. '*Arden of Faversham*, Swan Theatre, Stratford-upon-Avon – Review'. *Financial Times*, 7 May 2014.
Smith, Ian. *Race and Rhetoric in the Renaissance: Barbarian Errors*. New York: Palgrave MacMillan, 2009.
Smith, Peter J. 'Inaugurating the Complete Works (again): Shakespeare Nation, Doranism and Literalism in the Royal Shakespeare Company's 2014 Summer Season'. *Cahiers Élisabéthains* 89, no. 1 (2016): 58–73.
Smith, Steven R. 'The London Apprentices as Seventeenth-Century Adolescents'. *Past and Present* 61, no. 1 (1973): 149–61.
Spooner, Aaron. 'Shakespeare's Itinerant Soldiers and Foreign Wars: The Elizabethan Crisis of Debt in the Economy of Hal's England'. *Journal for Early Modern Cultural Studies* 12, no. 1 (2012): 49–84.
Stallybrass, Peter, and Allon White. *The Politics and Poetics of Transgression*. Ithaca: Cornell University Press, 1986.
Stanivukovic, Goran. 'The Language and Style of Early Shakespeare'. In *Early Shakespeare, 1588–1594*, edited by Rory Loughnane and Andrew J. Power, 76–101. Cambridge: Cambridge University Press, 2020.
Starner, Janet Wright, and Barbara Howard Traister. 'Introduction'. In *Anonymity in Early Modern Drama: "What's in a Name?"*, edited by Janet Wright Starner and Barbara Howard Traister, 1–10. Farnham: Ashgate, 2014.
Staub, Susan C. 'Bloody Relations: Murderous Wives in the Street Literature of Seventeenth Century England'. In *Domestic Arrangements in Early Modern England*, edited by Kari Boyd McBride, 124–46. Pittsburgh: Duquesne University Press, 2002.
Stern, Tiffany. *Making Shakespeare: From Stage to Page*. London: Routledge, 2004.
Stern, Tiffany. *Rehearsal from Shakespeare to Sheridan*. Oxford: Oxford University Press, 2000.
Stern, Tiffany. 'Shakespeare the Balladmonger?' In *Rethinking Theatrical Documents in Shakespeare's England*, edited by Tiffany Stern, 216–38. London: Bloomsbury, 2020.
Stern, Tiffany. '"This Wide and Universal Theatre": The Theatre as Prop in Shakespeare's Metadrama'. In *Shakespeare's Theatres and the*

Effects of Performance, edited by Farah Karim-Cooper and Tiffany Stern, 11–32. London: Bloomsbury, 2015.
Stewart, Alan. *Shakespeare's Letters*. Oxford: Oxford University Press, 2008.
Stodder, Joseph H. 'Three Apocryphal Plays'. *Shakespeare Quarterly* 38, no. 2 (1987): 243–8.
Stone, Lawrence. *The Family, Sex and Marriage in England, 1500–1800*. London: Penguin, 1977.
Sullivan, Garrett A., Jr. "Arden Lay Murdered in that Plot of Ground': Surveying, Land, and *Arden of Faversham*'. *ELH* 61, no. 2 (1994): 231–52.
Sullivan, Garrett A., Jr. *The Drama of Landscape: Land, Property, and Social Relations on the Early Modern Stage*. Stanford: Stanford University Press, 1998.
Swinburne, A. C. *A Study of Shakespeare*. London: Chatto & Windus, 1880.
Symonds, John Addington. *Shakspere's Predecessors in the English Drama*. London: Smith, Elder & Co., 1884.
Tarlinskaja, Marina. *Shakespeare and the Versification of English Drama, 1561–1642*. Farnham: Ashgate, 2014.
Taylor, Gary. 'Shakespeare, *Arden of Faversham*, and Four Forgotten Playwrights'. *Review of English Studies* 71, no. 302 (2020): 867–95.
Taylor, Gary, and Rory Loughnane. 'The Canon and Chronology of Shakespeare's Works'. In *The New Oxford Shakespeare Authorship Companion*, edited by Gary Taylor and Gabriel Egan, 417–602. Oxford: Oxford University Press, 2017.
Thacker, John. '*The Tragedy of Master Arden of Faversham* Review at White Bear, London'. *The Stage*, 15 August 2006.
Thomas, Philip. 'Military Mayhem in Elizabethan Chester: The Privy Council's Response to Vagrant Soldiers'. *Journal of the Society for Army Historical Research* 76, no. 308 (1998): 226–47.
Thompson, Ayanna. *Performing Race and Torture on the Early Modern Stage*. New York: Routledge, 2008.
Traub, Valerie. *Desire and Anxiety: Circulations of Sexuality in Shakespearean Drama*. London: Routledge, 1992.
Travitsky, Betty S. 'Husband-Murder and Petty Treason in English Renaissance Tragedy'. *Renaissance Drama* 21 (1991): 171–98.
Trewin, J. C. 'The World of the Theatre: Fun and Games'. *Illustrated London News*, 23 February 1963, 28.
Trewin, J. C. 'The World of the Theatre, Our Critic's First Night Journal'. *Illustrated London News*, 21 May 1955, 936.
Tynan, Kenneth. *Curtains: Selections from the Drama Criticism and Related Writings*. London: Longmans, 1961.

Vaughan, Virginia Mason. *Performing Blackness on English Stages, 1500–1800*. Cambridge: Cambridge University Press, 2005.
Vickers, Brian. 'Authorship Candidates for *Arden of Faversham*: Kyd, Shakespeare, and Thomas Watson'. *Studies in Philology* 118, no. 2 (2021): 308–41.
Vickers, Brian. 'Verbal Repetition in *Arden of Faversham*: Shakespeare or Kyd?'. *Notes and Queries* 65, no. 4 (2018): 498–502.
Wall, Stephen. 'Black Will and Shakebag'. *Times Literary Supplement*, 16 April 1982.
Walsham, Alexandra. *The Reformation of the Landscape: Religion, Identity, and Memory in Early Modern Britain and Ireland*. Oxford: Oxford University Press, 2012.
Walsham, Alexandra. 'Sermons in the Sky: Apparitions in Early Modern Europe'. *History Today* 51, no. 4 (2001): 56–63.
Wardle, Irving. 'Brutality as Genial Farce'. *The Times*, 1 April 1982.
Weimann, Robert. *Author's Pen and Actor's Voice: Playing and Writing in Shakespeare's Theatre*, edited by Helen Higbee and William N. West. Cambridge: Cambridge University Press, 2000.
Whigham, Frank. *Seizures of the Will in Early Modern English Drama*. Cambridge: Cambridge University Press, 1996.
Whipday, Emma. 'Everyday Murder and Household Work in Shakespeare's Domestic Tragedies'. In *Staged Normality in Shakespeare's England*, edited by Rory Loughnane and Edel Semple, 215–36. London: Palgrave, 2019.
Whipday, Emma. "Marrow Prying Neighbours': Staging Domestic Space and Neighbourhood Surveillance in *Arden of Faversham*'. *Cahiers Élisabéthains* 88, no. 1 (2015): 95–110.
Whipday, Emma. 'The Picture of a Woman: Roaring Girls and Alternative Histories in the RSC 2014 Season'. *Shakespeare* 11, no. 3 (2015): 272–85.
Whipday, Emma. *Shakespeare's Domestic Tragedies: Violence in the Early Modern Home*. Cambridge: Cambridge University Press, 2019.
Whipday, Emma. '"Thou Look'st Pale": Narrating Blanching and Blushing on the Early Modern Stage'. In *Playing and Playgoing in Early Modern England: Actor, Audience and Performance*, edited by Simon Smith and Emma Whipday, 37–56. Cambridge: Cambridge University Press, 2022.
Wickham, Glynne. 'Hell-Castle and its Door-Keeper'. *Shakespeare Survey* 19 (1967): 68–74.
Wiggins, Martin. *Journeymen in Murder: The Assassin in English Renaissance Drama*. Oxford: Clarendon Press, 1991.
Wiggins, Martin, with Catherine Richardson. *British Drama 1533–1642: A Catalogue*, vol. III. Oxford: Oxford University Press, 2013.

Williamson, Elizabeth. 'The Uses and Abuses of Prayer Book Properties in *Hamlet*, *Richard III*, and *Arden of Faversham*'. *ELR* 39, no. 2 (2009): 371–95.
Wren, Celia. '*Arden of Faversham*: Killing Time (and a Man) in an Entertaining Way'. *Washington Post*, 10 April 2015. Available online: https://www.washingtonpost.com/entertainment/theater_dance/arden-of-faversham-killing-time-and-a-man-in-an-entertaining-way/2015/04/08/eacbc186-dc84-11e4-b6d7-b9bc8acf16f7_story.html?utm_term=.e2c67b6d8850 (accessed 16 February 2022).
Youngblood, Sarah. 'Theme and Imagery in *Arden of Faversham*.' *Studies in English Literature, 1500–1900* 3, no. 2 (1963): 207–18.
Zeydel, Edwin H. 'Ludwig Tieck as a Translator of English'. *PMLA* 51, no. 1 (1936): 221–42.

INDEX

Abbey of Faversham 12, 31, 119, 177–80, 193–4, 197
absence 29, 98, 100
abuse (emotional/domestic) 28, 202, 204, 210, 216–18
Adams, Brandi K. 2, 8, 9, 206
Adams, Henry Hitch 29, 38, 212, 213
Adams, John Henry 75, 87
adaptation 19, 42, 57–60, 143, 145, 147, 152, 164
Admiral's Men 122
adultery 17, 36, 91, 98, 99, 111, 199
Aeschylus 175, 187, 188
Afghanistan 59
Africa 148–50, 167, 205, 206
Agamemnon 17, 175, 187
agency 28, 71, 76, 80, 81, 98, 105, 108, 110–12, 156, 179, 199, 200, 213
Agutter, Jenny 46, 62
Akhimie, Patricia 9, 160, 167, 207
Allde, Edward 4, 5, 18
Allde, Elizabeth 4, 18
Antidote to Venom 169, 170, 179, 183, 186
anxieties 7, 10, 24, 34, 107, 129, 153, 184, 197, 204, 208, 212
apocryphal plays 20, 22, 24, 36, 37, 50, 51, 81, 211, 213

apprenticeship 8, 95, 105, 109, 111, 115, 215
Archer, Edward 19
Archer, Ian W. 146, 165, 209
archives 148–53, 163–4, 166, 211
Arden, Alice. *See Arden of Faversham* characters
Arden, Thomas. *See Arden of Faversham* characters
Arden of Faversham characters
  Arden, Alice (character) 3, 6–8, 16–18, 24–8, 30, 32, 42–54, 57–9, 60, 68, 77, 79–80, 91–4, 96–101, 104–11, 126–7, 130, 131, 145, 157, 158–62, 173–7, 179–80, 182–3, 186–7, 200–3, 207, 210, 213, 217, 218
  Arden, Thomas (character) 5, 10, 26, 28, 31, 45, 47, 55–60, 69–71, 75, 93, 97–8, 100, 101, 104, 106, 120–4, 126–30, 132, 135, 143–7, 152, 155, 157–8, 174, 178–80, 182–3, 185–6, 193, 195, 196, 198, 200, 203, 205, 206, 212, 213, 216
  Arden, Thomas (historical figure) 2, 30, 68, 119, 137, 183, 188, 192–5, 203, 216
  Black Will 2–4, 8–9, 34, 46–88, 101–2, 104, 112, 119–28, 133, 135, 143–67,

INDEX

173, 176, 180, 184, 185, 206, 208–9
Bradshaw, George   3, 51, 106, 152–6, 176, 185, 208, 211
Cheyne, Lord   31, 153, 157, 180
Clarke (painter)   1, 48, 49, 52, 75, 93, 97–100, 103, 161, 213
Clifford, Lord   194
Ferryman   9, 42, 124–5, 127, 133, 135
Fitten, Jack   152, 153
Fowle, Adam   51, 106
Franklin   1, 12, 15, 31, 46, 54, 56, 60, 107, 120, 125–7, 129–35, 172, 173, 177
Greene   2, 3, 18, 28, 51, 56, 59, 60, 84, 100, 107, 132, 153–6, 158, 160, 178, 194, 196, 197, 203, 208
Mayor of Faversham   55, 110, 129, 130, 161, 162, 184, 210
Michael (Saunderson)   3, 51, 52, 56, 60, 77, 92, 93, 96–9, 101–11, 126, 132, 133, 155–7, 159, 161, 183–5, 196, 203, 213
Mosby, Thomas   3, 8, 10, 25, 26, 28, 32–4, 44–5, 47–8, 52–5, 57–8, 60, 70, 73, 76, 79, 86, 92–4, 96–101, 105–8, 110–11, 119, 126–7, 130–2, 158–62, 173–6, 178–9, 182–4, 193–4, 196, 200, 203, 206–7, 213, 217–18
Reede, Dick   45–6, 56, 132, 179, 194, 197, 199, 203–4, 210
Shakebag (also 'Loosebag'), George   2–5, 12, 34, 46–8,
50–1, 53, 55–7, 59, 60, 79, 101–2, 104, 112, 120, 122–4, 129, 131, 133, 135, 143–4, 154–8, 161, 163, 173, 176, 210
Susan   5, 8, 48, 52, 77, 91–115, 131, 141, 145, 185–6, 189, 196, 203, 213
Arraignment of Paris, The   19, 21
Atchyson, George   151
Atlanta Shakespeare Company   53
atmosphere   47, 49, 120, 123, 125–7, 129, 132, 133
authority   1, 7, 17, 28, 55, 72–4, 80, 91–6, 101, 103, 108, 109, 112, 185, 194, 201, 202, 204, 207, 212, 213
authorship   4, 6, 8–12, 19, 22, 24, 26, 35, 48–50, 59, 68, 80–4, 88, 89, 136, 169, 181

backgammon ('tables')   3, 5, 6, 70, 74, 104
Balizet, Ariane M.   73, 86, 105, 114
ballad   5, 6, 13, 17, 18, 41, 112, 113, 128, 195, 216
Barber, John   46, 62
Bars Closel, Régis Augustus   68, 69, 85
Bate, Jonathan   14, 53, 62, 82, 88, 140
BBC   43, 61
Beech, Master   4, 5
Beech's Tragedy   183
Belsey, Catherine   7, 13, 27, 29, 37, 38, 187, 201, 202
Best, George   207
betrayal   18, 92, 101, 103, 107, 120, 131, 155, 199
betrothal   96–101

Billington, Michael   76, 87
Birdseye, Cheryl   80, 88, 181, 188
Birth of Merlin, The   21
Blackborne, William   3
blackface   144
Blackfriars   57
Blackness   8, 143–67, 207–8. *See also whiteness*
blood/bleeding   1, 3, 16, 25–6, 28, 33, 35, 47, 55, 73, 74, 81, 92, 102–14, 129–30, 182–4, 207, 209–10
Bloom, Gina   70, 74, 85, 86
Blundeville, Thomas   38
blushing   26, 27, 99–100, 114, 145, 159, 165, 167, 210
Bluwal, Marc   48
Bodin, Jean   203–4
Bones, Ken   46, 62
Book of Common Prayer, The   96, 114, 201–2
bookshop shutter   144
Boulogne   153, 176, 208–9
Bourus, Terri   7, 14, 15, 52–3, 56, 63, 85
Bovilsky, Laura   201–2
boy actors   92–3, 96, 105, 108, 113, 114
Bradley, Kath   6–8, 11, 41–66, 76, 138
Bradshaw, George. *See Arden of Faversham* characters
Bradshaw, Richard   176
Brave Spirits Theatre Company   55
Breviat Chronicle   196
Brigandine, Robert   176
Bristol Revunions   49
Brodie, Elspeth   52
Brome, Richard   68, 138
Brown, Barbara   44
Brown, David Sterling   8, 13

Browne, George   4, 181
Bucharest   48–9
Burghley, William Cecil, Lord   151, 166
Burns, Beth   51, 63
Burton, Robert   126, 139, 140

Calverley, Walter   5
Canterbury   3, 18, 137
Capell, Edward   21
Carr, John Dickson   171, 184, 186–7, 189
Case is Closed, The   185, 189
Catholicism   128, 129, 177, 179, 182
Ceauşescu, Nicolae   49
Chakravarty, Urvashi   146, 165
Charon   9, 125
Cheyne (also 'Cheiny'), Lord Thomas. *See Arden of Faversham* characters
Christensen, Ann   70–1, 86
Christie, Agatha   183, 185, 189
Chronicles of England, Scotland, and Ireland (Holinshed, Raphael)   9, 14, 15, 28, 31, 35, 36, 41, 119, 121, 130, 137, 143, 146, 147, 152–4, 165–7, 193–5, 197, 200–1, 216
Ciccarelli, John   53, 54
Clark, Glenn   79, 80, 87
Clark, Sandra   79, 87, 140, 180, 181, 183, 188
Clarke. *See Arden of Faversham* characters
class   7, 31, 43, 46, 55, 56, 60, 100, 111, 154, 160, 200–1, 207
Classics on a Shoestring   44
Clifford, Lord. *See Arden of Faversham* characters
Clytemnestra   17, 175, 186, 187

Cocker, Joe   47
Coke, Sir Edward   201
Collier, John Payne   23
Comedy of Errors, The   42, 207
Comensoli, Viviana   38, 71, 72, 86, 213
community   2, 31, 71, 74, 144, 152, 154, 157, 160, 161, 164, 209, 212
Complaint and Lamentation of Mistresse Arden of Feversham of Kent, The. See ballad
conspiracy   30, 34, 45, 51, 52, 54, 101, 131–2, 161
contagion   146, 155
contamination   17, 21, 154
contracts   96–8, 100, 144, 148, 200
Court of Augmentations   31, 193
courtship   98, 103, 213
crime   3–5, 8, 13, 18, 24–5, 27, 29, 30, 73, 78–9, 81, 91–3, 101, 104–8, 142, 147, 154–5, 158, 161–5, 193, 195, 201–2, 205, 211, 216, 218
crime fiction   169–89, 215
crops   118, 198
Croydon, The 12.30 from   169–73, 183, 186, 187
Cruel Murder Done in Kent, A   15, 176
cruentation   73, 209–11
cuckoldry   28, 94
cues   95, 103, 125, 128, 148

Dalton, Michael   209
Daniel, Robert W.   7, 13
Dawson, Giles   138
Dawson, Lesel   210, 211

Deadly Wives (TV series)   215
de Certeau, Michel   69
Dekker, Thomas   5, 45, 124, 139
Dessen, Alan C.   122, 124, 126, 138–40
detective fiction   2, 9, 52, 168–89
deviance   192, 199–200
Dissolution of the monasteries   31, 176–8, 193
divine will or agency   9, 18, 45, 118–20, 125, 128, 130, 134–5, 210
divorce   27, 180
Doctor Faustus   125, 139, 180, 182, 186
Dolan, Frances E.   28–30, 38, 112, 113, 202, 205, 213, 216
domestic abuse   28
domestic tragedy   4, 6–8, 13, 19, 21, 29, 32, 38, 39, 43, 48, 49, 52, 53, 68, 70–5, 78–9, 81–2, 85–8
Donna Reed Show, The   53
Doran, Gregory   49, 61
dowry   97, 98, 159
dramaturgy   52, 71, 72, 76, 80, 81, 84, 95, 100, 103, 109, 120, 130
Duchess of Malfi, The   171, 172, 178, 188, 189
Durban, Kim   58, 64

Edward II   42
Edward III   21, 50
Eklund, Hillary   191–3, 218
Elizabeth I   17, 175
Elliott, Jack   83, 88
Em–Lou Productions   47, 62
Epilogue   1, 5, 12, 15, 16, 18, 19, 31, 45, 47, 54, 84, 129, 132, 133, 179, 199, 210

Erickson, Peter   145, 165
erotic desire   32, 201
Espinosa, Reuben   206, 207
Essex (county)   214, 215
Eure, Ralph, 3rd Baron   151, 166
executions   13, 29, 110, 184, 185, 211

fair/fairness   145, 158–60, 162
Fair Em   21
Faversham (Kent)   3, 20, 31, 42, 48, 69, 117, 122, 130, 134, 158, 161, 163, 176, 178–80, 193–5, 206
fear   17, 33, 44, 102, 103, 106, 129, 156, 181
feminism   7, 13, 27, 29, 43–6, 56, 60, 67, 76, 172, 216
Fenner, Dudley   94, 113
Ferryman. *See Arden of Faversham* characters
fictionalization   152
Fields, Barbara   206
Fields, Karen   206
film noir   52, 56, 57
Finch, Adrianne   43
Findlay, Polly   45–7, 49, 51, 52, 54, 60, 62, 67, 68, 76, 87, 182
Fitten, Jack. *See Arden of Faversham* characters
Flinders, Polly   172
Flower-de-Luce (inn)   51
Floyd-Wilson, Mary   75, 86, 211
Flushing (Vlissingen)   3, 162, 185, 196
fog (also 'mist')   2, 9, 49, 52, 117–41
footprints   103, 130–2, 134, 170, 172, 183, 184
'Fortune my Foe'   6
Fowle, Adam. *See Arden of Faversham* characters

Franklin. *See Arden of Faversham* characters
Freebury-Jones, Darren   83, 89
Friar Bacon and Friar Bungay   125, 139
friendship   156, 161
Froide, Amy   93, 113
Fuentes, Marisa   149, 166
Fulke, William   118, 121, 136–8

Galgoțiu, Dragoș   48–9
Garner, Ian   42
gender   2, 43, 44, 46, 55–6, 58–60, 72, 74, 80, 100, 111, 115, 165, 166, 199, 200, 207, 211
genre   4–10, 13, 24, 29, 52, 68, 70, 72, 75, 78, 113, 152, 181, 186, 192, 195, 211–14
Gillet, Louis   34
Goodbody, Buzz   44, 76
Gouge, William   72, 94, 95, 100, 113, 217
Gray's Inn   194
Great Gatsby, The (film)   51
Greatley-Hirsch, Brett   83, 88
Green, Douglas   56, 64
Greene. *See Arden of Faversham* characters
Greene, Douglas G.   171, 187
Greene, Robert   139
Griffin, Brett   53
Gruber, Elizabeth D.   69, 85
Grupo Filologica Inglesa   59, 65

Habib, Imtiaz   149, 166, 205–7
Hall, Kim F.   9, 146, 157, 158, 165, 167, 207
Hallett, Victor   46, 62
Halliwell, J. O.   23
Hamling, Tara   85, 104, 114
Hands, Terry   46–8, 62
Harris, Cheryl L.   157, 158, 167

Hartman, Saidiya   149, 166
Hayloft Project, The   58, 59, 64
Hazlitt, William   22, 37
Heal, Felicity   146, 165
Helgerson, Richard   30, 38, 78, 87, 88
hell   9, 123–9, 135, 156
Heng, Geraldine   206, 207
Henry IV   44
Henry V   181, 188
Henry VII   22
Henry VIII, 31, 119, 163, 176, 205, 208, 209
Heywood, Thomas   53, 196
Hidden Room, The   51, 56, 63
hierarchy   146, 207
Hirrell, Michael   84
HMS Griffin   150, 166
Hoadley, John   19, 42
Holinshed, Raphael   3, 4, 6, 14–18, 48, 119, 130, 131, 135, 137, 138, 140, 145, 146, 152, 165–7, 194, 200, 207
Holtier, Vittorio   49, 63
'Homicide'   4
homicide   10, 192, 204, 214–16
homosociality   77, 97, 161
Hoosier Bard Group   52
Hopkins, Lisa   2, 9, 186, 187
Hopley, Lizzie   45
Hornback, Robert H.   144, 165
hospitality   34, 74, 92, 147
household   7, 30, 31, 70–4, 81, 86, 92–7, 99, 101, 104, 108, 112–14, 121, 131, 133, 137, 169, 172, 174, 182, 193, 194, 202, 203, 205, 212–15
Hudson Shakespeare Company   53
Hughes, Michael   43
humour   6, 42, 47, 53, 125, 127, 163, 214

Huntingdon, 3rd Earl of (Henry Hastings)   197
huswifery   95
Hyman, Wendy Beth   191

Iamandi, Cristina   48
Iberia   10
identity   69–72, 76, 108, 111, 134, 147, 149, 151–3, 158, 159, 183
I'm with Her   57
injury   5, 54, 60, 104, 118, 144, 163, 184, 208
intimacy   72, 97, 154–6, 161, 216–18
Iphigenia   175
Islam   10

Jackson, MacDonald P.   33–5, 39, 58, 64, 82–3, 88, 89
Jacob, Edward   20, 21, 36
Jayawardena, Tony   47
joining of hands   96
Jonson, Ben   5, 22
Jovial Crew, The   68
Julius Caesar   181
justice   10, 45, 46, 85, 170, 184, 185, 191, 192, 200, 204, 205, 209–11

Kardashian, Kim   51
Keck, Emily Gruber   51
Kent   1, 3–5, 7, 15, 17, 20, 41, 48, 55, 56, 61, 71, 84, 91, 117, 119, 120, 122–5, 127, 135, 137, 138, 173, 174, 176, 196, 213
Kentish Post, The   42
Kewes, Paulina   146
King, Ros   93, 113
Kingsley-Smith, Jane   1, 6–8, 10, 12, 15–39, 68, 71, 83, 136, 137, 141

Kinney, Arthur F.   35, 83
Kirwan, Peter   11, 14, 21, 36, 47, 48, 62, 80, 88, 127, 140, 212, 213
Knight, Charles   23, 37
Knutson, Roslyn Lander   41, 60, 139
Kyd, Thomas   11, 50, 83, 84, 89, 125, 139, 141

Lake, Peter   119, 130, 136, 140, 141, 213
La Mama Experimental Theatre   57, 64
Lambarde, William   122, 123, 138, 139
land and land ownership   1, 7, 9, 12, 18, 22, 30–1, 45–6, 49, 56, 57, 68–71, 119, 132, 139, 147, 158, 161, 177–9, 193–4, 197–9, 203–4, 207
landscape   9, 30, 71, 85, 92, 119–24, 127, 133, 135–6, 160, 182
language   7, 23, 26, 32–4, 39, 60, 82, 156, 157, 159, 183, 184, 204
LaPerle, Carol Mejia   79, 80, 87, 88, 155, 167
Law, Phyllida   44
Lawrence-Mathers, Anne   134, 141
Lemnius, Levinus   126, 139
letters   97, 101, 127, 155, 185
Lillo, George   19, 42
Little Theatre   58, 64
Littlewood, Joan   43, 60, 76, 77
Liverpool   148, 150
locatedness   8, 68, 85
London   3, 4, 29, 31, 43–4, 57, 60, 69, 71, 84, 120, 127, 163–4, 181, 196

Loosebag, George (Shakebag). *See Arden of Faversham* characters
Loughnane, Rory   36, 83, 88, 113
Louis XII   177
Love's Labour's Lost   34, 167
Low countries   3
lust   1, 4, 6, 19, 35, 44, 49, 56, 74, 143, 146, 173, 203, 204
Lyly, John   84, 89, 175

Macbeth   8, 20, 25, 26, 33, 81, 127, 140, 170
Macbeth, Lady   25, 26, 33
McClellan, Bennett E.   50
Machyn, Henry   3, 12, 165, 196, 218
Mack, Gerhard   47, 62
Madelaine, Richard   108, 115
Manea, Aureliu   48
Margate Stage Company   43
mariticide   7, 160
Marlowe, Christopher   11, 50, 83, 84, 139, 174, 180
marriage   5, 7, 27, 52, 59, 91, 94, 96, 98, 100, 107, 110, 112, 145–6, 159, 171, 174, 177, 199–201, 203
marshes/marshland   121–3, 138
Mary Rose, The   176–7
masculinity (also 'manhood')   23, 77, 87, 108, 146, 164
Mayor, Lord. *See Arden of Faversham* characters
medical (also 'medical records')   123, 150, 151, 166
Mendoza, Kirsten N.   9–10, 191–218
Merry Devil of Edmonton, The   21, 51
meteorology. *See weather*

#MeToo 56
Metropolitan Playhouse. 54
Michael (Saunderson). *See Arden of Faversham* characters
Middlesex County Sessions records 214, 216
Middleton, Thomas 5, 13, 45
Midsummer Night's Dream, A 95
Minton, Eric 55–6, 64
Mirfyn, Alice 193
Miseries of Enforced Marriage, The 5
Miskimmin, Esme 172, 187
mist. *See fog*
Mitchell, Katie 44, 55, 76, 77
Morgan, Jennifer 149, 166
Morgan, Oliver 108, 115
Mosby (also 'Morsby'), Thomas. *See Arden of Faversham* characters
mourning 111
Mucedorus 21, 51
Munro, Lucy 35, 115, 130, 140
Murderous Michael 15, 137

Nashe, Thomas 127, 140
National Archives, Kew 148–50
neighbours 18, 28, 31, 45, 51, 52, 81, 104, 131, 133
Neill, Michael 32, 39, 112
New, Chris 44
Nicholl, Charles 13, 181–3, 188–9
North, 2nd Baron (Roger North) 176
North, Sir Edward 31
Northumberland archives 151, 166

obedience 72, 93, 95, 99, 112, 199, 201, 203, 207
O'Brien, Emily 4, 13, 136, 137

Odeon Theatre, Bucharest 48, 62
Orestes 175, 176
Orlin, Lena Cowen 30, 38, 71, 86, 132, 136, 137, 139, 141, 177, 187, 188, 199, 212
Othello 20, 161, 200–1
Overthrow of Stage-Plays, The 17
Ovid 173, 174, 176

Page of Plymouth 5
Painter (Clarke). *See Arden of Faversham* characters
parody 96, 99, 104
part (actor's) 95–110
Peake, Maxine 44
Pembroke's Men 41, 122–3, 138–9
Pericles 26
petty treason 30, 38, 91–2, 112, 113, 181, 187, 199, 201, 202, 216
Pintilie, Lucian 48
playgoers 120, 121, 124–6, 128, 129, 132, 133, 192, 195, 199
Ploieste State Theatre, Romania 48
plots 3, 9, 52, 57, 69, 70, 92, 94, 99, 101, 107, 110, 152, 158, 159, 176, 211–13
Plutarch 176, 194
Ponder, Cecily 3, 92, 93
Porter, Eric 44, 61
Postgate, Raymond 176
Potter, Samantha 44
practice as research 95
Preedy, Chloe Kathleen 9, 117–41, 179
Presley, Elvis 53
Prolusions, or, Select Pieces of Antient Poetry 21
property 10, 31, 32, 59, 73, 94, 158, 197–9, 201, 203, 204, 212, 213

props   74–7
providence   9, 118, 120, 134
PTSD   55
Puritan, The   50

Queen's Men, The   122, 138, 140
Questier, Michael   119, 130, 136, 140, 141

race   8–9, 143–67, 191–218
racialized language   144, 157, 164
racial otherness   8, 13, 145, 147, 150, 152, 154, 160
Raikes, Raymond   43
Rainolds, John   17, 125, 139, 187
rape   56, 202–4, 209
Rape of Lucrece, The   34
Rasmussen, Eric   53, 62, 82, 88, 139
Reede, Dick. *See Arden of Faversham* characters
Reformation, The   68, 75, 119, 127, 133, 176–8, 181, 186
repetition   16, 35
Resurgens Theatre Company, The   53
Richards, Jennifer   109, 115
Richardson, Catherine   6–11, 13, 42, 61, 67, 85, 86, 104, 113, 114, 123, 133, 136, 138–41, 144, 163–5, 167, 182–4, 189, 195, 214
Riddle, Nesta   172
Roaring Girl, The   45
Roberts, John   4
Robsart, Amy   175, 176
Roe, Alex   54, 64
Romney Marsh   122
Rose Theatre, Bankside   47, 62
Rowe, Nicholas   20
Rowley, Samuel   11, 45, 148, 162–4, 167

Royal Shakespeare Company   44–7, 49, 54, 60, 61, 67, 82, 87
rural life   49, 127, 206
Rydley (also Ridley) William   151–3

St. Valentine's Day   3
Salkeld, Duncan   1–14, 131, 141, 165, 214
Sanders, George   4, 181
San Francisco Bay Area   197
Satan   125
Schutzman, Julie R.   28, 29, 38
Scrope, Mary (Lady)   194
Serban, Andrei   57
service/servants   10, 51, 77, 92–112, 125, 142, 200–5, 210–16
sexuality   45, 111, 200, 206, 207
sexual transgression   32, 99, 201, 203, 212, 217, 218
Seymour, Jane   177
Shafer, Elizabeth   76
Shakebag. *See Arden of Faversham* characters
Sharpe, J. A.   214–16
Sharpe, Will   11, 14, 82, 88
Sheeha, Imam   7, 13, 73, 86, 93, 95, 99, 113, 114, 179, 188, 203, 205
Sheppey, Isle of   120, 122, 138
Short, John   151, 152
Shuttleworth, Ian   42, 61, 87
siblings   92–4
Simon, Zoe   44
Simpson, Jay   47
Simpson, Nicole   54
Simpson, O. J.   54
singlewomen   93, 113
Six Bookes of a Commonweale   203–4

Skin and Bones Theatre
  Company 44
slavery 148, 149, 165, 166
slut-shaming 217
Small, Sharon 45
Smith, Ian 9, 147, 166
Smithfield, London 3, 35, 196
smoke and fire 121, 124–6
snow 3, 9, 76, 103, 107, 119,
  120, 129–33, 170, 183, 184
social relationships 68, 198, 209
socioeconomic tensions 31, 173
Somerset, 1ˢᵗ Duke of (Edward
  Seymour) 177
Southwark 5, 12, 210
Spanish Armada 30, 134, 208
Speed, John 122, 138
Spevack, Melodee 50
Stafford, Elizabeth 3, 92, 93, 196
stage directions 5, 84, 105, 106,
  108, 109, 148
Starner, Janet Wright 10, 14
Stationers' Register 15, 18, 34, 137
Staub, Susan C. 104, 114
stereotypes 18, 68, 153, 200
Stern, Tiffany 5, 13, 35, 95, 109,
  113, 139, 140
Stilliard ('Steelyard'), the 163
Stockbury, Kent 117–19
Stodder, Joseph H. 50, 63
Stow, John 48, 130–2, 137, 141,
  196
Strange's Men 122, 138, 139
Sturgess, Keith 29, 34, 35, 38, 39
Sullivan, Garrett A. 31, 39, 68,
  86, 132, 136, 139, 141, 165,
  198, 199
Susan. *See Arden of Faversham*
  characters
Sussex's Men 122
'swart' 145–7, 152, 165, 200
Swinburne, Charles Algernon 23,
  25–7, 37, 183

tables (backgammon) 5, 104
Talking Heads, The 57
Taming of the Shrew, The 34,
  108, 115, 139
Tarlinskaja, Marina 82, 83, 88
Taylor, Gary 13, 14, 52, 53, 63,
  83–5, 88, 89
Taylor, John 36, 197
teaching (also 'pedagogy') 191–
  218
Thames Street 4
Theatr Clwyd Cymru 46, 62
Theatre de Ville, Paris 48
theatregoing. *See playgoers*
Theatre in Wales 46, 62
Thompson, Ayanna 9, 147, 166
Tieck, Ludwig 22, 37
Tragedy of Gowrie, The 5
Traister, Barbara Howard 10,
  14
trap-door 124
Trewin, J. C. 43, 61
true crime genre 4, 5, 13, 87, 91,
  136, 143, 147, 164, 181–4,
  188, 215
truth 1–3, 6, 12, 15, 73, 78, 129,
  147, 163, 179, 184, 193
Tucker Brooke, C. F. 24, 50
Two Lamentable Tragedies (cf.
  Beech's Tragedy) 4, 13,
  183, 185, 189
Two Noble Kinsmen, The 21, 24
Tynan, Kenneth 43, 61
Tyrrell, Henry 23, 25–7, 37

Unnatural Father, The 195

van Berg, Susie 172
Vaughan, Virginia Mason 138,
  153, 167
victimhood 26, 27, 111, 112,
  204, 205, 215, 218
villainy 18, 32–5, 68, 144, 208

violence   1, 13, 56, 59, 77, 103,
    111, 123, 163, 166, 179,
    191, 204, 209, 210, 214–18
von Schlegel, August
    Wilhelm   22, 37
vulnerability   93, 99, 120, 127,
    156, 197, 204

Walsham, Alexandra   118, 136,
    141
wardmote book, Faversham   12,
    48, 92, 137, 195
Warnes, Jennifer   47
Warning for Fair Women, A   4,
    23, 134, 135, 181, 189
Watch, the   107, 108, 184
Watson, Thomas   11, 84
weather (also 'meteorology')   9,
    10, 117–41, 178, 179
Webster, John   45, 188
Weever, John   178, 188
Weimann, Robert   111, 115
Wentworth, Patricia   187, 189
What You Will Theatre
    Company   42
*When You See Me You Know
    Me*   148, 162–3, 167
Whigham, Frank   28, 31, 32, 34,
    38, 39, 68, 137, 188, 194,
    195
Whipday, Emma   2, 7, 8, 30, 42,
    44, 61, 81, 88, 92–115, 131,
    134, 141, 159, 165–7, 170,
    185, 186, 189, 213
White, Edward   4, 15, 121

White, Martin   35, 49, 61, 63, 85
White Devil, The   45
whiteness   8, 13, 145–6, 156–62,
    164, 167, 206–7
widowhood   180
Wiggins, Martin   39, 41, 61, 74,
    85–7, 136, 138
Wilkins, George   5
Williamson, Elizabeth   75, 86
Willing Suspension
    Productions   50, 54, 63
Wills Crofts, Freeman   169–73,
    179, 180, 183–6
Wine, M. L.   12, 34, 35, 41, 113,
    123, 136
witchcraft   75
Witch of Edmonton, The   21,
    45, 51
Withers, Bill   57
*Woman Killed with Kindness,
    A*   29, 53, 85, 87
Women's Liberation
    Movement   43, 172
Worcester, 3rd earl of (William
    Somerset)   194
Worcester College, Oxford   43

Yarington, Robert   4, 13
Yorkshire Tragedy, A   5, 13, 24,
    29, 181
Youngblood, Sarah   32, 33, 39,
    187

Zeland (Zeeland)   196
Zürich   47, 62

www.ingramcontent.com/pod-product-compliance
Lightning Source LLC
Chambersburg PA
CBHW071822300426
44116CB00009B/1401